Dutch Graphic Design

Dutch Graphic Design

Kees Broos
Paul Hefting

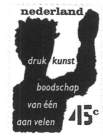

Phaidon Press Ltd
2 Kensington Square
London W8 5EZ

First published in Great Britain 1993
© 1993 V + K Publishing, Laren,
The Netherlands

Jacket design © 1993 Phaidon Press Ltd

ISBN 0 7148 3450 5

A CIP catalogue record for this book is
available from the British Library.

Printed in the Netherlands

7   Introduction

16   Decorative art and rationalism

42   Expressionism and classic typography

58   Type, line and form

76   New typography and photomontage

92   Functionalism and decoration

114 Depression, emigration and occupation

136 Freestyle images and austere design

158 Formal arrangement and variation

170 Free approach vs. grid

196 The recent past

215 Biographies and selected bibliography

219 General bibliography

221 Index of names

223 Acknowledgements

Contents

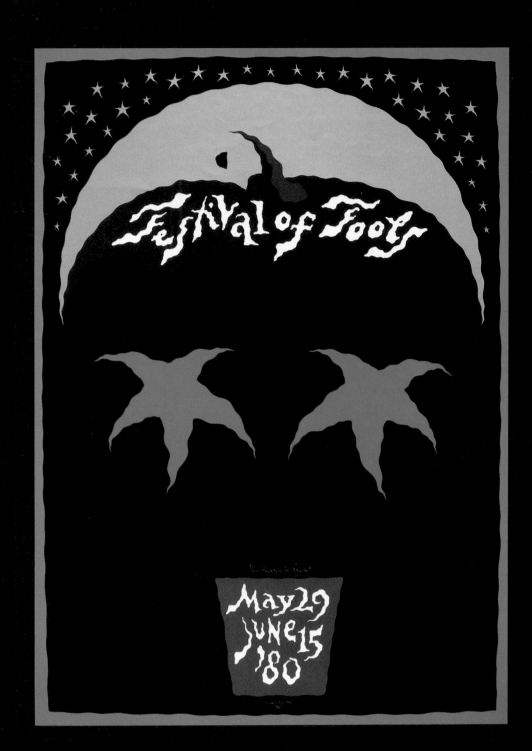

In 1976 the Dutch Postal, Telegraph and Telephone Service (PTT) issued a stamp designed by Willem Sandberg to mark the anniversary of the Dutch printers' organisation. Sandberg designed books, catalogues and posters, was a writer and collector of fine art and printed matter, and also commissioned work from other designers as a former museum director. The slogan with which he adorned the stamp was: 'Printing – a message from one person to many'. It was a typically pithy and idealistic message from this Jack-of-all-design-trades.

But who is this 'one person' that he referred to? It could be a painter who heads now and then for the etching or lithographic press to reproduce his or her visual ideas for a wider public. Or it could be a pacifist screenprinting anti-nuclear posters, with their robust symbols and forceful content, to be flyposted on walls and hoardings. Both artist and activist are printing messages that they hope will reach 'the many'. However, the pacifist's work lies, strictly speaking, outside the artistic sphere and is referred to as graphics, which serve a broader purpose in society than a purely artistic one.

Then there are words alone. A poet may write his verse in a notebook or, these days, on a portable computer screen. If he should run into a sympathetic publisher, his poems are in the bookshops a year later thanks to the art of printing – again a message from one person to many. That is not all. Six months later the same anthology is displayed at an exhibition showing the annual 50 best-designed books in the Netherlands. The jury's report pays tribute to the book's designer, praising the lovely embossing, the precise balance between margins and type area and the sensible paper choice. We are now in an area where a second messenger – the graphic designer – is involved. The publisher of the anthology is also mentioned in the report, although we are uncertain about the nature of *its* message. It could be an indirect one about erudition and good taste. The printer, who made an extra effort to turn out a flawless edition, is also included among the messengers. And let us not forget that the type in which the poems were set was once created by a typeface designer.

In short, any sample of printed matter – passports and postage stamps, pamphlets and paperbacks – can be, as Sandberg says, the message of one individual. More often, however, it is the result of a collaboration between many, each contributing their speciality to the finished product. Depending on the purpose of the printed matter, one specialist's name may be more prominently associated with the final product than another, whether it is the writer, graphic designer, photographer or typeface designer. In many instances, however, they remain anonymous. This book deals with the whole range of specialists who have been or are involved with the designing of printed matter, even if it is not their main profession, and regardless of whether they were credited for the work or not.

Printed matter fulfills numerous functions, thus the visual content is endlessly varied. Here we are concerned with its design; the letters and images as conceived, created and arranged by designers and printers. Not that content is unimportant. On the contrary, the balance between form and content has continually been at the heart of numerous discussions on design during the 20th century – discussions between innovators and traditionalists, amateurs and professionals, establishment figures and anarchists, clients, students and interested observers from the general public. Issues such as the role and style of decoration, the relative merits of drawings and photographs, fashions in typefaces, the best way to communicate clearly and the designer's right to take a political stand, have all been argued over. Thus, an overview of a hundred years of graphic design also provides an overview of prevailing ideas, a summing up of changes that occurred within a few years, a reflection on shifting opinions about letters and images, a report about dissension between the younger and the older generation, and a rollcall of the quirky or more accommodating personalities.

Introduction

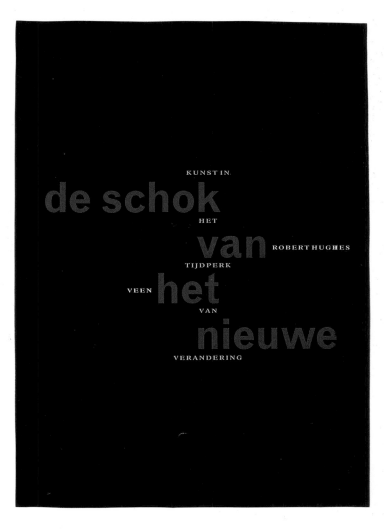

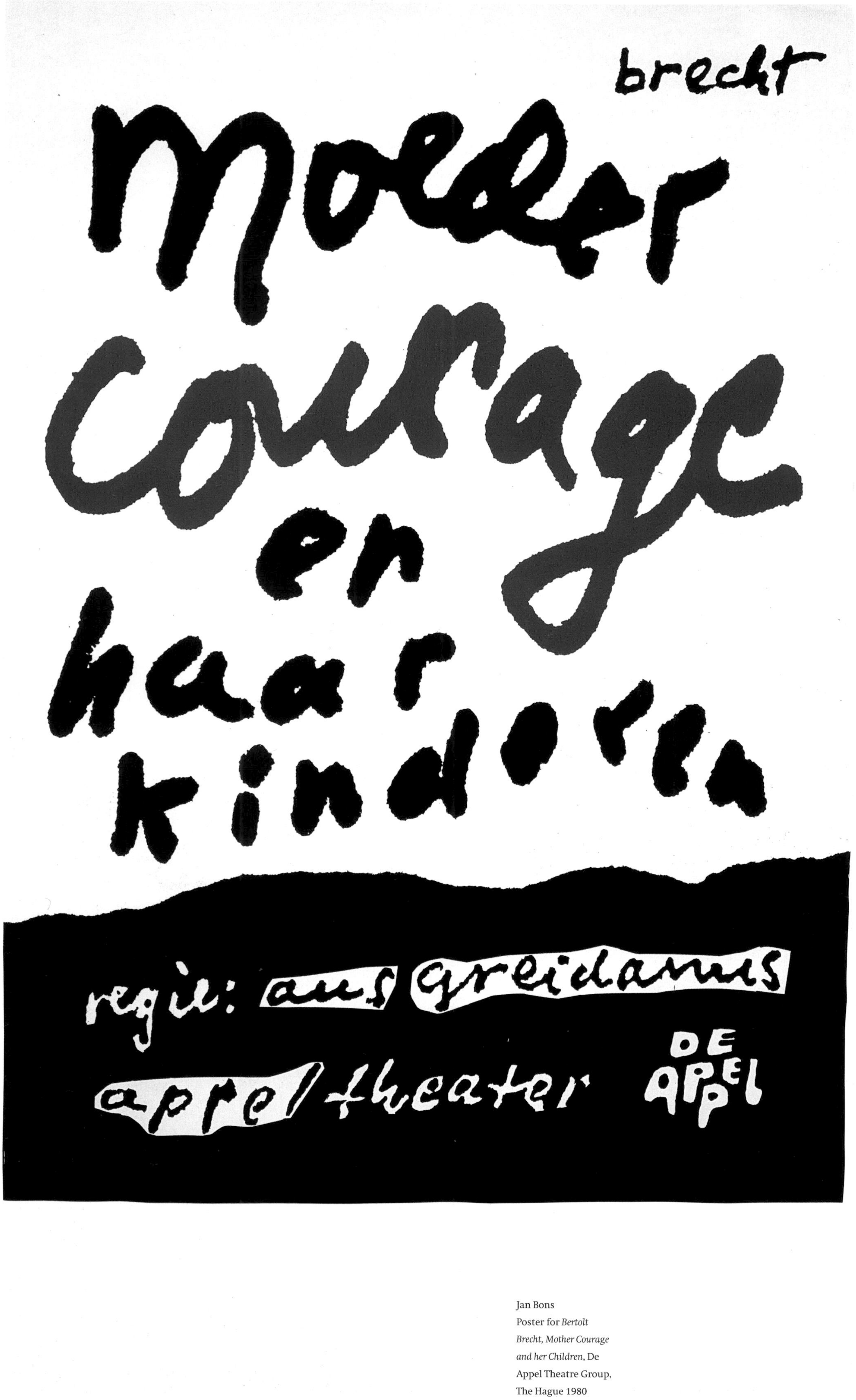

brecht

Moeder courage en haar kinderen

regie: aus greidanus

appel theater DE APPEL

Jan Bons
Poster for *Bertolt
Brecht, Mother Courage
and her Children*, De
Appel Theatre Group,
The Hague 1980

Graphic art can be appreciated for its visual form – the purpose of this book – but that is just one way of viewing it. Collectors of printed matter may be interested in it for other reasons, and may or may not want to know all the details of its design. The philatelist may wish to know that his 1925 unfranked postage stamp of a flying dove was made by the graphic designer, Chris Lebeau, but what philatelist groups stamps according to their designer? The chances are that Lebeau's name is better known by the fanatical collector of posters.

Just as designers of printed material have specialised during the 20th century, so enthusiastic collectors have developed their own preferences and expertise. One collector may have a sharp enough eye to distinguish Jan Van Krimpen's Romulus typeface from his Romanée, and have only scorn for the typographer who dared use the sans-serif Nobel for an anthology of poems. Anyone in the 1950s who spoke in revered tones about the wood engravings of John Buckland Wright in the fine books published by De Roos Foundation could expect to be dismissed by a later generation, who preferred the contemporary photographs of Ed van der Elsken and the typography of Jurriaan Schrofer. We do not know whether a collector of fine books bought the poems of J.H. Leopold because he liked the poet, or because Jan van Krimpen did the typography, or both. It may seem odd to acquire a book simply because the cover is a fine example of graphic design, especially when there may be a splendid book within. However, it is no more strange than the collector who buys stamps, not to send on letters but to store them unused in a special album.

For a century now Dutch presses have been turning out a mass of printed matter, although this momentum is slowing down. Nevertheless, much still remains from the past – in libraries, museum archives, attics and market stalls. To attempt an overview – even from the limited perspective of graphic design – is a daunting task.

The destiny of printed matter lies in the hands of a few of the many who received a message. We may save snippets of paper which prove worthless, or which may become pieces of history. History does not create itself. It is defined by people who have to make do with what remains from the material relics of an earlier age. They are dependent on what others have been interested in or chosen to keep; upon the balance between collecting mania and the destructive urge within society. What one person throws carelessly away, another searches for painstakingly for years.

It was only after the Second World War that graphic design became recognised as a profession in the Netherlands and was taught in the academies. Before this, the work was done by architects, painters and typographers. It was an applied art and belonged to the broad field of industrial design, for which the first special courses had been established a century before. Designers of posters and postage stamps from the first half of the 20th century were from various backgrounds. Some had undergone architectural training in Delft or Amsterdam, while many came from the Institute for Industrial Art Education or the Rijksacademie in Amsterdam, the academies in The Hague and Rotterdam, the Industrial Arts School in Haarlem or the School for Graphic Disciplines in Utrecht.

In the 1930s, the teaching of applied art in the Netherlands received a new impetus. The subject was combined with the contemporary medium of photography, and at the academies in The Hague and Rotterdam as well as the New Art School in Amsterdam, it was now being taught in the Advertising Department. This was the beginning of an independent discipline within graphic design, and its pioneers adopted a militant attitude.

Wim Crouwel
Exhibition poster
*The New Architecture –
Amsterdam*, Stedelijk
Museum, Amsterdam
1983

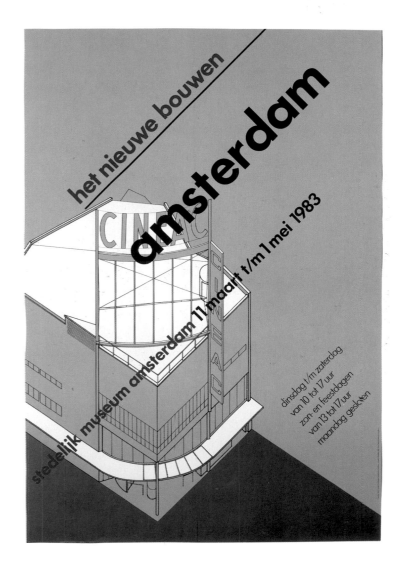

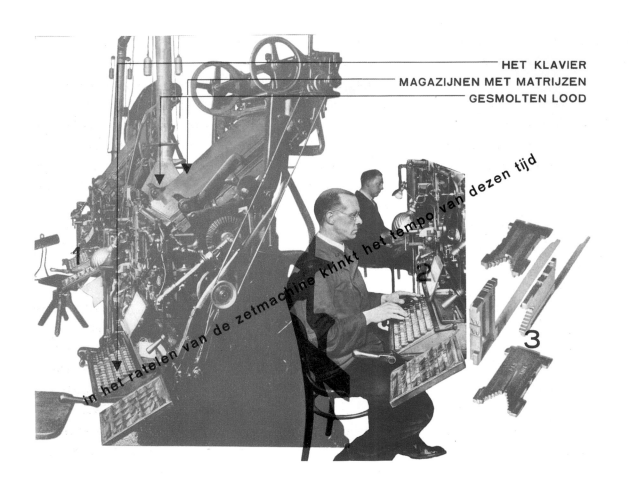

HET KLAVIER
MAGAZIJNEN MET MATRIJZEN
GESMOLTEN LOOD

in het ratelen van de zetmachine klinkt het tempo van dezen tijd

Piet Zwart
Page from an
advertising booklet
for *Nijgh en Van
Ditmar*, Rotterdam
1931

H.N. Werkman
Double-page spread
from *The Next Call*,
no. 9, Werkman,
Groningen 1925

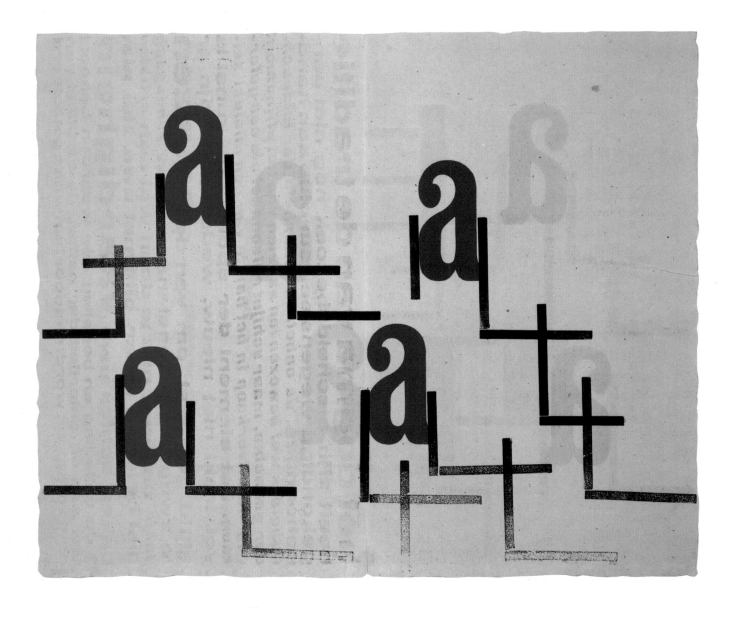

Over fifty years later, graphic design has become a multi-disciplinary subject, and also covers lettering for buildings, signage and exhibition design. It has come full circle: the architect H.P. Berlage had designed posters and calendars, and nowadays graphic designers are themselves involved with three-dimensional space. We have restricted this book to two-dimensional graphic design, however, and included only work that was printed on paper.

While influences from Britain, Germany, Russia, Switzerland and France have been present in various periods of Dutch graphics, particularly during the 1920s when international contacts with avant-garde designers conveyed the feeling of belonging to one large family, nonetheless a fairly exceptional situation has always existed in the Netherlands. This came about initially through the equal standing of the fine arts, architecture and industrial art, which meant that the typographer or graphic artist was not plunged into anonymity. Moreover, it was architects and painters in particular who gave graphic art its first impulse to renew itself.

From the beginning of the 20th century, this climate has also been sustained by the fact that a number of company directors have taken an enormous interest in Dutch culture and therefore in good design. These directors were personally involved in commissioning designers, often for the idealistic purpose of adopting a contemporary image for their company. The most prominent between 1910 and 1940 included C.H. van der Leeuw of the Rotterdam Van Nelle coffee and tea company, P.M. Cochius of the Leerdam Glass Manufacturers, J.C. van der Marken of the Dutch Oil Company (NOF) in Delft, F. Kerdijk of the Trio printing firm in The Hague, J. de Leeuw of the interior firm Metz & Co and J.F. van Royen of the Dutch Postal, Telegraph and Telephone Service (PTT). As spokespersons for the external image of their companies they were all prepared to take risks. In addition, they also held key positions on various cultural boards of the time.

There has also always been a very open-minded attitude in the Netherlands towards the art of printing, in which tradition and innovation have gone hand-in-hand. Especially in the 1920s, references to, and a conscious reaction against, traditional modes were noticeable at the same time. The publishing firm of the brothers W.L. and J. Brusse in Rotterdam, for instance, had its books designed by both the classic typographer Sjoerd de Roos as well as the functionalist innovator Piet Zwart. During the first decades of the 20th century there was also a feeling of responsibility towards society. Socialism and a striving for a just distribution of material and spiritual goods led in the Netherlands to a wish for communal art – beautiful design available to all – even in graphic design.

During the 1920s the approach to this ideal took two different directions. The élitist attitude to typography, aimed at producing fine books, had such advocates as the typeface designers Jan van Krimpen and Sjoerd de Roos, and clashed with the proletarian approach towards design of typographers who thought in broader terms than 'the book'. For the latter, typography was no longer a 'holy' matter. It embraced everything that was printed, and the design of such printed material was judged by designers like Piet Zwart and Paul Schuitema according to its effect on the reader or viewer. The result was that a division arose between book typography and 'the rest': a division which, incidentally, is not reflected in this book.

The early diversity that had occurred spontaneously due to the various training backgrounds of typographers and non-typographers, now began to disappear because of new techniques and changes in training. Typography was taught increasingly at the art academies, and what the typesetter had in the past done for himself was now prescribed by the graphic designer.

From 1945, during the period of post-war reconstruction, new ideas flourished once again. In America, graphic designers and clients were developing new concepts, and gradually the idea of the exceptional graphic image that drew attention to a company or product was born. It became the basis of the concept of a house style. By the 1960s the government, its various ministries and the Dutch railways had discovered graphic designers and were making use of their services. It is curious that a government style for printed matter never evolved, although in the Netherlands of today, with its strange mix of collectivism and individuality, this would no longer be appreciated.

Another instrinsic difference between Dutch graphic design and that of other countries is the distinction made between graphic design and advertising design, which is reflected in Holland's two professional trade organisations, the Association of Dutch Designers (for designers working mainly for the non-commercial sector) and the Art Directors Club Nederland. Here, diametrically opposed interests are at play; on the one side the autonomy and freedom of the graphic designer, and on the other, the idea that design is dictated by advertising and thus aimed at a broader public. Whenever this situation is discussed, however, Dutch designers tend to argue for the independence of design from purely commercial considerations.

The fine arts and architecture as well as social and political developments have always inspired Dutch graphic design. Elements from Expressionism, Dadaism, Constructivism, Art Nouveau and New Functionalism have been effortlessly incorporated into the graphic arts. This close intertwining of art and design has been its most characteristic feature. Much of what this book presents has to do with the natural affinity that graphic designers have with Dutch cultural life: its museums, theatres, festivals and concert halls. It is in this inspirational climate that the most appealing or innovative designs are often produced.

The political involvement of Dutch designers in the 1930s in such causes as the Spanish Civil War and Nazi persecution, and much later in the typically Dutch Provo movement of the 1960s, has also left its mark on design. Socially committed or coolly objective; these two polarities have clashed with one another over a long period. Even today, the question of what role a graphic designer should play in society is still a valid one. There has never been a clearly formulated theoretical basis for the profession in the Netherlands, although the influence of international debate makes a strong case for one. In the Nethelands, however, one factor that enters all discussions is a sense of social responsibility. In addition, the need for tradition or innovation, for freedom or engagement is still apparent – for typographers, purely functionalist designers, and to those quirky individuals who regard experimentation as a *conditio sine qua non* and who adopt an independent attitude towards those clients unsure of their own taste.

The increasing demand for design has led in recent years to a greater number of freelance designers and design studios. This has led to a more varied approach to style, but at the same time has created a certain mediocrity. Or perhaps we should interpret it as a general language of form that has developed many dialects. The transition from letterpress to full-colour lithography has greatly contributed to the impression of mediocrity because much of what is produced tends to look the same. And in the general bombardment of images from both printed matter and the competing television screen, those images appear to be sinking into a uniform morass. At the same time, the advent of the computer and desktop publishing has left the image of graphic design less clear. These criticisms should not be seen as cause for pessimism, however. For creative designers, the mass of media

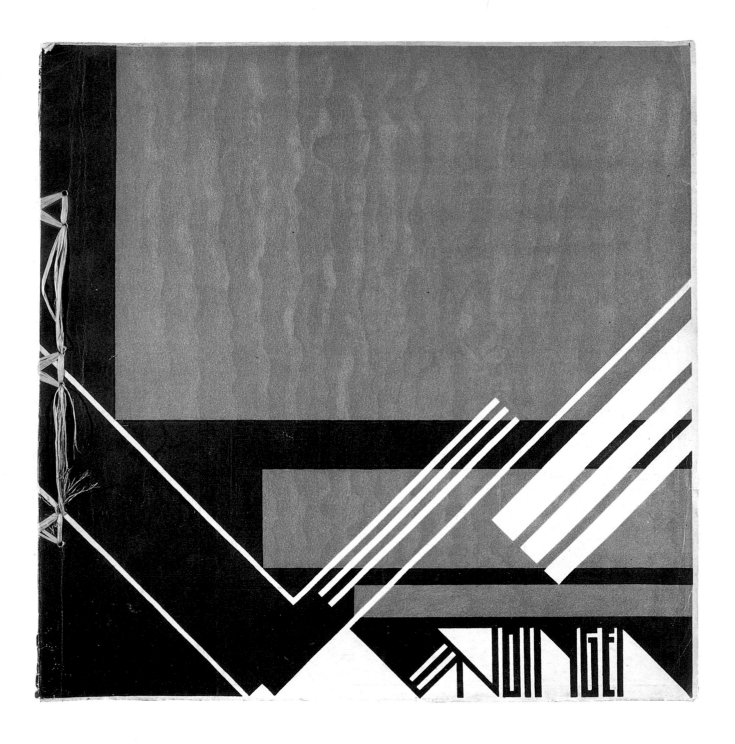

B. Bijvoet and
J. Duiker
Cover of *Wendingen*,
vol. 4, no. 12,
C.A. Mees, Santpoort
1922. The issue was
devoted to the
winning design for a
Rijksacademie for the
visual arts

images is a challenge. Even in the past, the most inventive designers have always gone one step further than was thought possible.

This book is about one hundred years of graphic design in the Netherlands. It can thus only give a broad overview of the wealth of printed matter designed since 1890. Within this limitation, however, it possible not only to discuss individual Dutch designers, from Jan Toorop to Gielijn Escher and from Jan van Krimpen to Gerard Unger, but also to to draw attention to contributions from related areas – clients in industry and public service and publishers and printers who stimulated the development of Dutch graphic design and helped it to flourish. The short chapters, illustrated with well-known and lesser known examples of design, chart the ever-changing course of design through the century.

The ultimate selection of material for inclusion in *Dutch Graphic Design*, especially that from recent years, is inevitably subjective. But no book is ever definitive while pleasure and interest in the subject remain. What it clearly demonstrates, however, is the way in which both pure typography and letter and image combinations have visually reflected the diverging spiritual, material, cultural and technical developments of the last hundred years.

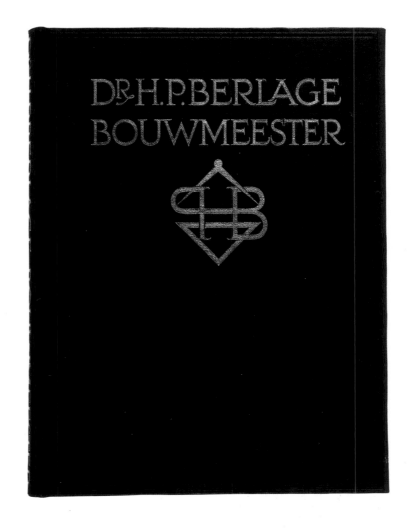

S.H. de Roos
Cover embossing for
*J. Gratama, Dr H.P.
Berlage Bouwmeester*
(Dr H.P. Berlage,
Architect), W.L. and
J. Brusse, Rotterdam
1923

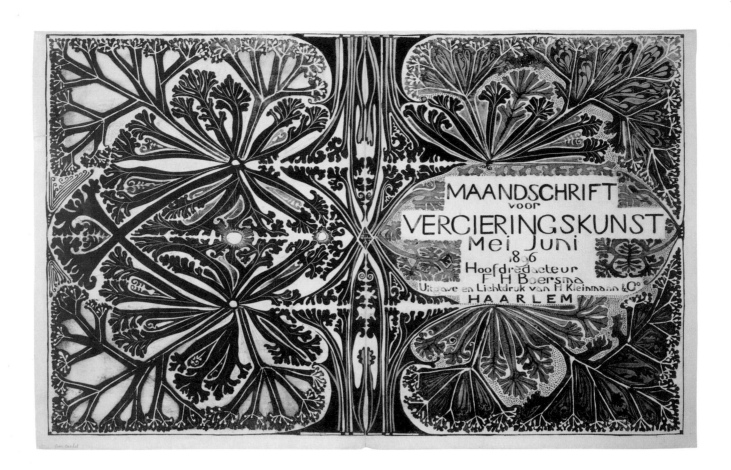

C.A. Lion Cachet
Front and back cover
of *Maandschrift voor*
Vercieringskunst
(Decorative Art
Monthly),
F.H. Boersma ed.,
H. Kleinmann & Cie,
Haarlem, May-June
1896

H.P. Berlage
Poster for the *North
Holland Tram Company*,
Amsterdam 1893

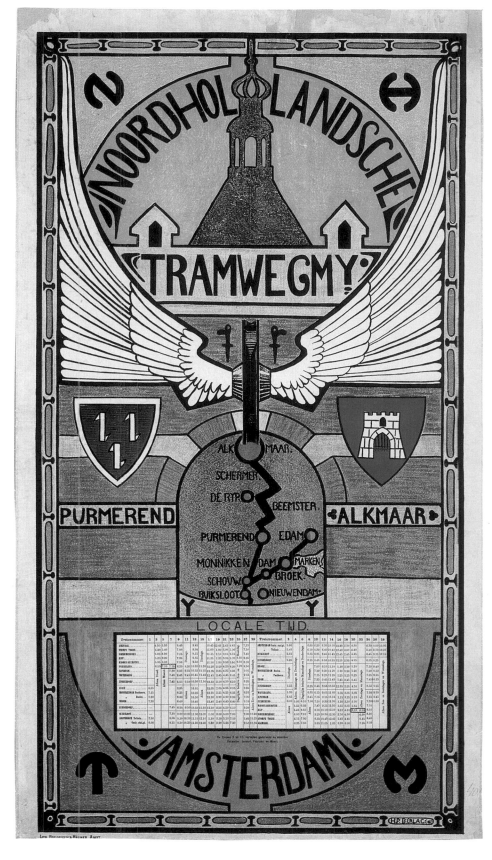

Decorative art and rationalism

A wave of innovation in the fields of the visual arts, architecture, graphic design and industrial art in general spread through Europe from the latter half of the 19th century. With regard to the industrial arts, Britain in particular led the way. It was there that William Morris and Walter Crane in the 1860s-70s began an offensive against machine-made uniformity. Imitation was sinful; the aim was towards individual and original designs. These could be based on tradition, but not on the arbitrary copying of the forms and embellishments of past styles.

The guild system of the Middle Ages appeared to Morris and Crane an ideal base on which to build their romantic dream of a group of artists working for society, creating good-quality, well-conceived objects with an emphasis on fine craftsmanship. By so doing, they thought, humankind could undoubtedly be comforted in a bleak world. Art could play a social role in the home; its furnishings, utensils, books, clothes – everything would emanate a warmth and love for the crafts. Mass-produced industrial goods should make way for the handmade.

To a lesser degree this paralleled developments taking place in Vienna, particularly evident in new city architecture and the work of the Wiener Werkstätte, a group of artisans and designers that quickly made a name for itself with exciting modern – but also industrially manufactured – objects.

There was another aspect to the concern for fresh design ideas. The well-to-do classes were tired with the gewgaws masquerading as fine craftsmanship that had the pseudo-status of 'classical' or 'Empire' styles imposed upon them, or were else puffed up as being stately 'Empire'. At the 1851 Great Exhibition in London these wares were displayed as the high-quality products of the new industrial society. Yet this famous showcase also prompted an awareness that there were other ways of giving form to the human environment.

From the 1860s on, designers were experimenting with new and unusual ideas and forms, which would eventually give rise to 20th-century modernism. Their objective was to find a 'contemporary' vision for design of all kinds, designs that could be manufactured industrially, if necessary, and which would emanate a fresh élan and youthful vigour. The search was on for the new: hence the popularity of Art Nouveau (or Jugendstil, as it was known in Germany) at the turn of the century.

In the Netherlands, innovation in the graphic design of books, posters and illustration began around 1890. In literature of the period a distinction was made early on between the decorative tradition and 'rationalism'. In book design the decorative was expressed in an artistic approach to layout, illustration and cover decoration. However, posters, calenders, advertising and other forms of graphic material intended for the general public were also given a decorative treatment. The creators had for the most part been trained as artists, but some were architects who, according to the prevailing fashion, were involved with everything to do with design.

Another interested group emerged at this time, from the printing world. Their concern was with typography and the development of new typefaces, and they aimed at a contemporary layout for all type matter whatever its purpose – the rationalist approach. These designers were each in their way convinced that clear, good-quality printed matter would have a favourable effect on the observer and would develop in him or her a feeling for the beauty of contemporary design. Dutch publishers such as L.J. Veen and Kleinmann, and printers like Berend Modderman, encouraged these new ideas.

In the Netherlands decorative tradition and rationalism existed side by side: the freedom of the one style alongside the functional and ordered precepts of the other; the drawn, fanciful letter alongside the manufactured, stylised letter and formal embellishment – precise in size and layout. These two movements, in fact, have influenced Dutch graphic design ever since.

Frequently, however, no such clear distinction was made and both forms were used together, even in the work of one artist. Line, colour and shape as autonomous means of expression were exuberantly manifest in elements of new art, from the patterned to the virtually abstract. In architecture an emphasis on clarity and purity of construction emerged, particularly in the work of H.P. Berlage and K.P.C. de Bazel, but the new decorative style, which was making itself felt in other types of crafts, could not be ignored. And from painting, forms associated with Symbolism, which was a dominating force in European art at the time, are clearly evident in the applied art of Jan Toorop and Johan Thorn Prikker.

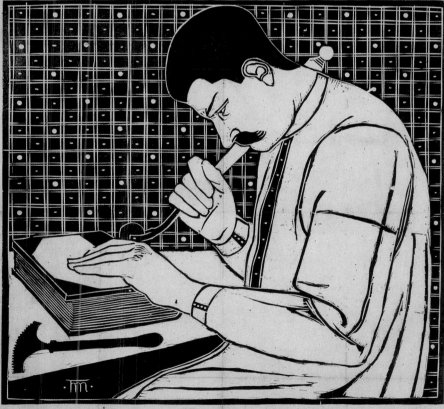

J. Thorn Prikker
Magazine poster
*Revue bimestrielle pour
l'art appliqué*,
Kleinmann, Haarlem
1896

C.A. Lion Cachet
Advertisement flyer
for the March issue of
the magazine *Revue
bimestrielle pour l'art
appliqué*, Kleinmann,
Haarlem 1896

C.A. Lion Cachet
Scroll for the
*Municipality of
Apeldoorn*, 1898, to
mark the coronation
of Queen Wilhelmina,
and commissioned as
a symbol of loyalty to
the resident of the
Het Loo summer
palace

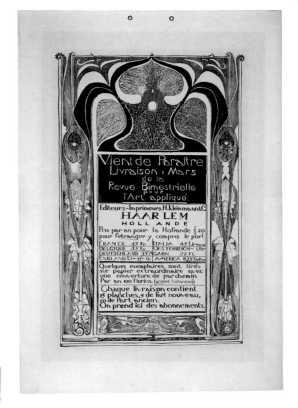

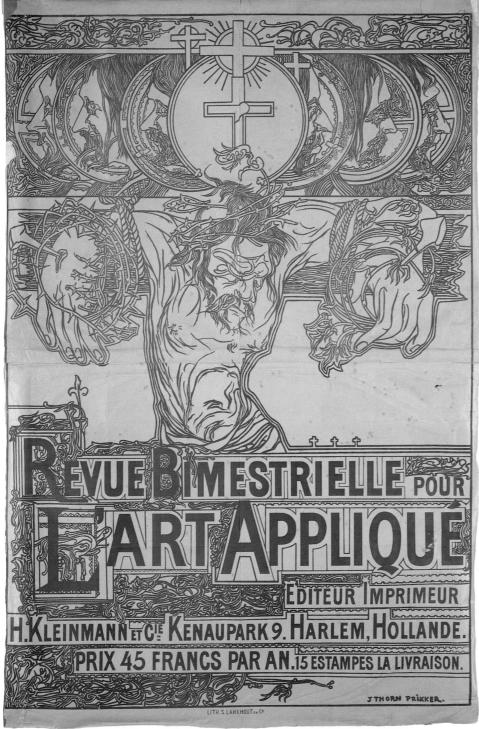

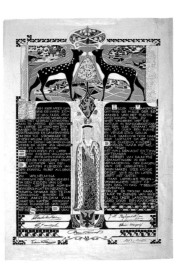

G.W. Dijsselhof
Diploma for the
*International Exhibition
of the Book Trade and
Related Subjects*, 1892.
An association to
promote the book
trade had invited
Dijsselhof, Cachet and
Nieuwenhuis to
produce a design.
Dijsselhof came up
with a woodcut
depicting stylised
peacock feathers and
palms, surrounded by
a Buddha and other
figures

C.A. Lion Cachet
Diploma for the
*International Exhibition
of the Book Trade and
Related Subjects*, 1892.
Incorporated into the
decoration are Greek,
Persian and Hebrew
letters

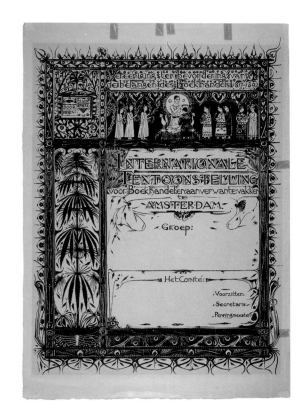

Art Nouveau

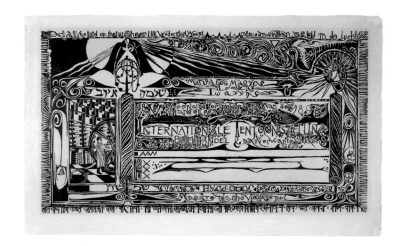

Art Nouveau caught on in the Netherlands around 1890. An awareness of
the equal merit of both fine art and the applied and industrial arts, largely
inspired by William Morris's ideas on the social function of design, resulted
in a growing attention to form in everyday life that had nothing to do with
academicism. The essays of Lewis F. Day, such as *Everyday Art*, and those of
Morris and Crane appeared around this time in Dutch translation, and
various societies were established to foster new developments in art and
industrial design. These included Arti et Industriae, Labor et Ars, the Hague
Art Circle and, in 1940, the Netherlands Association for Crafts and Industrial
Art (VANK). The latter dedicated itself to cultivating a 'harmonious link
between artistic trade practices and mechanised technique'.

International contacts with, among others, Les XX in Brussels and the
Wiener Werkstätte in Vienna increased the need to break new ground in the
Netherlands also. In industrial art, too, stylised forms, the inner structure of
nature and the geometric starting points of a new decorative art were to be
found. Together, they constituted the beginnings of abstraction: the use of
line, form and colour for their own sakes, independent of clear and
recognisable representation.

These elements were used with great freedom in the graphic and
decorative arts: sometimes applied in a willowy, curvilinear style or sometimes in a formally arranged way. They were used as borders, for eye-catching
effect, or as grids. Motifs from other cultures, such as Egypt, Arabia, Japan
and India were studied and adopted, while the symbols of rediscovered
religions, old and new philosophies or fashionable sects were used in either a
pure or abstract form. Existing sources from all over the world were applied
in every conceivable manner, particularly in graphic design.

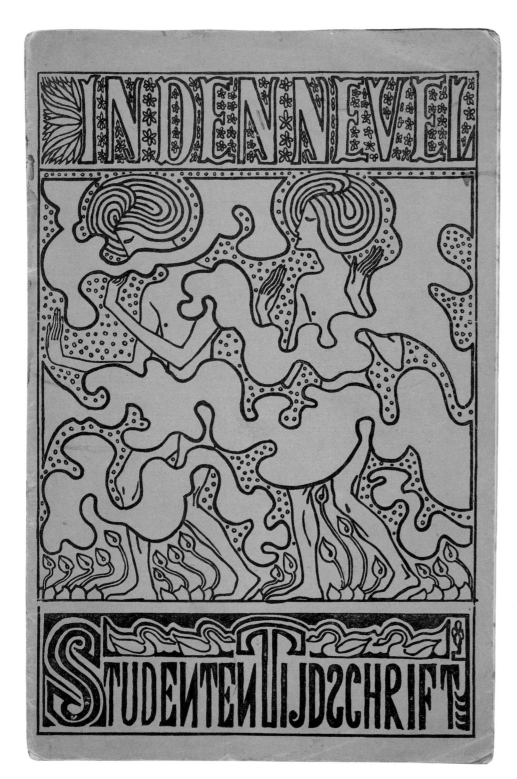

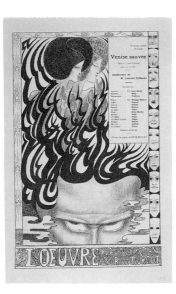

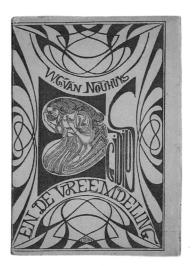

Jan Toorop
Cover of the student
magazine *In den nevel*
(In the Mist), used
between 1896 and
1899; J. Waltmann
Jnr., Delft. From 1895
Toorop's woodcut was
printed in a different
colour every year

Jan Toorop
Poster for *Venise
sauvée*, performed by
the Théatre de
l'Oeuvre, Paris 1895.
This was a French
adaptation by Gil
Pène of a 17th-
century play written
by Thomas Otway
that was also staged
in the Netherlands in
1895 and 1896.
Toorop was
commissioned
through the graphic
artist Philippe Zilcken
in Paris

Jan Toorop
Cover design for *W.G.
van Nouhuys, Egidius en
de vreemdeling* (Egidius
and the Stranger); De
Erven F. Bohn,
Haarlem 1899. The
design was inspired
by the work of
William Morris,
which Toorop had
seen in Oxford in
1899

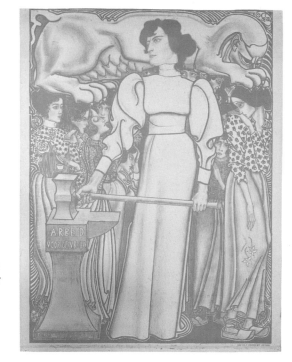

Jan Toorop
Work for Women
poster, Amsterdam
1898. It was designed
for a national
exhibition that aimed
to give 'an overview of
the female workforce
in the year in which a
young woman will
ascend to the Dutch
throne'

The style of Jan Toorop

The painter and graphic artist Jan Toorop – who in his work moved first from sombre naturalism to pointillism, then to the linear style of Art Nouveau and on through Symbolism to arrive at a stylised, pious realism – received numerous commissions after 1890 to design posters, book covers and magazine illustrations.

Every Dutch person from around the turn of the century was familiar with Toorop's poster, *Delftsche Slaolie*, which he designed in 1894 for the Dutch Oil Factory (NOF) in Delft. Owing to this poster, depicting two female figures with curling hair overflowing into the swirling salad oil being advertised, Art Nouveau became dubbed the 'salad oil' style in the Netherlands.

Despite the fact that the drawn line of Symbolist painting was adopted by many designers as an abstraction for feeling or movement, the schematised lines of Toorop's work during the early 1890s were his trademark. The cover of the Delft student magazine *In den Nevel*, the poster for 'The Shipwreck' by Dutch composer Johan Wagenaar, and all his graphic art of those years show the same decorative style: the same women with wavy hair that he had introduced in 1892 in the study for his well-known painting *The Three Brides* (1893). The ponderous symbolism of Good and Evil in this painting was apparently easily translated a year later by Toorop into suggesting flavourful salad oil. The female image, even then, was a compulsory and successful aspect of product advertising.

Around 1896 Toorop developed a new form of stylisation and a severe compositional style in his poster *The High Land at Beekbergen* and for the poster he designed for the Arnhem Insurance Company, which preceded the monumental work he was to introduce to Berlage's Stock Exchange in Amsterdam five years later.

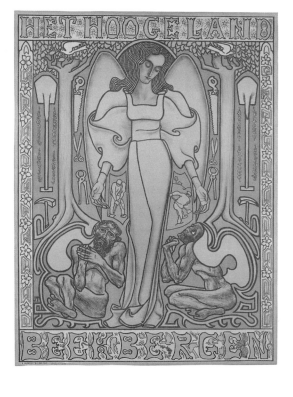

Jan Toorop
Poster for the charity
organisation *Het
Hooge Land –
Beekbergen*, 1896.
Depicted are the tools
used by the residents.
Toorop's sister, Janet
Hall, posed for the
female figure

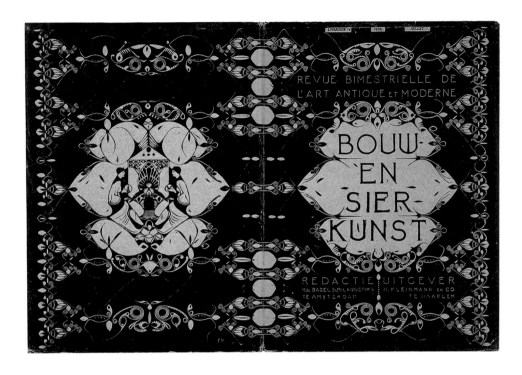

The architect as designer

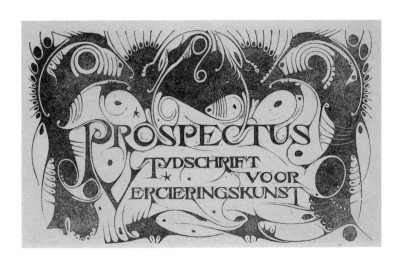

In architects such as H.P. Berlage, K.P.C. de Bazel and J.L.M. Lauweriks we find men whose work went beyond the mere design of buildings. The entire decoration of the interiors, including furniture, glass and lighting, wood-work, and graphic elements such as nameplates, signs and numbering, were designed by the architects themselves and executed under their supervision. This manner of working led to buildings with a great sense of unity and harmony in the overall design, evident down to the tiniest detail.

Such architects were also commissioned from time to time to design posters, calenders, bookplates and book covers. They also took on the decorative layout of magazines to which they were affiliated or had themselves set up, such as *De Architect* and *Bouw- en Sierkunst* (Architecture and Decorative Art).

Besides Berlage's many decorative and architectural drawings, we know he designed two posters, for the North Holland Tram Company and for the Dutch railways, in 1893. The advertisement for the timetable for the Hook of Holland-Harwich crossing is an extravaganza of typographic and decorative elements, with a train as the central image. The Art Nouveau elements displayed in this poster are not those of the rationalist Berlage. Despite the details and the almost hidden timetable, his Amsterdam to Alkmaar poster is more stark and therefore carries more impact. Here there are clear similarities to his architectural drawings of the period, for instance to those for the De Algemeene (bank) building on Amsterdam's Damrak. In his decorative design Berlage also worked according to theosophical principles: the mystical transformation of matter into the purely spiritual, represented by geometrical figures. Whether he employed such 'spiritual' concerns for the aforementioned posters is unlikely, but from around 1900 spiritual matters played an important role in his work.

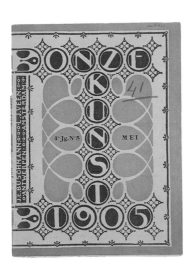

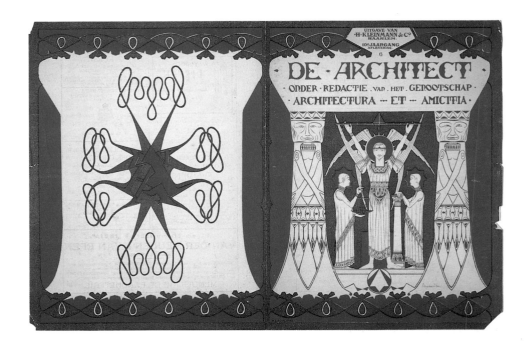

For De Bazel, too, religious symbolism was an essential component of his work. His woodcuts for the theosophical publication *Licht en Waarheid* (Light and Truth) reveal largely emblematical and allegorical representations. Designs for covers or title pages of architectural magazines like *Bouwkundig Weekblad*, *Architectura* and *Tijdschrift voor Vercieringskunst* show not only influences from Egyptian art, Roman decoration or Eastern batik, but also such motifs from nature as butterfly wings. Much of the design is resolved in geometric patterns, repeated, altered and reversed. In the main the typography is elaborately decorative and thus difficult to read. This decorative influence can also be seen in the work of G.W. Dijsselhof, Chris Lebeau and Duco Crop. De Bazel was also responsible for the first Dutch postage stamp designed in the new style: a set of Jubilee stamps issued in 1913. They are reminiscent of the postage stamps created by the Austrian, Koloman Moser, which had appeared a few years earlier.

J.L.M. Lauweriks' decorative style was based on theosophical ideas similar to De Bazel's. Whereas at first he used floral motifs, later the work became more abstract and severe. The layout for Lauweriks' magazine *Ring*, founded in 1908 in Düsseldorf, is linear and systematic. The decoration is often made up of typesetting elements such as typographers' letters, emblems and bars – a new and revolutionary method that would have its imitators. Lauweriks' typographic method of working can be seen in H.T. Wijdeveld's magazine *Wendingen* (Directions) and in Theo van Doesburg's alphabet of 1918.

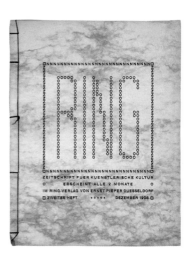

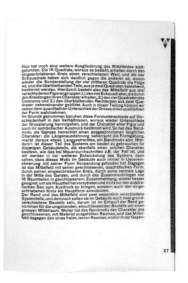

VANDEN VOS REINAERDE

Willem, die den Madoc maecte,
Daer hi dicke omme waecte,
Hem vernoyede so haerde,
Dat davonturen van Reinaerde
In Dietsce onghemaket bleven,
Die hi hier hevet vulscreven
Dat hi die vite dede soeken,
Ende hise naden walscen boeken
In Dietsce dus hevet begonnen.
Atant i vint la reine Bramimunde:
Jo vus-aim mult, Sire, dist ele a l'cunte,
Kar mult vus preiset mis sire e tuit sihum
A vostre femme enveierai dous nusches:
Bien i ad or, matistes e jacunces,
E valent mielz que tut l'aveir de Rume;
Vostre emperere si bones n'en vit unkes.
Jamais n'iert jur que de l'mien ne vus dunge
Guenes respunt: E nus vus servirument.
Il les ad prises, en sa hoese les butet.

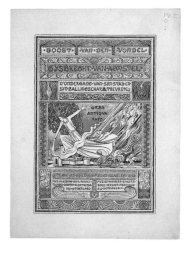
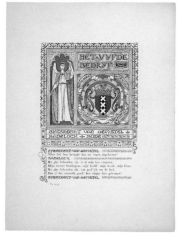

A.J. Derkinderen
Book decoration for
the deluxe edition of
Joost van den Vondel,
Gysbrecht van Aemstel,
with an introduction
by Leo Simons, music
by Bernard Zweers
and theatre décor
designs by H.P.
Berlage; De Erven F.
Bohn, Haarlem 1893-
1900. The book was
published in 20 loose-
leaf issues between
1893-1900, and both
letterpress and colour
lithography were
used

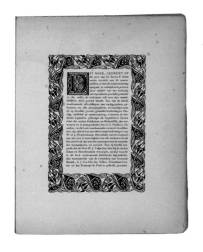

W.O.J. Nieuwenkamp
and J.G. Veldheer
Page from the book
Oude Hollandsche steden
aan de Zuiderzee (Old
Towns of the Zuider
Zee), De Erven F.
Bohn, Haarlem. Both
designers were
clearly influenced by
William Morris's
Kelmscott typography.
Veldheer

produced the title
page and border
decoration in
woodcut, while
Nieuwenkamp
executed the
drawings using
blocks

G.W. Dijsselhof
Text in woodcut for
Vanden Vos Reynaerde
(an old Dutch fable),
1898, one of
Dijsselhof's attempts
to compose his own
faces under the
names Klei-type, Hei-
type and Wei-type.
Although the story
was intended for
publication it was
never used

G.W. Dijsselhof
Book decoration for
the deluxe edition of
Walter Crane, Kunst en
samenleving (Art and
Society) after Crane's
Claims of Decorative Art,
1892. The Dutch
version is by Jan Veth;
Scheltema and
Holkema's Boekhandel,
Amsterdam 1894

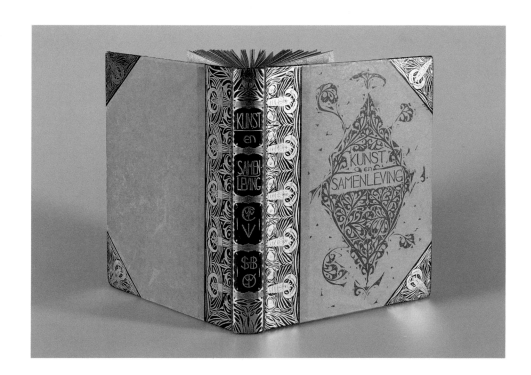

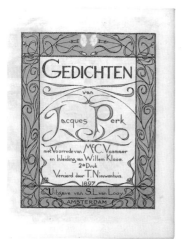

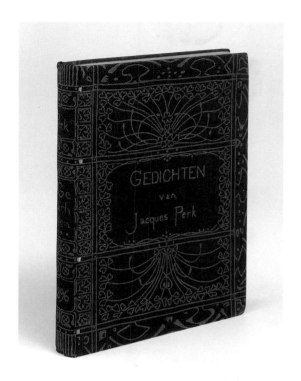

The new book

The Netherlands was justly proud of its fine book publishing traditions. Type founders, engravers and printers had built on a trade dating back to the last quarter of the 15th century, although for masterly type, illustration and binding, the 17th century was a Golden Age. For those living at the end of the 19th century, however, and aware of the heroic past, their own age seemed to have degenerated into typographic bad taste, imitation and vulgar foreign examples; in short into styleless, crass commercialism. It was in such terms that the critic Jan Kalf and the portrait artist Jan Veth censured the decline of the book as an art form in the second half of the 19th century.

The English Arts and Crafts Movement, however, provided a great inspiration for Dutch youth. An important example were the books on crafts published by the Kelmscott Press, founded by William Morris in 1890. Because of these, new viewpoints on a book's appearance gained currency, and the book came to be considered as a piece of design in its own right, to be constructed in correct proportions of paper to inked surfaces. Typeface and decorated initial letters flowed harmoniously together with border decoration and woodcut illustrations.

The first brave attempt to publish a book of this nature in the Netherlands was Vondel's *Gysbrecht van Aemstel* by A.J. Derkinderen, which appeared in 1893 but was not wholly successful. The publication, which in itself could be a monument to decorative art, contains a mixture of styles: on the one hand the text was printed in a light letterpress with heavy lithographic decoration in four-colour and gold with soberly designed music sheets, while on the other the illustrations were stage sets drawn like architectural models by H.P. Berlage. Derkinderen's richly decorated pages mainly resembled scaled-down ornament taken from the neo-Gothic churches of the day.

The following year G.W. Dijsselhof demonstrated a superior approach with his skilled and elegant design for Walter Crane's *Kunst en Samenleving* (Art and Society). Each stitched and bound edition was different in appearance, but each showed a flawless unity of text and image using symmetrical, decorative woodcuts as opening and closing vignettes. For the text the designer made do with a meagre Caslon typeface, thus it is no wonder that Dijsselhof made several attempts to design his own typefaces, ones that would be in keeping with his woodcuts, such as the Hei, Klei and Wei faces.

In 1895 Roland Holst published *Sonnetten en Verzen in Terzinen* (Sonnets and Poems in *Terza Rima*), a book that pointed to a new soberness in future design. The richly decorated page that Morris preferred, however, had its Dutch equivalent in a book by Wijnand Nieuwenkamp with illustrations by J.G. Veldheer. For a book by Jacques Perks entitled *Gedichten* (Poems), T. Nieuwenhuis was responsible for decorative borders executed with a lighter touch and more colourful variations.

Jan Toorop
Cover of *Louis
Couperus, Psyche*.
The repetitive
swirling lines used to
illustrate this
fairytale are
characteristic of
Toorop's work around
the turn of the
century; Veen,
Amsterdam 1898

R.N. Roland Holst
Cover of *Louis
Couperus, Majesteit* ,
Veen, Amsterdam
1893. The novel is one
of the first examples
of Art Nouveau in
Dutch book decoration

Theo Neuhuys
Cover for the novel in
four parts *Louis
Couperus, De boeken der
kleine zielen* (The Books
of Small Souls), Veen,
Amsterdam 1901-1903

Jan Toorop
Cover of the prose
poem *Louis Couperus,
God en goden* (God and
Gods), Veen,
Amsterdam 1903.
This is one of the
most extravagant
covers Toorop
produced for Veen
and has virtually
abstract decoration

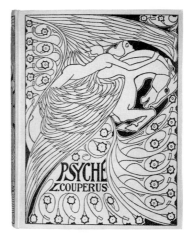
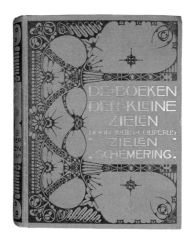
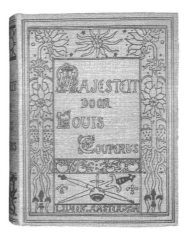
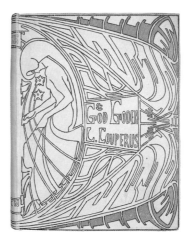

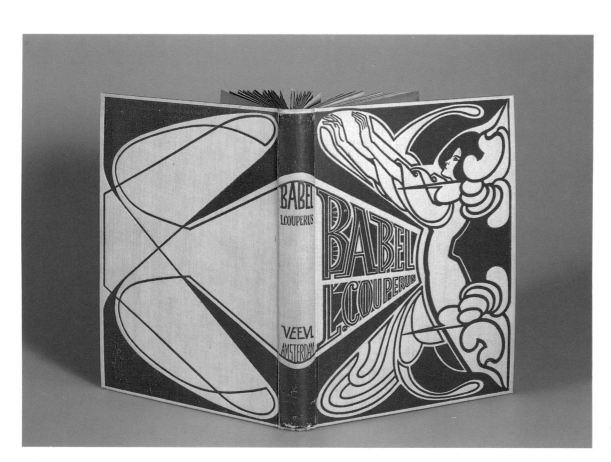

Jan Toorop
Book for the
symbolical story *Louis
Couperus, Babel*; Veen,
Amsterdam 1901.
Toorop chiefly used
female figures to
depict spiritual
aspects in art and
literature

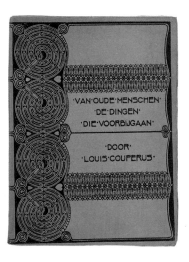

Chris Lebeau
Cover of the novel
Louis Couperus,
Van oude menschen de
dingen die voorbij gaan
(The Things that Slip
by Old People), Veen,
Amsterdam 1906. The
spare, structural
arrangement of this
cover closely
resembles the
patterned decoration
of the damask table
linen that Lebeau
designed in 1905

During the 1890s various publishers were quick to see the commercial possibilities of the new style in applied art. The work of young decorative artists lent itself well to fine-quality books, providing striking covers and daring illustrations. By the turn of the century, a flourishing market had developed, both economically and culturally, with Amsterdam in the lead. Important publishers such as H.J.W. Becht, C.A.J. van Dishoeck, S.L. van Looy, Van Holkema & Warendorf, P.N. van Kampen, W. Versluys and L.J. Veen encouraged what they saw as an affinity between literature and the visual arts. As a result they commissioned a new generation of designers to create the latest novels and poetry anthologies of a young generation of writers.

L.J. Veen was an Amsterdam publisher with a very eclectic list, from technical and scientific books and schoolbooks to novels and magazines like *Onze Kunst* (Our Art). A man with broad cultural interests he was friendly with Amsterdam artists such as Jan Toorop and Roland Holst. In 1893 Veen published his first book by Louis Couperus, a writer of symbolistic, naturalistic and historic tales. For this novel, *Majesteit*, the young Roland Holst designed a cover in the new decorative style. It became a bestseller and new Couperus titles followed regularly, with covers and illustrations designed by such decorative artists as Jan Toorop, Chris Lebeau and Theo Neuhuys, or architects H.P. Berlage and L.W.R. Wenckebach. Toorop's covers and illustrations were the most outstanding. His compositions, replete with female figures, paralleled the symbolic content of such novels by Couperus as *Psyche* and *Babel*. Toorop's treatment of the letterforms, stretching them like elastic, was also highly unconventional. The book titles were sometimes illegibly jumbled up with the lavish linear decoration, inspired by traditional Eastern patterns. Louis Couperus later preferred a more austere decorative style, requesting of his publisher in 1912, 'Please, anything but a *modern* style!'. He thought Toorop's designs done for his own and for other publishers looked too much alike.

Couperus waxed lyrical in 1900, however, about Chris Lebeau's batiked velvet cover for the luxury edition of his Indonesian novel, *De stille kracht* (The Quiet Strength): 'It is just like the wing of a butterfly', he wrote to Veen, 'we are ecstatic about it!'.

Young Dutch artists had by this time discovered the art and architecture of the Far East. They embraced Indonesian decorative art as an anti-academic source of inspiration and praised exotic techniques, such as 'batik', for decorating textiles. As a reaction to Toorop's extravagance, the covers created by Lebeau and Theo Neuhuys showed that simpler forms of decorative art could also merit attention.

The publisher L.J. Veen

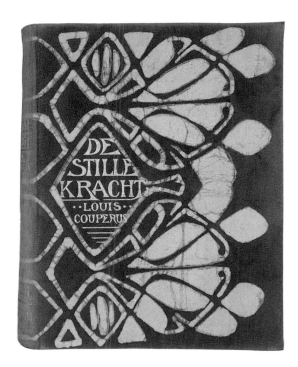

Chris Lebeau
Cover of the novel
Louis Couperus, De stille
kracht (The Quiet
Strength), Veen,
Amsterdam 1900.
The Javanese batik
technique was
extremely popular in
the Netherlands and
used in applied art in
many different forms

Theo van Hoytema
Cover and two pages
from *The Happy Owls* ,
H. Henry & Co,
London 1896. The
book was an English
translation of *Uilen-
geluk* by Tine van
Hoytema, C.M. van
Gogh, Amsterdam
1895

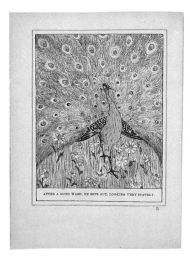

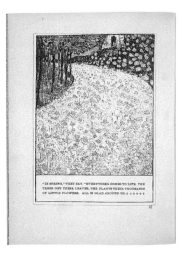

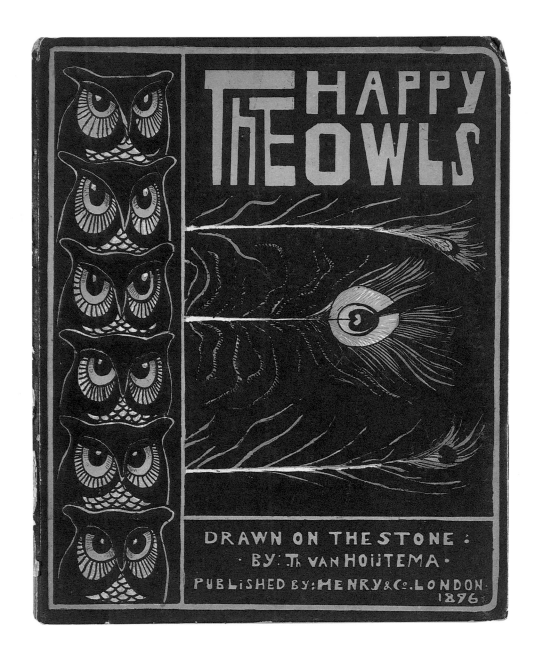

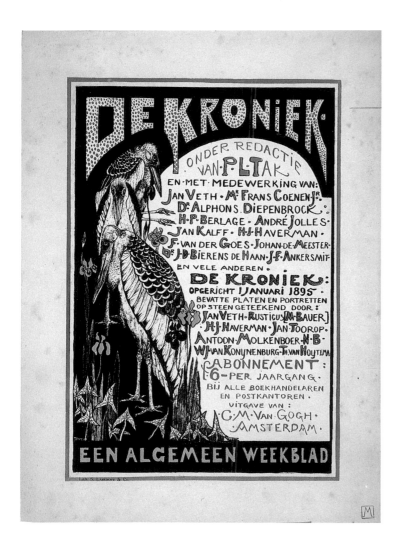

Theo van Hoytema
Advertising flyer for
the journal *De Kroniek
– Een Algemeen
Weekblad* (The
Chronicle – a General
Weekly), published
between 1895 and
1907 and edited by
P.L. Tak; C.M. van
Gogh, Amsterdam
1895

Theo van Hoytema:
birds in colour

Theo van Hoytema was a born draughtsman and illustrator, renowned in his day for his spirited and quirky depictions of animals, especially sundry feathered birds. Using a large and continually increasing collection of studies from nature, he designed murals, decorative screens and furniture in Art Nouveau style and made numerous series of lithographs in black and white and colour.

Following his academic training, he began his career by illustrating a scientific publication for the Museum of Natural History in Leiden. He learnt to make lithographs, drew some political cartoons, and in 1891 began working on a series of five children's picture books. The example and success of British children's books in full colour by Walter Crane, Randolph Caldecott and Kate Greenaway were undoubtedly an inspiration. Van Hoytema did not work with a trained lithographer, as was the practice, but drew on the lithographic stone himself. Initially his style was studiously naive, but later as he became more accomplished in the art of multi-colour printing, unexpected and complex images began to appear. As opposed to commercial chromolithographic practice, where the copyist often composed his pictures from red, yellow and blue dots, Van Hoytema used an unorthodox, direct technique in the manner of French poster artists like Toulouse-Lautrec. He drew with a crayon, a fine pen and a broad brush alternately onto the stone, using a knife to scratch out unwanted detail. The refined lines of Japanese prints and the unusual way the image is cut have here and there left their traces in Van Hoytema's children's books. Occasionally he drew both the text – mainly short pieces – and illustration on the stone, so that word and image formed a harmonious whole.

Van Hoytema's version of Hans Christian Andersen's fairy tale *The Ugly Duckling* (1893) consisted of 31 four-colour lithographs. Its daring design, with its asymmetrical compositions and pictures cut away, made it a unique and unexpected phenomenon in the book world. An English edition appeared a year later in London. His next book, a fairy tale written by his wife Tine, entitled *Uilengeluk*, was also published in London under the title *The Happy Owls*. When Van Hoytema designed an advertisement for the distinguished and progressive magazine *De Kroniek* published P.L. Tak, which had little to do with biology, he could not resist including plants and animals. A final example of his book design was Andersen's fairy tale *Two Hens*, for which Van Hoytema chose a horizontal format. The cover is powerfully eye-catching, drawn with broad lines, while the illustrations show his mastery of a wide range of lithographic drawing techniques.

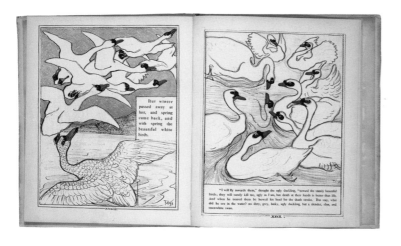

Theo van Hoytema
Spread from *The Ugly
Duckling*, H. Henry &
Co, London 1893. This
was an English
version of the Hans
Christian Andersen
tale, published by
C.M. van Gogh,
Amsterdam 1893. In
the Dutch version,
also illustrated by
Van Hoytema, the
text was drawn by
hand on the
lithographic stone

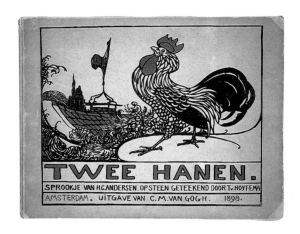

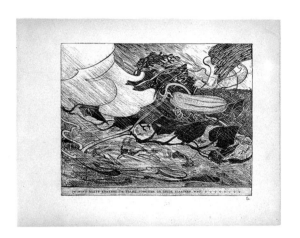

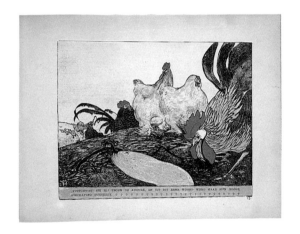

For the short-lived cultural magazine *De Tuin* (The Garden), published by Kleinmann in Haarlem, publishers who attempted to launch numerous titles on new decorative art, Van Hoytema designed a remarkable cover whereby the quite naturalistically drawn illustration ran asymmetrically over the front and back. The banner of the magazine was much more stylised – done in the manner of Lion Cachet.

Theo van Hoytema became extremely popular by dint of his annual calendars, which he began producing in 1902. He first published these himself, but after 1910 an Amsterdam wine merchant brought them out as a promotional gift. Each elongated page comprised a number of fixed elements: a drawn calendar month, an illustration of an animal in its natural habitat and, to tie it altogether, a decorative border of flora and fauna motifs – whimsically drawn and without recourse to the excessive geometric stylisation current at the time. The calendars are typical of a period in which a great interest in nature was fostered by idealists like Jacob P. Thijsse, author of the 'Verkade' biscuit fine-sticker albums, the first of which appeared in 1906. After 1910 Van Hoytema's poster designs were laid out in a more finely detailed manner, and although more monumental in conception, they became more static in appearance.

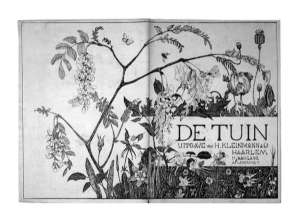

Theo van Hoytema
Cover and two pages
from *Twee hanen –
Sprookje van H.C.
Andersen* (The Two
Cocks – a Fairytale by
H.C. Andersen), C.M.
van Gogh,
Amsterdam 1898

Theo van Hoytema
Cover of the
magazine *De Tuin*
(The Garden), an
illustrated monthly
on art, literature,
music, politics, social
sciences and social
work. Edited by art
critic Albert
Plasschaert, it
appeared six times
during 1899;
Kleinmann, Haarlem
1899

Theo van Hoytema
Poster for a *Biological
exhibition in The Hague
Zoo*, Dutch Natural
History Society and
the Royal Zoological
and Botanical
Association, 1910

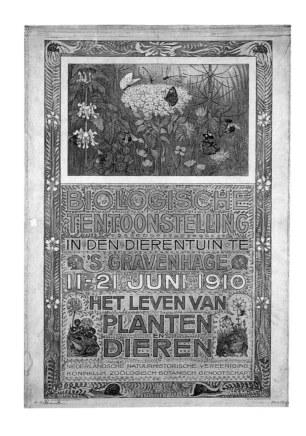

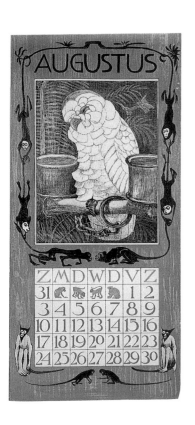

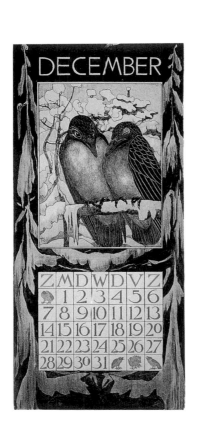

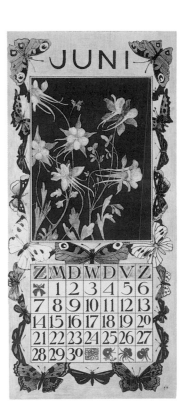

Theo van Hoytema
Calendar pages for
*August and December
1902 and June 1903*,
published privately
by Van Hoytema

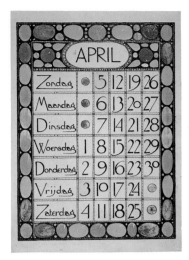

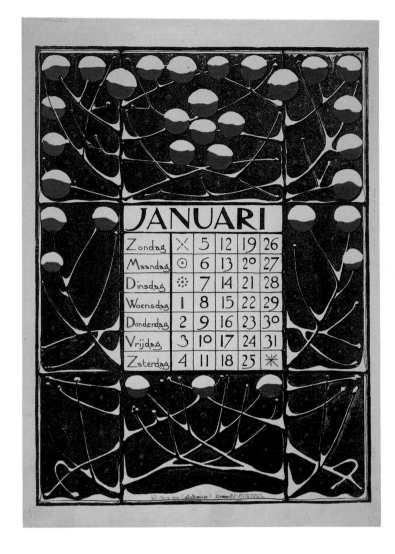

Calendars with decorative months

In the Netherlands the business world was growing apace. The modern office, with its personnel, desks, typewriters, telephones and cabinets, was an important pivot on which internal communication hinged. The number of printers responsible for letterheading, invoices and advertising matter grew correspondingly. It was customary for many printers to send their clients a calendar as a New Year's token, designed in-house and often displaying feats of typographic or printing prowess – four-colour reproductions of old masters, for instance – as evidence of their ability.

In 1895 Scheltema & Holkema's Boekhandel en Uitgeverij, an Amsterdam book retailer and publisher that had gained credibility by publishing Walter Crane, commissioned the artist T. Nieuwenhuis to design a calendar. The 1896 calendar in multi-colour lithography – Nieuwenhuis applied himself to this technique after experimenting with woodcuts in 1894 – was a fine example of the use of new art. Scheltema & Holkema continued to publish decorative calendars for many years. Their 1899 calendar was designed by Nieuwenhuis, C.A. Lion Cachet and G.W. Dijsselhof, who were each responsible for illustrating four months. All three were once pupils in the art ateliers of the neo-Gothic architect P.J.H. Cuijpers, who gave a vital boost to the revival of Dutch craft skills in the 19th century.

This calendar, however, no longer reminds us of the Gothic Middle Ages, as each of the three artists appears to have crystallised a language of form that display similarities but are individually quite different. In part their forms were developed from their decoration: Lion Cachet and Dijsselhof designed batiked, stretched wall coverings with starkly stylised flora- and fauna-like motifs, while Nieuwenhuis used woven wall decoration. The calendars were effortlessly in keeping with this.

The decorative wall calendar became all the rage as a new and acceptable form of advertising. Many artists exercised their creative powers on them, and exciting experiments with lettering and numerals as well as with decoration took place. Lithography provided illustrators with a great degree of freedom. H.P. Berlage not only built the offices of the life insurance company De Nederlanden van 1845, but each year between 1897 and 1905 designed a calendar for the company as well. The graphic artist, Georg Rueter, designed calendars for banks and printing companies and in 1900 launched his own series, which continued well into the 1920s. The earliest were published by 't Binnenhuis, an Arts and Crafts-inspired foundation of which Berlage was one of the founders. In the final analysis, the most popular were Theo van Hoytema's nature calendars.

C.A. Lion Cachet
Calendar page for
January 1900

T. Nieuwenhuis
Calendar page for
February 1900
Each designer
produced six calendar
months. Lion Cachet
confidently and
inventively combined
letterforms with
decoration, while
Nieuwenhuis forsook
his severe design
approach in order to
be more consistent
with Lion Cachet's
freer style

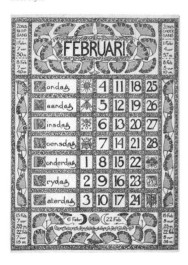

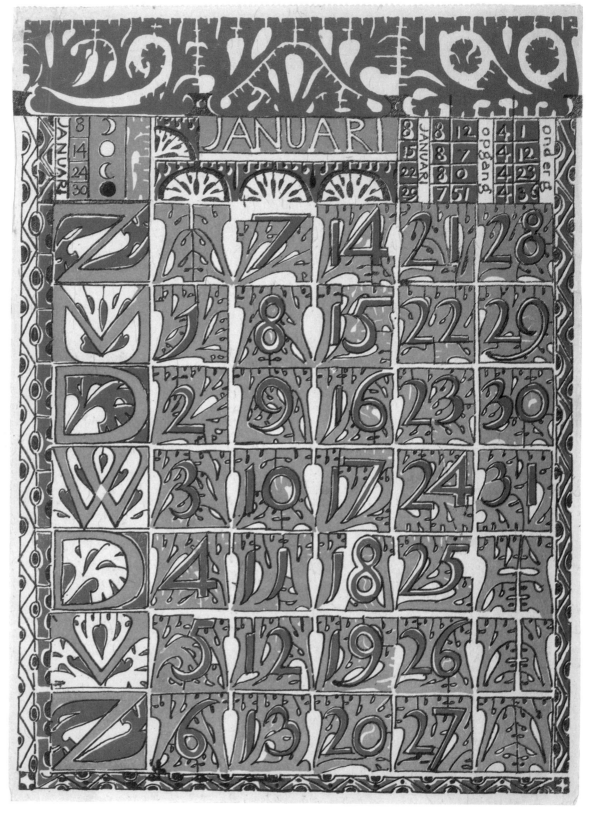

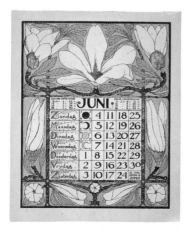

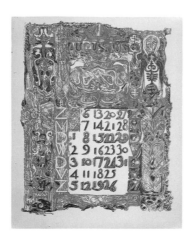

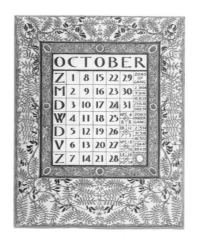

T. Nieuwenhuis
Calendar page for
June 1899

C.A. Lion Cachet
Calendar page for
August 1899

G.W. Dijsselhof
Calendar page for
October 1899
Nieuwenhuis, Lion
Cachet and Dijsselhof
produced four
calendar months each
for 1899

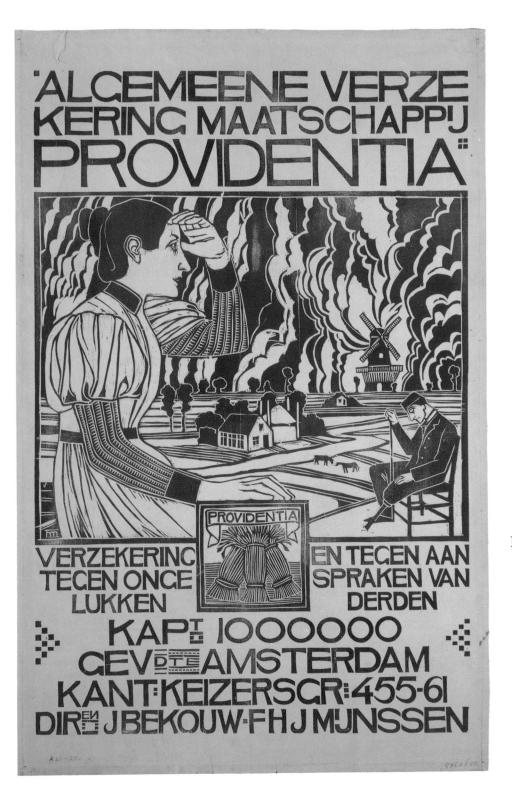

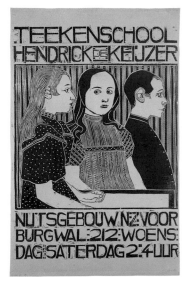

Posters

Theo Molkenboer
Poster for the
*Providentia General
Insurance Company*,
Amsterdam c.1895

Theo Molkenboer
Poster for the
*Hendrick de Keyser
Drawing School*,
Amsterdam 1894.
This is a fine early
example of the
effective use of
woodcut for a poster

Willem van
Konijnenburg
Poster for *Fop Smit
boat trips*, 1901. The
artist worked from
1896 to 1905 for the
Fop Smit & Co
Shipping Company in
Rotterdam

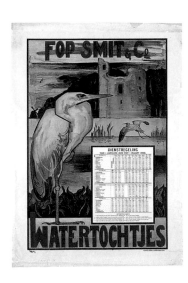

The phenomenon of the poster was developed in the mid-19th century in Europe's major cities. Special walls and poster pillars were erected in London, Paris and Berlin to advertise the circus, theatre, sporting events, exhibitions and industrial products. Whereas typographic posters were the standard manner in which to praise products or trumpet a cultural event, after 1890 imagery was also important. The technical development of colour lithography and photolithography, together with new concepts in fine art and the influence of Japanese prints, contributed to the poster becoming a serious form of applied art in the 1890s. Famous names like Henri de Toulouse-Lautrec, Jules Chéret, Théophile Steinlen, Eugène Grasset, Will Bradley, Thomas Theodor Heine and Bruno Paul were all associated with it. Posters were exhibited as works of art and collecting them gained in popularity.

Jan Toorop's salad-oil poster of 1894 was one example of how artists regarded the poster as an interesting area for experiment. The younger generation, whether gripped by the ideal of community art or enchanted by the commercial aspects of advertising, also had their chance.

Theo Molkenboer discovered new possibilities for design in the large-scale woodcut. He avoided the excessively decorative styles of Dijsselhof, Lion Cachet and Nieuwenhuis, and settled for monumental, stylised forms, with huge areas of colour and a strong contrast between black and white. His lettering is lucid and spare, without frills or ostentation.

The work of painter and architect Johann Georg van Caspel was strongly influenced by French examples. From 1896 to 1903, he designed numerous posters and other forms of advertising for the printers Steendrukkerij Senefelder in Amsterdam. His style was somewhat inconsistent: typographic posters alternating with naturalistic representation and images of muses, virgins and goddesses. Stylistic inconsistency is also characteristic of the posters designed by Jacques Zon, who was inspired by the work of the Czech-Austrian painter, Alphonse Mucha. Other painters and architects who designed posters from time to time were Johan Braakensiek, Joseph Israëls, Marius Bauer, Georg Rueter, Willem van Konijnenburg, Ferdinand Hart-Nibbrig and Johan Thorn Prikker.

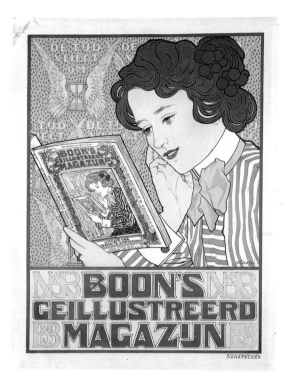

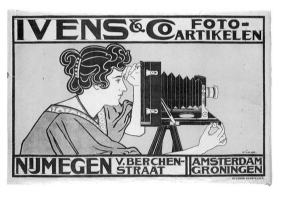

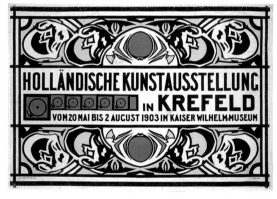

J.G. van Caspel
Poster for *Boon's Illustrated Magazine*, 1900, which first appeared in 1899 from Boon Publishers, Amsterdam

J.G. van Caspel
Poster for *Ivens & Co: Photographic Goods*, Nijmegen and Amsterdam 1899

J. Thorn Prikker
Poster for the *Holländische Kunstausstellung* (Dutch Art Exhibition), Krefeld, Germany, 1903. The whimsical and expressive abstract decoration complements Thorn Prikker's well-known batiked fabrics

F. Hart-Nibbrig
Poster for an exhibition of *Paintings and studies by F. Hart-Nibbrig*, 1901. Hart-Nibbrig was an artist who incorporated colour lithography into his graphic work

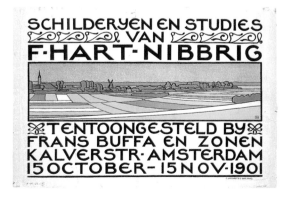

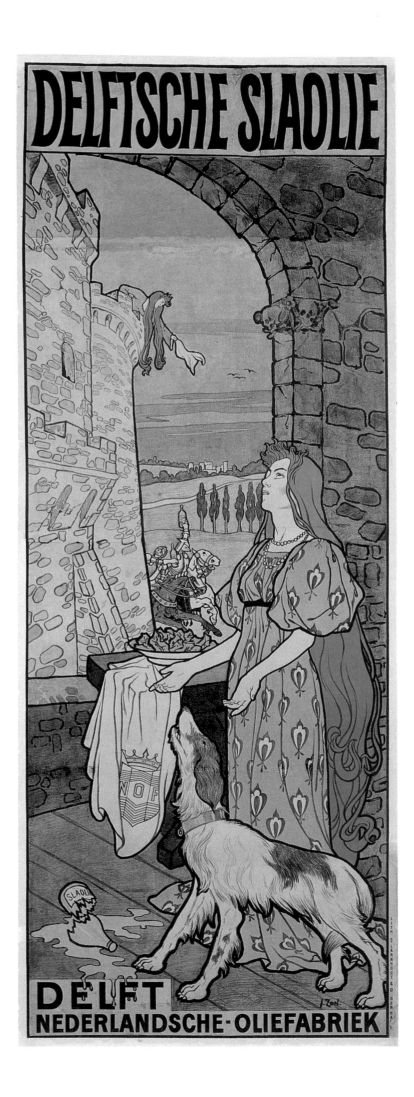

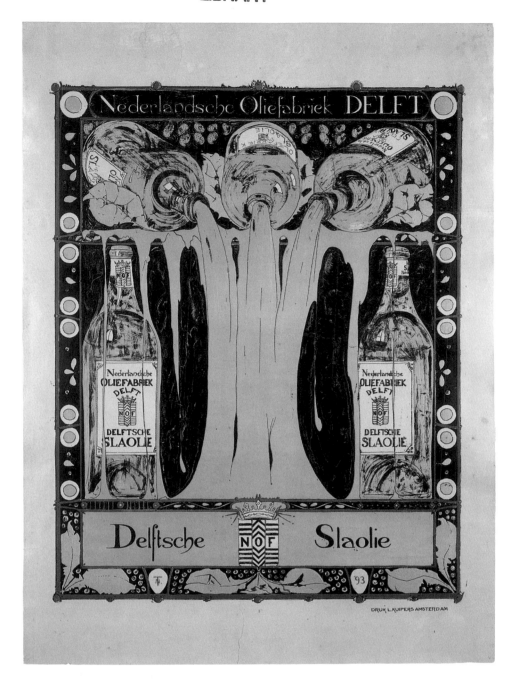

Jacob Zon
Poster for *Delft Salad
Oil*, Dutch Oil Factory
(NOF), Delft c.1895

T. Nieuwenhuis
Poster for *Delft Salad
Oil*, Dutch Oil Factory
(NOF), Delft c.1893

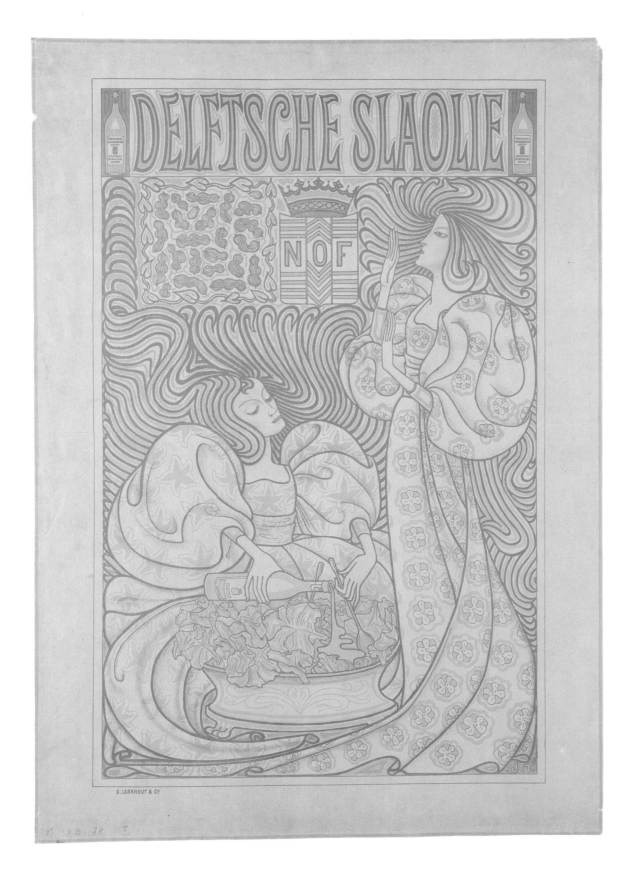

**Posters for
an oil company**

Jan Toorop
Poster for *Delft Salad*
Oil, Dutch Oil Factory
(NOF), Delft c.1893

By around 1900 the new style and everything related to it had caught the interest of industry. Company directors were made aware of socially responsible design, together with the concept that a good product could only be achieved when there was proper cooperation between employer and employee. Congenial working conditions and decent social provisions were translated by J.C. van Marken, director of the Dutch oil company (NOF) and the Dutch Gist & Spiritus Company of Delft, in the motto 'With each other, for each other'. He built a garden village for his employees and enlisted well-known artists to make 'artistic pictures', which would also be of educational value to the general public, to advertise his products.

From the series of posters produced for both factories after 1895 we can deduce the ideas people then held about advertising. The main criterion was a beautiful picture in which a story might be hidden; sometimes the image of a woman or a decorative device played a role. The posters of J. Zon bear witness to this style. Theo Nieuwenhuis displayed his decorative talent in one of the first NOF posters ever designed. Its depiction of a painting of horses by the artist G.H. Breitner caused fierce criticism from fellow designers, who derided the lack of any link whatsoever between the painting and the product it advertised. Jan Toorop also used a Symbolist work for an NOF poster, adopting it to fit the purpose.

The company's main concern with this type of advertising was to employ an artist with a reputation which would guarantee the quality of the art work, rather than to embrace the avant-garde. It was for this reason that the popular illustrator Anton Pieck was later hired (in 1947), and he produced work that followed the company line. Nevertheless, these NOF posters contributed to new trends within Dutch visual arts becoming more widely known.

Other firms besides the two Delft factories commissioned artists to create seductive works for their poster advertising. However, for more genuine advertising – that is to say, where the product was central to the poster and where illustration, colour and typography formed a unity – companies increasingly hired designers such as J.G. van Caspel and T. Molkenboer, who understood the aesthetics of commerce. In general this created a divide between a 'genuine' artist and artists who worked for companies.

R.N. Roland Holst Scroll for *Calvé, Delft*, presented to employees to mark their years of loyal service with the company, Delft 1924

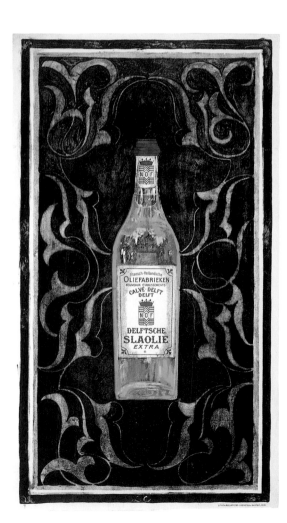

C.A. Lion Cachet Advertisement flyer for *Delft Salad Oil Extra*, Dutch Oil Factory, Calvé, Delft c.1900. For Lion Cachet this was an extremely subdued, almost naturalistic rendering

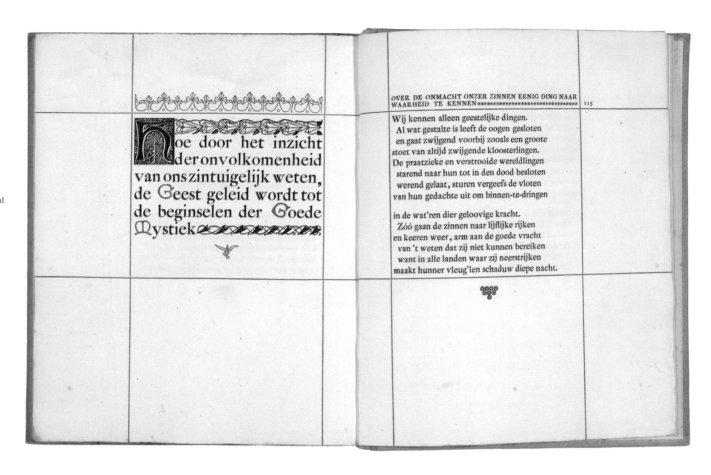

The monumental decoration of Richard N. Roland Holst

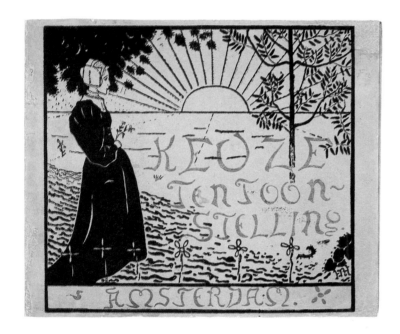

Richard N. Roland Holst was trained at the Amsterdam Rijksacademie and began by painting Impressionist-style landscapes. Inspired by the work of Vincent van Gogh and by his friend Jan Toorop, Roland Holst became more aware of the expressive potential of line and colour. He went on to concentrate on drawing, and learnt lithography. His literary bent brought him into contact with writers and poets of his own generation. In 1895 he illustrated an anthology compiled by the poet Henriëtte van der Schalk. Entitled *Sonnetten en Verzen in Terzinen*, it was extremely plain in concept. Red lines marked off the type area – harking back to the lines of a Middle Ages manuscript – and the decoration was limited to hand-cut initials and typographic flourishes.

During the winter of 1894-95 Roland Holst spent a few months in London and was befriended by Walter Crane, whose book *Claims of Decorative Art* had just been published in Dutch translation by Jan Veth. He also met William Morris's friend, T.J. Cobden-Sanderson, later the founder of the Dove Press, and he became close friends with Charles Ricketts and Charles Shannon, whose Vale Press (1896) contributed greatly to the private press movement. Their formal typographic book style, spare in decoration, is reflected in Roland Holst's own work. However, when he was not utilising letterpress but creating his own covers and posters in four-colour on stone, he reinstated decoration in abundance. Similar to Crane, he combined a socially motivated, idealistic symbolism with a monumental, decorative language of form.

Roland Holst's commitment to socialism went hand in hand with a sound technical knowledge of design, and he became particularly known for his monumental murals and his stained glass windows. This is well illustrated in his murals of 1907 in Berlage's building for the Dutch General Diamond

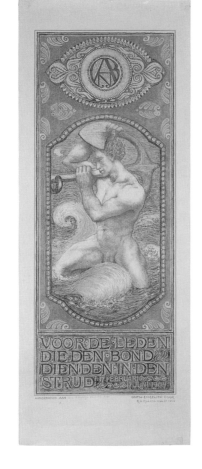

R.N. Roland Holst
Commemorative
poster for the *Dutch
General Diamond
Cutters' Federation*
(ANDB), Amsterdam
1904. The well-
organised ANDB,
under Henri Polak,
was celebrating its
10th anniversary.
The monogram is by
H.P. Berlage

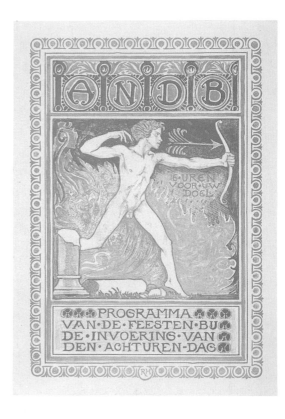

R.N. Roland Holst
Programme in
celebration of the
*Dutch General Diamond
Cutters' Federation*
achieving an eight-
hour working day,
Amsterdam 1919

Processors Union, where the human form represents abstract concepts
of 'Solidarity', 'Militancy', 'Hope' and 'Zeal'. He used the same schematised
figures in his later lithographic posters, magazine covers and
commemorative scrolls, usually combined with a wealth of decoration.
These are stylistically associated with his stained glass windows, murals and
tapestry designs.

As director of the Amsterdam Rijksacademie and a practical publicist,
Roland Holst's views greatly influenced graphic design in the Netherlands
well into the 1920s, as is evident in the work of young designers like Walter
van Diedenhoven, Jaap Jongert and Jaap Gidding.

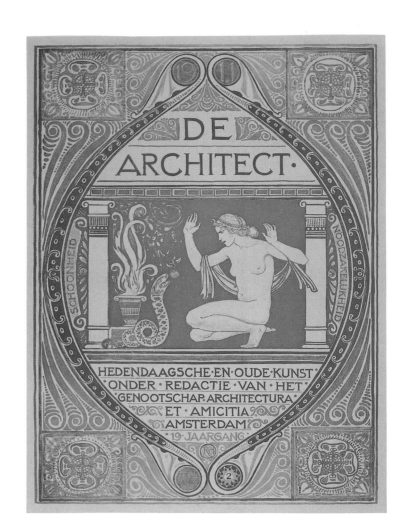

R.N. Roland Holst
Cover of *De Architect*,
vol. 18, no. 2,
Kleinmann, Haarlem
1911

Expressionism and classic typography

The combination of decorative and rational modes present in the graphic arts from the end of the 19th century persisted in various forms until the late 1920s. Embellishments might consist of Art Nouveau type, stylised decoration or picturesque, expressive forms derived from current fashions in the fine arts, as in Jan Sluijters's graphic work. Berlage's rational, architectonic style ultimately evolved into a form of Constructivism influenced by post-revolutionary changes in Russian art. In the 1920s everything was thrown into confusion, and it is often difficult to attach a date to certain art works. Hence many examples of 1930s decoration appeared to have been executed before 1920.

It was an age of eclecticism, an accumulation of ever-increasing new design possibilities largely adapted from the fine arts and architecture, from which sprang the Amsterdam School, Symbolism, Cubism, Expressionism, Constructivism and New Objectivity. Practitioners in the field of typography naturally looked at events abroad, although these were interpreted in a typically Dutch manner. Designers in the Netherlands displayed great potential in this area.

Alongside the experimentation and new opportunities, the preference for the art of classic book typography remained very strong. It was a tradition upheld, for instance, by the Joan Blaeu Society, which propagated fine-quality books printed in limited editions for book lovers. There was also the World Library, which widely disseminated finely produced and uplifting books among the Dutch reading public. Here, too, great care was taken with the typography.

In the meantime, printing techniques improved and expanded. As well as the existing hand-drawn and commercial type, more typefaces were designed and made available. As far as the image was concerned, the standard graphic techniques of wood engraving, woodcut, linocut and the drawn lithograph were used, and figures and settings still remained largely allegorical.

Traditional decoration remained as much as ever 'artistically' present as did experimental, functional, pragmatic and informative design. These two directions, the one stemming directly from the graphic craft and printing and the second influenced by painting and architecture, are visible in their various changing forms to the present day.

J.F. van Royen
Pamphlet for the
*Committee to Elect
Independent Members of
Parliament*, The Hague
1922. In this election
pamphlet Sjoerd de
Roos's typeface,
Hollandsche
Mediaeval, is used

COMITÉ VOOR DE VERKIEZING VAN ONAFHANKELIJKE KAMERLEDEN

MANIFEST

DE VERWORDING VAN DEN STRIJD der politieke partijen — in Nederland toch reeds gegroepeerd naar verouderde en dus onwerkelijke scheidingslijnen — heeft bij ons volk de opvatting bevorderd, dat behartiging van economische belangen om hun zelfs wil een begeerlijk einddoel is.

Deze averechtsche opvatting werd de bodem, waarop de politiek der huidige partijen met haar scherp gevoerde onderlinge concurrentie kon tieren. Deze bestaat voor een groot deel uit het tegen elkaar opbieden om groeps- en andere kleine belangen te behartigen, omdat dit den luidsten weerklank vindt in den tegenwoordigen geestestoestand, die met stoffelijke wenschen is overvuld. Groote richtingslijnen zijn in deze politiek teloor gegaan. En de geestelijk belangrijke, doch in getal kleine groepen van kunstenaars en intellectueelen zijn van deze politiek meer en meer het slachtoffer geworden.

Wij achten het in 's lands belang, dat, nu aldus het materieele overmatig sterk naar boven is gekomen, de juiste verhouding van stoffelijke en geestelijke waarden worde hersteld.

Noodig oordeelen wij hiertoe, dat in de volksvertegenwoordiging afgevaardigden worden gebracht, die, los van knellend partijverband of -program, in de aangelegenheden van staatsbestuur zelfstandig zullen oordeelen en handelen, hierbij geleid en uitsluitend gebonden door de overtuiging, dat in laatste instantie de GEESTELIJKE VERHEFFING van een volk het einddoel van alle politiek is.

Ook wij achten economische welvaart een met alle kracht, ook in het staatsbeleid, na te streven goed. Die welvaart kome ten bate van alle lagen der bevolking. Wij ontkennen echter, dat dit een einddoel zou zijn, en oordeelen het noodzakelijk, dat de overweging van elken economischen maatregel van deze waarheid uitga, dat economische welvaart vooral van waarde is als een der voorwaarden voor den opbloei eener krachtige beschaving.

De politiek zal, juist in deze jaren van maatschappelijke en zedelijke depressie, van noodzakelijke sterke beperking der uit-

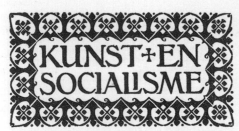

KUNST + EN
SOCIALISME

HET DOEL EN STREVEN DER
HEDENDAAGSCHE ENGELSCHE
✠   SOCIALISTEN   ✠
LEZING GEHOUDEN VOOR HET
ANTI-KLERIKAAL GENOOTSCHAP TE
✠ LEICESTER, 23 JANUARI 1883 ✠

Mijne vrienden, ik verzoek u een blik te
werpen op de verhouding tusschen de
Kunst en den Handel, waarbij ik dit laatste woord bezig in zijn meest gebruike-
lijken zin, nl. dien van het concurrentie-
stelsel, in waarheid den eenigen vorm,
waaronder men zich tegenwoordig den Handel denkt.
Terwijl er tijdperken zijn geweest in de wereldgeschie-
denis, toen de Kunst den schepter zwaaide over den
Handel, toen Kunst een zaak van gewicht was en Handel, zooals wij het woord opvatten, weinig beteekende,
zal men nu integendeel algemeen erkennen, dat de
Handel van zeer groot en de Kunst van zeer weinig
belang is. Ik zeg, dat men dit algemeen zal erkennen,

105

S.H. de Roos
Book decoration for
*William Morris, Kunst
en maatschappij*
(Art and Society),
translated by M.
Hugenholtz-Zeeven
and with a profile of
Morris written by
Henri Polak; A.B.
Soep, Amsterdam
1903. De Roos used
the French typeface
Grasset (1898) for the
text, and the drawn
decoration and
initials were designed
to tie in with this

S.H. de Roos
Cover designs for a
series of books
translated from the
Greek by P.C. Boutens:
*Aischylos – Agamemnoon,
Platoon – Phaidros,
Aischylos – Smeekelingen,
Platoon – Drinkgelag.*
The titles were
published in 1915,
1923, 1930 and 1931
respectively; W.L. &
J. Brusse, Rotterdam.
The texts were set in
Hollandsche
Mediaeval, Erasmus
and Grotius

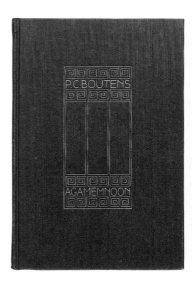

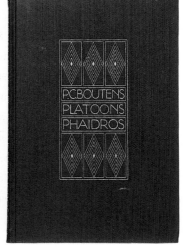

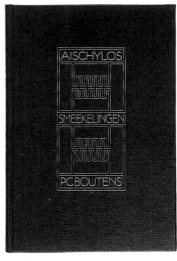

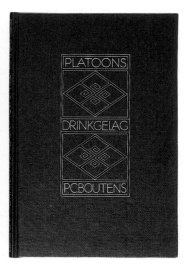

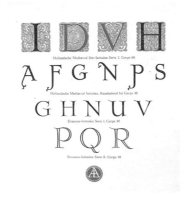

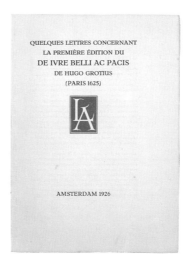

Sjoerd H. de Roos and formal decoration

Sjoerd H. de Roos was one of the most important Dutch typeface designers and writers on typography. He trained at the Rijksacademie, Amsterdam, and subsequently worked at 't Binnenhuis for Van den Bosch and Berlage, and at the same time for a tin-can manufacturer in Wormerveer. His earliest book designs appeared between 1900 and 1907. In 1907 he was appointed designer and creative advisor by the Amsterdam Type Foundry where, among other things, he designed the Bilderdijk Initials – capitals with stylised and often symmetrical floral motifs, inspired by William Morris. De Roos was greatly influenced by the ideas on art and society of Morris and Crane. In 1903, Morris's *Art and Society* was published in Dutch translation and designed by De Roos. In De Roos's decorative style can be discerned the influence of Berlage and De Bazel.

For De Roos, the typographer, the task lay in creating well-designed type and clearly defined layout. He was concerned with the 'book beautiful', expressing the hope that 'public appreciation would assist in making the work of the book printer an actual art form again'. He aimed for balance, harmony and unpretentious floral decoration. He spoke of 'the spiritualisation of the material', stating: 'It is the duty of the decorative artist through his creative ability to elevate the raw material to a high state'. This was the general purpose of community art at the time, which De Roos realised in his designs. The name of his type Hollandsche Mediaeval (1912), the first comprehensive family of Dutch typefaces of the 20th century, referred to the principles of the English Arts & Crafts Movement, which was in turn inspired by the Middle Ages. 'Mediaeval', however, was also at that period the name of a letterform based on the Venetian typeface of Nicolas Jenson and Aldus Manutius from the last quarter of the 15th century.

In 1914 Roos's new letter type was joined by Hollandsche Mediaeval Initialen, which could be used in text as coloured decorative capitals. A little later De Roos added a variation with Hollandsche Mediaeval Sier-Initialen, which harkened back to the richly decorative Bilderdijk Initials. In 1915 he designed Zilverdistel (Silver Thistle) for the Zilverdistel Press, founded by P.N. van Eyck and J.F. van Royen.

Later typefaces designed by De Roos are Erasmus (with initials) and Grotius (1926), both much used as book type by, among others, the master printers Nypels and Boosten & Stols. He also designed Meidoorn (1927), produced for the Heuvel Press, and Egmont (1932-34). De Roos published many articles with selected decorative capitals in the *Typografische Mededeelingen*, a typographic house magazine from the Amsterdam Type Foundry. And in 1914 he initiated the founding of the Typographic Library at the Amsterdam Type Foundry, which was opened to the general public with the objective of demonstrating 'everything important to do with our trade'.

DE ZILVERDISTEL WIL BOEKKUNST GEVEN. ¶ IN DEZE VERSCHIJNT HET BOEK ONS ALS EEN EENHEID, WELKE HET BUITEN HAAR niet bereikt en die het nochtans, wil het een kunstwerk zijn, bereiken móet. Deze eenheid is die van geest en materie, bepaald door de uit het begrip 'boek' af te leiden wetten en door het karakter van den geschreven inhoud. Vrucht eener kunstarbeid, is het boek in dit saamtreffen van geest en materie een nieuwe schepping, een nieuwe persoonlijkheid, die door de volmaaktheid van haar lichaam te beter de volmaaktheid van haar innerlijk doet erkennen. Als zoodanig moet het in de eerste plaats voor de constitutieve vereischten der soort eene technisch en aesthetisch op het volmaakte gerichte verwer-

2

kelijking vinden; in de tweede plaats dient Over Boek- het, als species van zijn soort, persoonlijk be- kunst. paald te zijn. Deze persoonlijke bepaling kan slechts het gevolg zijn van een zorgvuldige aanvoeling en verbeelding van datge- ne, welks middelaarschap de bestemming van het boek is: het wezen van den geschre- ven inhoud. Slechts dàn, wanneer in een boek tegelijkertijd de technische en aesthe- tische eischen van het boek op zichzelf be- vredigd zijn en de persoonlijkheid der door den inhoud bepaalde species harmonisch belichaamd is, mogen wij ons over een goed en schoon boek verheugen. ¶ Alleen op de- zen grondslag kan men spreken van boek- kunst, omdat alleen hierbij sprake is van een geestelijk voorstellen en van een vormend verwerkelijken dezer voorstelling door den maker. De geestelijke voorstelling omvat in de boekkunst chronologisch vooreerst een inzicht in het wezen en de saamstellende

3

J.F. van Royen and P.N. van Eyck Opening spread of *Over boekkunst en de Zilverdistel* (Book Design and the Silver Thistle), De Zilverdistel, The Hague 1916. It demonstrates the first use of De Roos's Zilvertype (1915); the initial was hand-drawn

Private presses

The private presses established in Britain and Germany at the end of the 19th century did not have many imitators in the Netherlands. In 1935 A.A.M. Stols, a publisher, lamented the fact that there were so few lovers of fine books in the Netherlands. He estimated the total at no more than 50, which he asserted was the reason why the Dutch illustrated book had never really flourished and why there were so few private printers in the country. It could be argued, however, that many commercial publishers such as Stols himself, as well as Nypels, Brusse and Veen, had already fulfilled this task to a great extent.

Nonetheless A.A.M. Stols, who established the Halcyon Press in 1927 to produce limited editions of books, was a great book lover. Jan van Krimpen worked on several of his special editions, though he was philosophically opposed to fine books and never viewed these editions of Stols as such. This point is illustrated here by two pages from *Dante Gabriel Rossetti, Hand and Soul*, one designed by Van Krimpen (Halcyon Press), the other by De Roos (Heuvel Press), in which the contrast in typographic viewpoint is clearly evident: the austere as opposed to the decorative. To a lesser degree, this contrast can also be seen in two pages from *François Villon, Oeuvres*, designed by Van Krimpen and Van Royen respectively. From this it is evident how Van Royen liked to pull out all the stops.

Alongside his work for the Dutch Postal, Telegraph and Telephone Service (PTT), Jean Francois van Royen devoted much of his free time to printing. From 1913 to 1922, together with P.N. van Eyck, he was at the helm of the fine book publishing firm De Zilverdistel (The Silver Thistle), at that time the only private press in the Netherlands, founded by the writers J. Greshoff and J.C. Bloem, for whom De Roos designed a special type and initials. At first Van Royen used the presses of the Enschedé firm in Haarlem and those of

J.F. van Royen Spread from *J.H. Leopold, Oostersch,* Kunera Press, The Hague 1923-24. These poems after Persian and Arabic poets were set in Disteltype, a calligraphic Roman letter by Lucien Pissarro. The title and initials were by Van Royen. This was the fourth book from the Association of Fifty, which included the decorative artist Richard Roland Holst among its members

OOSTERSCH,

DE DAUW HANGT PARE-
len aan takken en aan blaren
in kettingen en snoeren.
de kusmond van den
wind, als hij ze aan wil roeren,
doet ze ontstellen, sidderen zonder bedaren
en stort ze allen neer, de wankelbaren.

De beek is een velijnen blad,
een boek, een open letterschat,
een gulden labyrinth, waarin
de vogels komen lezen, dat
de wind beschrijft,
de wolk, die overdrijft,
zet er de stippen en de zittelteekens in.

Mijn boom heeft kweeën tegen ooft,
dat glanzend was en honingzoet.
De top is over en het pad
ligt afwaarts voerend voor mijn voet.

Gedronken is wat van den wijn
de klare opperbloesem is.
Er rest mij nu nog eene slok,
een slok, die niets dan droesem is.

4

Een lichte lente is de jeugd,
een winter is de ouderdom,
Maar is een winter zonder meer
en brengt geen nieuwe lent' weerom.

Waar zijn de vrienden van voorheen
in fleur en frischheid hunner jaren?
Waar zijn de bruiden met de krans
en de juweelen in de haren?

Onder de aarde hebben ze al
hun tent gebracht en heengebeurd
En nu de zefir spelend heeft
de winterwa vaneengescheurd.

Nu tilt de eerste amandelbloem
een hoofdje popelend en stout.
Een tenger, zilveren vrouwenlijf
te voorschijn uit het doodkischout.

En de violen zijn een lok
van zwart en muskusgeurend haar,
Dat viel, o liefste, liefste, en zeeg
onder der dagen valsche schaar.

Ik meen, de lelie is een kind,
een feeënkind en opgeleid
Tot hooge kieschheid van gevoel
en adel van welsprekendheid.

5

G.W. van der Wiel & Co, an Arnhem printers. But then in 1915 he bought
an Albion press in England and from then on maintained close contact
with some of the private publishers there, such as the Eragny Press, owned
by Lucien Pissarro, and the Dove Press belonging to T.J. Cobden-Sanderson.

In 1922 Van Royen himself began publishing fine books for book lovers
under the name Kunera Press, the only other Dutch private press. Van Royen
contributed significantly to typography and the 'book beautiful'. He wrote
copiously about the subject and demonstrated his talent for management in
the worlds of art and the industrial arts. In 1926 Sjoerd De Roos established
his Heuvel Press, for which he developed a new type, Meidoorn (Hawthorn).
He ran it for nine years before transferring the press to Duwaer, an
Amsterdam printer, in 1935.

Jan van Krimpen
Spread from *François
Villon, Oeuvres*, 1929,
a volume from the
fine book series first
published in 1927 by
A.A.M. Stols and
printed by Enschedé
in Haarlem for the
Halcyon Press. Van
Krimpen used a 15th-
century Gothic letter
by an unknown type-
cutter from
Enschedé's historic
collection. The titles
and initials were
hand-drawn

J.F. van Royen
Spread from *François
Villon, Oeuvres*, set in
Pissarro's Disteltype;
Kunera Press, The
Hague 1926

Jan van Krimpen
Spread from *Dante
Gabriel Rossetti, Hand
and Soul*. This fantasy
about an Italian artist
named Chiaro
dell'Erma dating from
1850 was often
reprinted in fine book
form; Enschedé for
the Halcyon Press,
Haarlem 1928. The
initials are hand-
drawn

S.H. de Roos
*Dante Gabriel Rossetti,
Hand and Soul* set
in Meidoorn with
a drawn initial
coloured in blue;
Heuvelpers,
Hilversum 1929

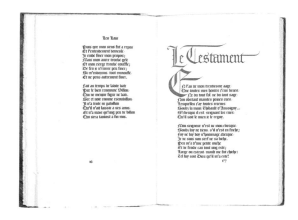

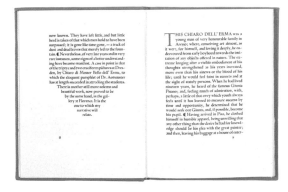

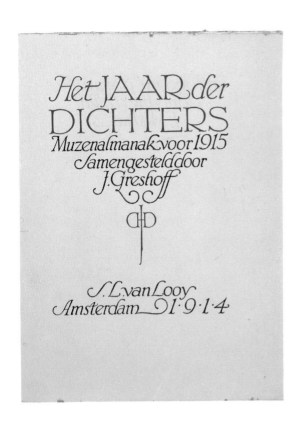

Jan van Krimpen
Title page for *Jan Greshoff, Het jaar der dichters, Muzenalmanak voor 1915* (The Year of the Poets: an Almanac of the Muses for 1915), S.L. van Looy, Amsterdam 1914. This was the fifth edition of the yearbook, which had a German-inspired, hand-drawn title page

Jan van Krimpen

Jan van Krimpen was an internationally recognised Dutch typeface designer. He began his career in 1912 as typographer and a contributor to *De Witte Mier* (The White Ant) journal, published by De Zilverdistel, the private press of the writers Greshoff, Bloem and Van Eijck. The publication aimed to inform and draw attention to good typography. Van Royen, a later client of Van Krimpen's, also wrote in the journal, attacking the standard of office government printed matter. In 1915 Van Krimpen began working for himself as a typeface designer and bookbinder, while in 1920 together with Bloem, Greshoff and Van Nijlen he formed the editorial staff working on a series of publications distributed under the *Palladium* title. In these he supported the notion of the well-designed book, printed on high-quality paper with beautiful typefaces, without undue decoration or any deliberate aesthetic intentions. He was in short an orthodox thinker and against typographic experimentation.

By way of commissions to design the typography for postage stamps – the most famous of which was the number stamp he designed in 1946 – he came into contact with the printing firm of Joh. Enschedé & Son in Haarlem, which asked him to design a type. This resulted in Lutetia, named after the Latin for Paris, where it was shown at the Art Deco exhibition in 1925. It was Enschedé's first book type of the century, and in 1925 Van Krimpen was taken on by the company. Other typefaces followed, including Romanée (1929) and Romulus (1931). In 1926 Van Krimpen became friendly with the English typographer, Stanley Morison, who suggested that he should write an essay, 'Typography in Holland', for *The Fleuron* (no. VII). Van Krimpen set down his ideas on the craft and criticised the work of De Roos as being too decorative. His opinion in this essay is clear: 'the book is really a book only when it has

shaken itself free from the influence of the decorative artist'. In 1947 a monograph by John Dreyfus was published on Van Krimpen's work. Despite the graceful decoration, designed by Van Krimpen, the typeface chosen for the text was spare. However, it had an evident practical function with regard to legibility, and a pleasing appearance on the page.

Jan van Krimpen
Pages from the
Palladium Series of
books, edited by J.C.
Bloem, Jan Greshoff
and Jan van Nijlen;
Hijman, Stenfert
Kroese & Van der
Zande, Arnhem 1917.
Printed by G.J. van
Amerongen,
Amersfoort.
Illustrated here are
André Jolles, Idylle,
1924, and *P.N. van
Eyck, Inkeer*

(Repentance), 1922.
The series was typeset
in Caslon with hand-
drawn titles and
initials

THE
POEMS OF
M·A·R·Y
QUEEN OF
SCOTS

DE PEN OP PAPIER

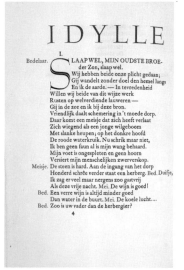

IDYLLE

INKEER

Jan van Krimpen
Cover of *The Poems of
Mary Queen of Scots to
the Earl of Bothwell,*
Enschedé, Haarlem
1932. Set in Van
Krimpen's Romanée,
which Enschedé
introduced in 1929

Jan van Krimpen
Page from *Martinus
Nijhoff, De pen op papier*
(The Pen on Paper),
set in Lutetia and
Lutetia Italic;
Enschedé, Haarlem
1927

L'ART HOLLANDAIS
À L'EXPOSITION INTERNATIONALE
DES ARTS DÉCORATIFS
ET INDUSTRIELS
MODERNES
PARIS
1925

Jan van Krimpen
Title and page from
*L'Art Hollandais à
l'Exposition
Internationale des Arts
Décoratifs et Industriels
Modernes*, Paris 1925.
Van Krimpen's
Lutetia is here used
for the first time – in
the same year as
Enschedé introduced
it. The open capitals
were hand-drawn

C'EST de 1880 qu'en Hollande on fait partir
la grande rénovation artistique. Elle
fut surtout sensible à cette date dans le domaine de
la littérature, mais un mouvement parallèle dans les
arts industriels s'était déjà dessiné en Angleterre
sous l'inspiration de William Morris, et ne tarda
guère à se répandre en Europe.
Il convient toutefois de signaler un courant précurseur: le rationalisme, dont Viollet-le-Duc fut l'initiateur en France et Cuypers l'in-
troducteur en Hollande. En architecture ce rationalisme, utilisant
les formes gothiques traditionnelles, fut confusément interprété.
On prêta en effet plus d'attention à l'expression formelle du go-
thique qu'au solide principe de construction rationnelle sur lequel
il s'appuyait. Cuypers notamment remit en vogue la voûte et cher-
cha en outre à obtenir de nouveau dans les divers métiers une pure
exécution du détail.
C'était là une tâche fort difficile, exigeant de nombreuses années de
préparation, ne permettant d'ailleurs pas d'espérer la possibilité
de porter la pratique professionnelle au degré de perfection qu'elle
atteignit au moyen-âge. Cuypers ne la poussa pas plus avant parce
que, s'il faisait lui-même les dessins, il n'exécutait pas de ses propres
mains. Elle fut reprise par des artistes œuvrant dans diverses branches des arts industriels et qui s'inspirèrent des idées de William
Morris et de Semper. Les sculpteurs taillèrent eux-mêmes leurs
statues dans le bois ou la pierre, les céramistes moulèrent et tour-
nèrent leurs vases, procédèrent à leur émaillage et à leur cuisson,
les fresquistes et les peintres verriers exécutèrent leurs travaux,
les artisans du batik, les graveurs, les imprimeurs, les tisserands et
les reliurs étudièrent leur métier, se familiarisèrent avec les maté-
riaux et la technique et consacrèrent toute leur activité à l'exercice
8

Posters for art and industry

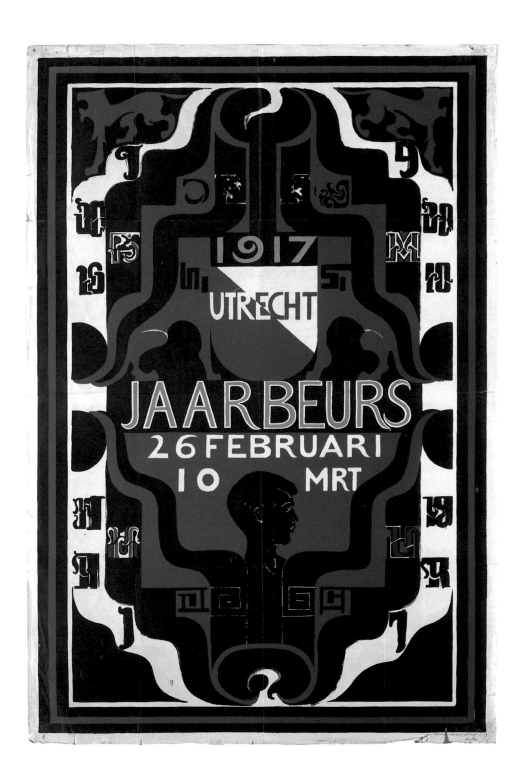

C.A. Lion Cachet
Poster for the *Trade Fair*, Utrecht 1917, in which the swirling, semi-abstract shapes are a late echo of Art Nouveau

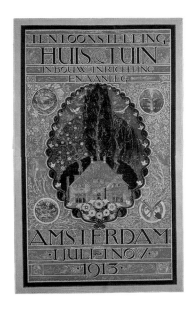

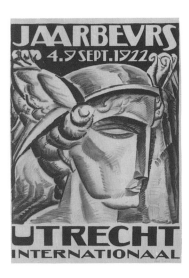

Walter van Diedenhoven
Poster for an *Exhibition on homes and gardens*, Amsterdam 1913. In this symmetrical composition, letter, decoration and romantic illustration are all given equal emphasis

Leo Gestel
Poster for the annual Utrecht *Trade Fair*, 1922. Here Mercury, the god of commerce, has been treated in the Cubist style of the Bergen School of North Holland

While the 1900s saw great diversity of style in poster art, partly due to the use of techniques such as lithography or woodcut, and partly due to the many stylistic viewpoints of the designers concerned, by the second decade of the twentieth century design had begun to stagnate. On the one hand were the highly decorative effects of the industrial arts, on the other the much freer approach of the painters. Roland Holst's influence is present everywhere; for example, in the work of Walter van Diedenhoven and others, text and flat representation are symmetrically embedded in an all-embracing, finely detailed and drawn decoration. Roland Holst was also known for his well-designed letterforms and in art education increasing attention was paid to calligraphy, following the foreign influences of Edward Johnston and Anna Simons, who reinstated the Renaissance letter, and Rudolf von Larisch, who was dedicated to a more decorative viewpoint.

The typographic posters of Johan Briedé and Jaap Gidding are examples of divergent viewpoints on the function of type. With Briedé, who had studied at the academies in Rotterdam and The Hague, we see a personal variation on classic type design, separated from border decoration and similar to book typography. With Gidding, who studied both in Rotterdam and Munich, there is a tendency to make the type a decorative element in itself and to manipulate the foreground and background after the example of Alfred Roller and Koloman Moser of the Wiener Werkstätte.

In 1917 the Royal Dutch Trade Fair opened its doors. Its first poster, the result of a closed competition, was by Lion Cachet and showed his familiar swirling, almost abstract decoration. Five years later Leo Gestel produced a poster with an allegorical portrait of the god Mercury, a theme that such other designers as Louis Raemaekers, P.A.H. Hofman and Henri Pieck would also take up. As a painter Gestel worked in a modified version of Cubism, similar to that adopted in the Netherlands under the influence of the painter Le Fauconnier, particularly among the so-called Bergen School of painters to which Gestel belonged.

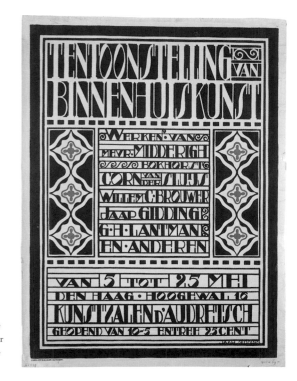

Jaap Gidding
Poster *Exhibition of Interior Design*, D'Audretsch Art Rooms, The Hague 1919. Gidding unites positive and negative letterforms with their background to create a decorative weave

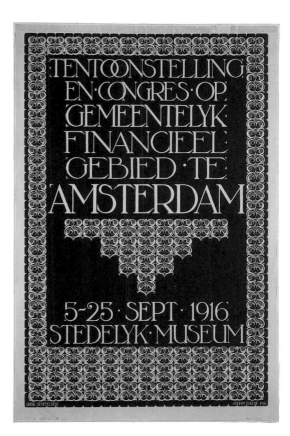

J. Briedé
Poster for an *Exhibition and conference on municipal finances in Amsterdam*, Stedelijk Museum, Amsterdam 1916. Briedé concentrates on drawn letterforms and a repetitive flat decoration

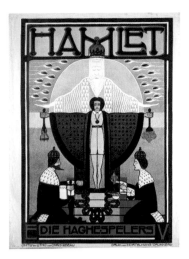

Chris Lebeau
Poster for *Shakespeare,
Hamlet*, 1914, for the
third production by
Eduard Verkade's Die
Haghespelers theatre
group. Lebeau also
created his first
theatre décors for
this play

Chris Lebeau
Poster for *Shakespeare,
Hamlet*, 1915. An eye-
catching poster and
one of several Lebeau
designed for Eduard
Verkade for the 1915-
1916 theatre season

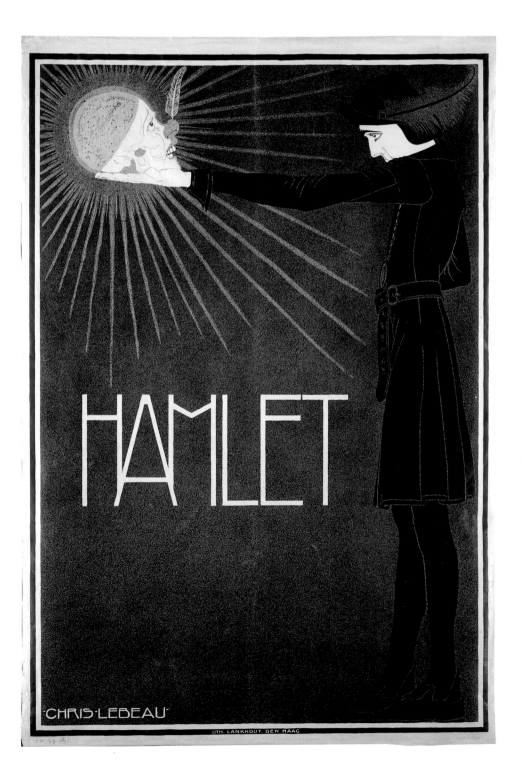

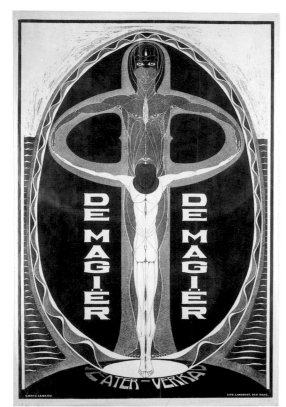

Chris Lebeau
Poster for *Chesterton*,
De Magiër (The
Magician), 1915, for
Eduard Verkade's
theatre group. An owl
is depicted on the
chest of the magician
as a symbol of
wisdom

Chris Lebeau was a multi-talented artist and artisan. Originally from an anarchist and socialist working-class family, he expressed his political convictions in his work. On leaving school, Lebeau was trained in decorative painting at Quellinus, the Amsterdam school for art and design. In 1899 he took drawing lessons at the Vâhana School, partly founded by Lauweriks and De Bazel, where the teaching of skills and crafts were given a theosophical basis, or were started from strictly geometric principles. All of Lebeau's further work revealed the influence of his quasi-mystical training.

Lebeau's career was distinguished by the many commissions he received for batik printing. Following this period, Lebeau designed carpets and later, from 1903 onwards, damask for the Van Dissel firm in Eindhoven. He also designed the company's catalogues and other advertising material. After 1914 he created posters and décor for Eduard Verkade's theatre group, with whom he travelled to Indonesia, once the Dutch East Indies. Lebeau illustrated books, produced posters, designed wallpaper, glass and ceramics and decorated the wedding hall of Amsterdam's town hall with paintings, stained glass windows and fabrics. A popular graphic work was his postage stamp depicting a dove – a clear political statement for governmental printed matter – designed for the Dutch post office in 1924 and which continued in use for 24 years. Having had other designs turned down in a competition in 1920, these were then accepted for an airmail stamp issued in 1921, and already show the dove. In 1928 Lebeau produced two more airmail stamps depicting the portraits of Koppen and Thomassen, two Dutch aviation pioneers. He was also a well-established portrait artist.

Lebeau's graphic work, including his two-dimensional designs for wallpaper and damask, was characterised by decorative elements or figures that were always incorporated into a geometric pattern. Hence his work was frequently close to that of De Bazel or Berlage, although in its sometimes overly decorative and thus illegible typography it also bears similarities to the Amsterdam School. His work demonstrates an enormous consistency and constraint that over the years began to seem old-fashioned, especially in relation to new developments, but this was not unusual in the Netherlands of the 1920s and 1930s.

Chris Lebeau
Postage stamp *The
Flying Dove*, PTT (Post
Office), The Hague
1924

Chris Lebeau

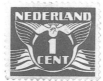

Chris Lebeau
Poster for the *William
Brok Fine Art Gallery*,
Hilversum 1919,
depicting a visitor
looking through his
hands at a painting

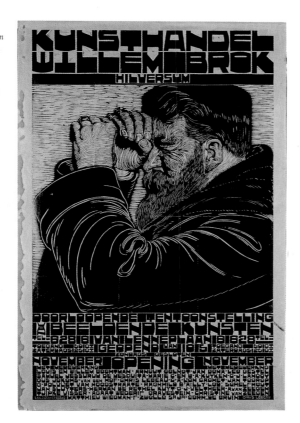

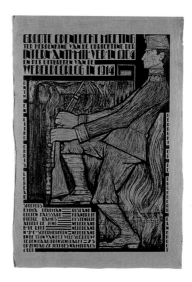

Chris Lebeau
Poster for the *Large
open-air meeting to
mark the founding of
the International Anti-
Military Society in the
Netherlands*
Amsterdam 1924.
In this monumental
print, the anarchic
Lebeau gives
prominence to the
image of a broken
rifle

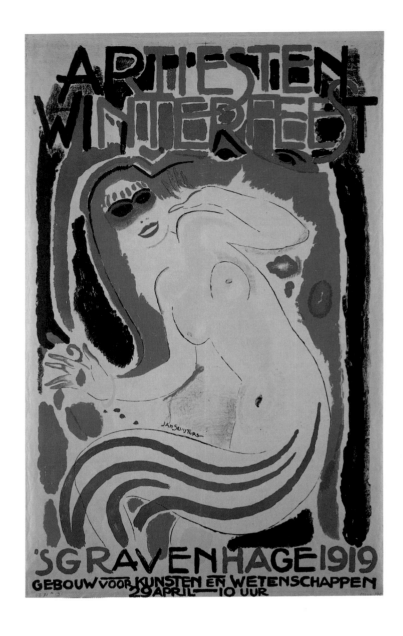

Posters by painters

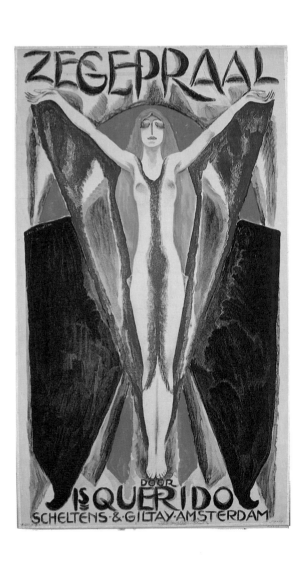

Jan Sluijters
Poster for the *Artists'
Winter Party*,
Amsterdam 1919.
A playful and
decorative
composition from the
period when Sluijters
was becoming
renowned for his
erotic naked figures

Jan Sluijters
Poster to mark the
second reprint of
Israël Querido's novel
Zegepraal (Triumph),
Scheltens & Giltay,
Amsterdam 1923.
The author was an
early admirer of
Sluijters' work

In courses similar to those given at the Amsterdam Rijksacademie, the division between fine art and applied art was evidently becoming greater under Roland Holst's influence. Graphic art, however, was by no means confined to decorative artists. Painters like Jan Sluijters, Willy Sluiter and Piet van der Hem, for instance, produced political cartoons for the newspaper *De Nieuwe Amsterdammer* as well as covers and illustrations for books, magazines and posters.

Sluijters's work betrayed his preference for French painting, for such artists as Toulouse-Lautrec and Van Gogh, and for the rich colours of Fauvism – all of which found expression in his posters. His lithographic poster, *Artists' Winter Party*, in particular shows a masterly use of swirling lines and expressive colours. The same fluency is evident in the posters he designed for the Amsterdam publishers Scheltens & Giltay: monumental-symbolic posters like *Triumph*, as well as slightly more vulgar ones for a series of novels by Is. Querido about Amsterdam's oldest neighbourhood, the Jordaan. Less masterly, but having a certain fashionable lightheartedness, were the posters of the somewhat older painter, Willy Sluiter, and the caricature illustrations of Piet van der Hem.

The Brussels painter Raoul Hynckes was among the many Belgian artists who sought exile in neutral Holland at the outbreak of the First World War. He was a painter of luminous landscapes who, in the 1930s, became celebrated as a Magical Realist with a preference for depicting skulls. During the last years of the war and shortly thereafter, the Amsterdam lithographers Kotting commissioned a series of lithographic posters. Hynckes's first posters were caricatures, but he soon arrived at a linear style with large colour shapes that sometimes suggested great depth, as in *The Westlands Steam Train*, or flat surfaces as in the *Regata* poster. He also designed theatre posters and illustrated children's books and magazines for the Workers' Youth Federation, which revealed a certain affinity with the decorative style and pastel shades of Art Deco.

Raoul Hynckes
Poster for *The Westlands steam train*, 1920

Willy Sluiter
Exhibition poster for an *Exhibition at the Hotel Hamdorff, Laren, 1916*; the hotel was famous for its exhibitions and parties for artists

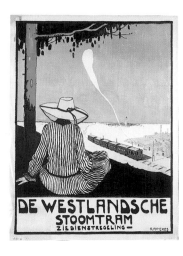

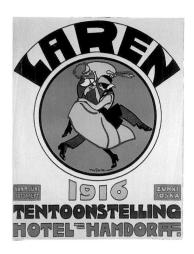

Raoul Hynckes
Poster for *Regata: An exhibition of advertising and graphic work*, Amsterdam 1919

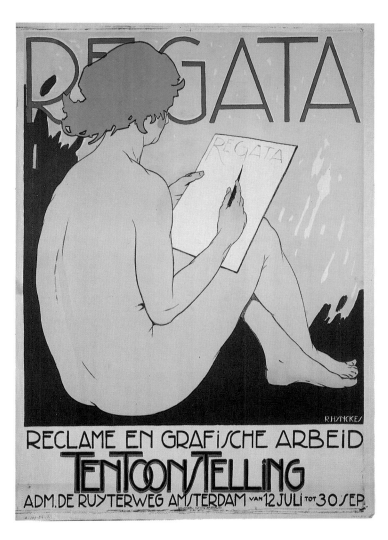

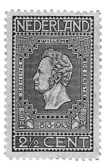

K.P.C. de Bazel
Jubilee stamp, PTT (Post
Office), The Hague
1913, copper
engraving by J.J.
Aarts. One of a set of
12 postage stamps
depicting four
monarchs, designed
to commemorate
the centenary of the
kingdom of the
Netherlands

Van Royen and the Dutch PTT

M.W. de Klerk,
S.H. de Roos,
N.J. van der Vecht
Three *Postage stamps*,
PTT (Post Office), The
Hague 1923, winners
of a competition

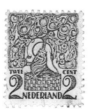

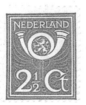

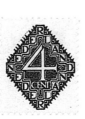

Early in the 20th century and after studying law, Jean François van Royen worked for Martinus Nijhoff, a publisher in The Hague, and there he became greatly interested in new book design and the printing trade, which he was later to practise so fervently. He kept abreast of developments in literature, the fine arts and industrial design, and this laid the foundation for his search for harmonious relations between aesthetics and intellectualism. For him, life's moral obligations went hand in hand with a moral obligation towards good design. In 1904 he began working as a lawyer for the Staatsbedrijf der PTT (the state-run Postal, Telegraph and Telephone service) and saw there was much to improve in aesthetic terms. Accordingly he championed an attractive working environment, believing that this would produce better results, and that the company as well as individual workers would be placed on a higher plane. At the PTT Van Royen acted as an intermediary between the company and numerous artists, who through him received many commissions for graphic and industrial design.

In 1912 Van Royen criticised the government's standard typefaces and a year later attempted to introduce the recently designed Hollandsche Mediaeval from De Roos. This effort failed, but he did bring in a new design policy for postage stamps. In 1913 a series of Jubilee postage stamps designed by the architect K.P.C. de Bazel were issued to commemorate the centenary of the Kingdom of the Netherlands. It was a victory for Van Royen, who wrote to the designer: 'It is fine to think that we now at last have something beautiful in this field'.

Following the First World War, Van Royen, as general secretary of the board of directors, was able to bring about further improvements within the PTT in terms of better graphic design of stationery, annual reports, advertising and lettering on delivery vans and buildings. Moreover, he helped improve the look of postboxes, signage, office interiors and furniture and also influenced the architecture of new PTT buildings, which after 1920 were built by the Ministry of Housing and Construction. The latter were chiefly designed by architects of the so-called Amsterdam School. In 1919 Van Royen became a member of the Netherlands Association for Crafts and Industrial Art (VANK) and in 1922 was appointed its chairman. In this duel capacity he was very important to the PTT and to Dutch industrial art in general. He exercised his fine aesthetic judgement and managerial qualities on many other committees and boards in the field of the fine arts and industrial design. However, Van Royen's biggest passion was for beautiful books and for the art of printing. Despite his openness towards new movements in art and industrial design in the 1920s, Van Royen remained attached to an aesthetic typified by Morris and Crane.

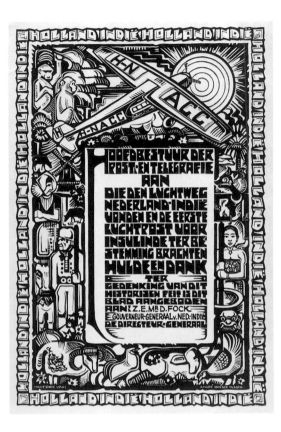

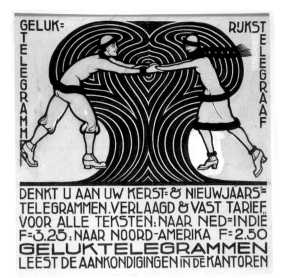

Chris Lebeau
Advertisement flyer
for *Greetings telegrams*,
PTT, The Hague 1927

André van der Vossen
Poster to celebrate
the first airmail flight
from *Holland to the*
Dutch East Indies, PTT
(Post Office), The
Hague 1924

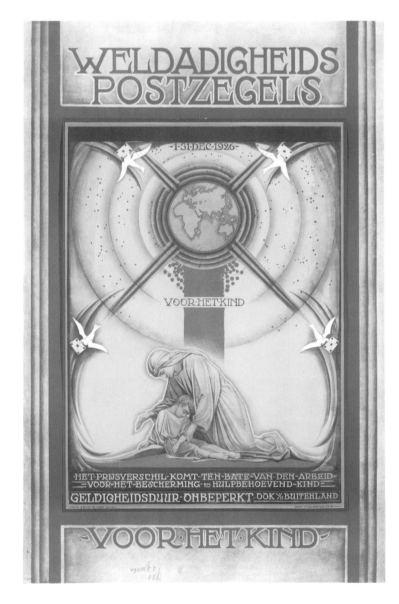

Anton Molkenboer
Advertisement flyer
for *Child Welfare*
Postage Stamps, PTT,
The Hague 1927

Type, line and form

Even before the First World War poets and painters were expressing disapproval of the academic tradition in literature and the fine arts, and this had far reaching consequences for the Dutch reading and viewing public. Poets like Mallarmé, Marinetti and Apollinaire, painters like Picasso, Duchamp and Picabia and many other iconoclasts and thinkers initiated a creative process of destruction and renewal in which the boundaries between painting, architecture, literature and music became blurred. The growing number of new media and graphic techniques such as photography, film, book and magazine typography and advertising, were also involved.

The war years made international links between artists virtually impossible. The fact that in 1916 the German writer Hugo Ball had set up his Cabaret Voltaire in Zürich, which quickly became an international gathering point for avant-garde painters and poets, dawned very slowly on the neutral Dutch. It was printed matter in the form of pamphlets and one-man publications like *Cabaret Voltaire* and *Bulletin Dada* that finally disseminated the new ideas throughout Europe.

In 1917 and 1918 the first issues of two magazines, entitled *De Stijl* and *Wendingen*, appeared in the Netherlands and promised to be a yardstick for the new developments. A manifesto published in *De Stijl* magazine in 1918 by the painter Theo van Doesburg, called for an 'international oneness in Living, Art and Culture'; and for individualism and a new vision to set against prevailing dogmas. These new concepts were already visible in the paintings of Piet Mondrian, Bart van der Leck and Vilmos Huszár, and were extended eventually to architectural form. Through a return to the most elementary shapes and colours, a new purified vision and new spatial concepts were brought into force. These precepts were also applied to poetry in an attempt to attain a 'constructive oneness regarding content and form'.

The journal *Wendingen*, published by the architect H.T. Wijdeveld, proposed no such plan of action. It adhered to the views held by the Amsterdam School architects, which Van Doesburg so detested, and which were breathing new life into the decorative aspects of the architectural reform of a previous generation. *Wendingen* was also a sumptuously produced reflection of the many contradictory movements and opinions that typified the 1920s. For instance in the autumn of 1922, Theo van Doesburg published as a full *De Stijl* issue El Lissitzky's *Suprematisch worden van twee kwadraten* – the Dutch version of an experimental picture book that had already appeared in Berlin, with a lithograph by Lissitzky on the cover.

The post-war years made travelling around Europe easier and Van Doesburg's international contacts quickly increased. In 1919 he became familiar with French and German Dadaist publications and between December 1920 and November 1921 he made an extended trip through Germany, Belgium, France and Italy, where he made contact with numerous young artists. The outcome was the publication of his own Dadaist magazine, *Mécano*, in which he introduced to the Netherlands the work of such artists as Kurt Schwitters, whose anarchistic way with word and image influenced future graphic design.

In the 1920s magazines like these were an important means of communication for the visual arts. Even a loner such as H.N. Werkman could be part of the international network with his publication *The Next Call*. In such journals as *Pasmo*, *Ma*, *G*, and *Merz*, an international movement that dubbed itself the New Typography emerged. It included Jan Tschichold, László Moholy-Nagy, Kurt Schwitters, Karel Teige and Piet Zwart, and was to change radically the image of typography.

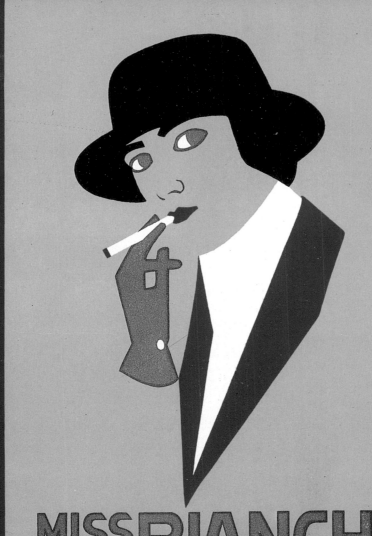

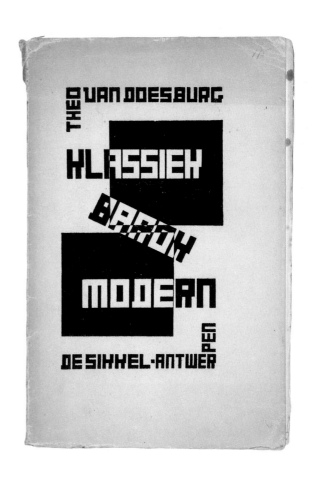

Theo van Doesburg
Cover of a booklet
Theo van Doesburg,
Klassiek Barok Modern,
De Sikkel, Antwerp
1920

Theo van Doesburg, Vilmos Huszár and De Stijl

Theo van Doesburg
and Vilmos Huszár
Cover of *De Stijl*
– a monthly for
contemporary visual
arts, vol. 1, no. 2;
Leiden 1917. The
'block' letters of the
masthead are in
keeping with
Huszár's abstract
compositional style

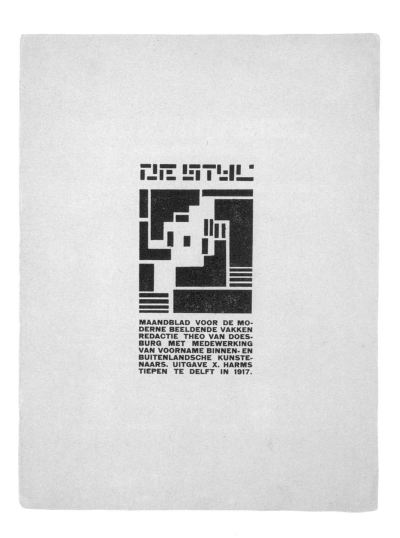

In 1917 Theo van Doesburg stepped into the limelight as editor-in-chief of the new magazine *De Stijl*, which until his death in 1931 was the international mouthpiece of the avant-garde. This avant-garde embraced a wide variety of styles. There was Mondrian's Neo-Plastic paintings, El Lissitzky's Constructivist Utopian works, Kurt Schwitters' Dadaist collages and poems and Gerrit Rietveld's chairs. The cover of the first issue was accompanied by the following text: 'The typographic decoration between title and cover text is by the Hungarian artist Vilmos Huszár. It is borrowed from a woodcut, which though intended to be purely fine art has been used here to form an aesthetic and harmonious whole with the printing.' Thus type and image were consciously attuned.

Vilmos Huszár settled in the Netherlands in 1919. As a painter he experimented with all sorts of modern styles and in 1916 tried to paint abstract compositions in the manner of Van der Leck. An example of this is the vignette that he designed for the cover of *De Stijl*, the publication with which he was involved from its inception. More so than Van Doesburg, he took risks and bridged the gap between the fine and applied arts by designing exhibition stands, a lamp, a clock, marionettes, interiors and fabrics with coloured areas and horizontal and vertical lines. Huszár also designed type matter for such artistic associations as the VANK, The Hague's Kunstkring and Filmliga, as well as for commercial advertising – largely posters, murals, advertising vehicles and billboards for the Miss Blanche cigarette brand. In these, geometric forms and lines took a semi-abstract or stylised figurative shape that was frequently close to Van der Leck's work.

Van Doesburg's elementary upper case alphabet, designed for his own use, has a basic grid of 5 × 5 units. He regarded the fundamental shape of the type as capable of being stretched in a horizontal or vertical direction. This was in marked contrast to classic typography, in which the proportions of the basic form are unassailable and at best can only be enlarged or made smaller in its totality. By changing the square grid into a rectangle, sometimes to a 2:3 ratio and then to one of 5:4, he was able to press long and short lines of text into a rectangular frame, while at the same time creating a visually unified image. His alphabet was a starting point when he designed the cover for the booklet *Klassiek Barok Modern*, and he also adopted it for some posters.

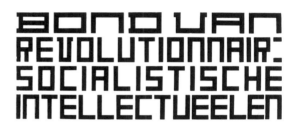

Theo van Doesburg
Letterhead for the
*Union of Revolutionary
Socialists*, 1919. Van
Doesburg designed a
series of capitals
based on a grid of
5 × 5 rectangles,
which could lie, stand
or form a square and
thus form a series of
letterforms varying
from narrow to wide

Theo van Doesburg
Mailing wrapper for
De Stijl, 1921. During
its fourth year, the
magazine was given a
new, dynamic
typography, with a
'De Stijl NE' (New
Images) logo on the
cover

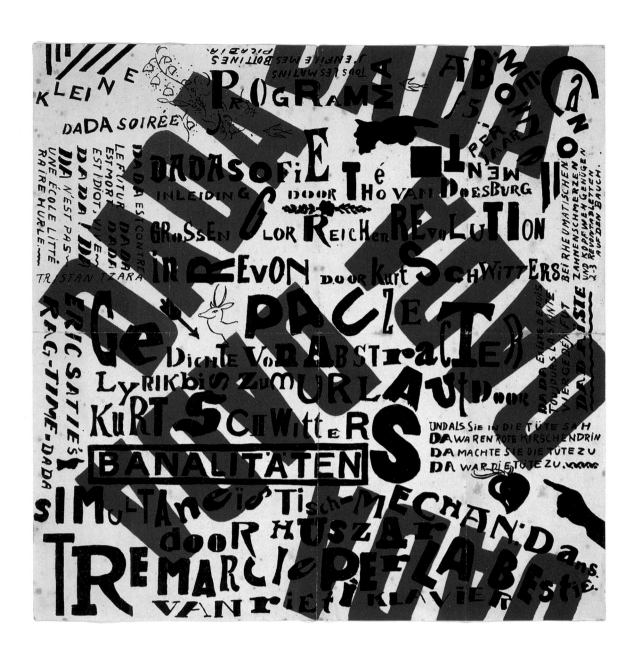

Theo van Doesburg
and Kurt Schwitters
Programme/poster
for a *Dadaist Evening in
The Hague*, advertising
the renowned Dada
performances given
by Schwitters and
Theo and Nelly
Doesburg on a tour
of the Netherlands in
1923

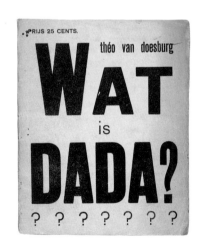

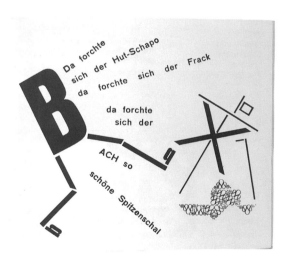

Theo van Doesburg
Cover of the booklet
Wat is Dada? (What is
Dada), De Stijl, The
Hague 1923. Van
Doesburg's vivid use
of printed letters
became an
increasingly
important ingredient
in his Dadaist work

Theo van Doesburg,
Kurt Schwitters,
Käthe Steinitz
Page from *Die Scheuche
– Märchen*, Aposs
Verlag, Hannover
1925. Schwitters had
already worked with
Steinitz on Dadaist
illustrated books.
Inspired by El
Lissitzky's example,
Van Doesburg
suggested that the
illustrations should
be constructed of
typographic material

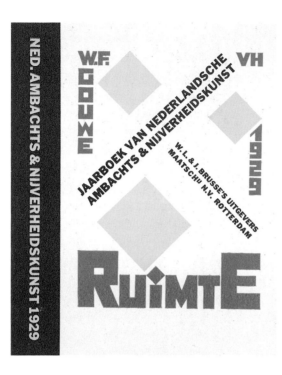

In his use of typography Van Doesburg demonstrated the Constructivist as well as the Dadaist side of his personality. In 1921 *De Stijl* was redesigned, which appears to be symbolic of Van Doesburg's striving for the pure, spatial structures that he envisaged for future architecture and urban development. He pressed on with open, elementary type matter for writing paper and other printed material that *De Stijl* used.

Van Doesburg also immersed himself in the expressive opportunities of typography. In 1923, together with Mondrian and Anthony Kok, he published in three languages a manifesto on literature. He wanted 'to give the word a new meaning and new powers of expression' and create 'a constructive oneness regarding content and form'. What he meant is evident in the poem *Letterklankbeelden* (Type-sound images), which he published under the pseudonym I.K. Bonset. The positioning and size of the letters and words on the page were used to bring out the poetical content of the text, while typographic elements were incorporated so that the text could be correctly rendered, as in a musical score. Van Doesburg included similar visual sound poems by Raoul Hausmann and Kurt Schwitters in his Dadaist magazine *Mécano* and thereby formed a chain in a tradition that stretches from Mallarmé and Marinetti to the concrete and visual poetry of the 1960s.

Van Doesburg's interest in the theatre was expressed in 1923, the year of the Dada expedition through the Netherlands with Kurt Schwitters. They designed provocative posters and programmes for the soirées and matinées. In the lithographic drawn compositions as well as in the posters composed of typographic material, they allowed the different-sized type to dance across and off the surface and thereby ridicule legibility and 'good taste'. In 1925, as a continuation of these lively experiments, Schwitters, Käthe Steinitz and Van Doesburg put together a children's book *Die Scheuche* (The Scarecrow), an inventive and humorous example of the visual use of typographic elements. The inspiration for this book was the sensational typographic design El Lissitzky had used for *Dja Golossa*, an anthology of poems by Vladimir Mayakovsky. In this book El Lissitzky established new relations between word and image, where the simplest typographic elements such as type and line, together with a sparing use of colour, combined to produce maximum visual effect. The influence of *Dja Golossa* can be seen either directly or indirectly in much of the printed matter produced during the mid-1920s.

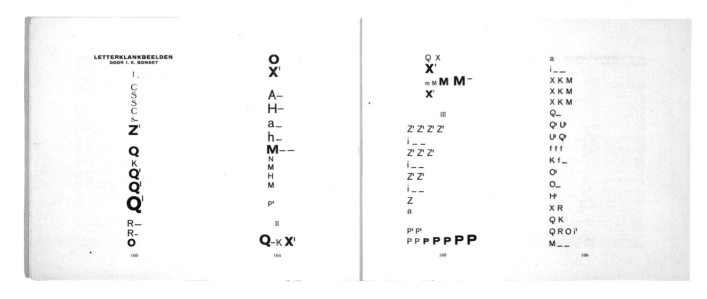

Bart van der Leck and
P.J.C. Klaarhamer
Pages 3 and 24 from
the deluxe edition of
*Het Hooglied van
Salomo* (The Song of
Solomon), W. Versluys,
Amsterdam 1905. The
entire book was
drawn in two colours
directly onto the
lithographic plate

Bart van der Leck
Poster for the
*Rotterdam-London
Batavia Line*, 1916.
Thanks to the warm
contact he had with
Mrs Kröller-Müller,
who collected his
paintings, Van der
Leck received many
commissions from
Müller & Co
Steamship Company

Bart van der Leck

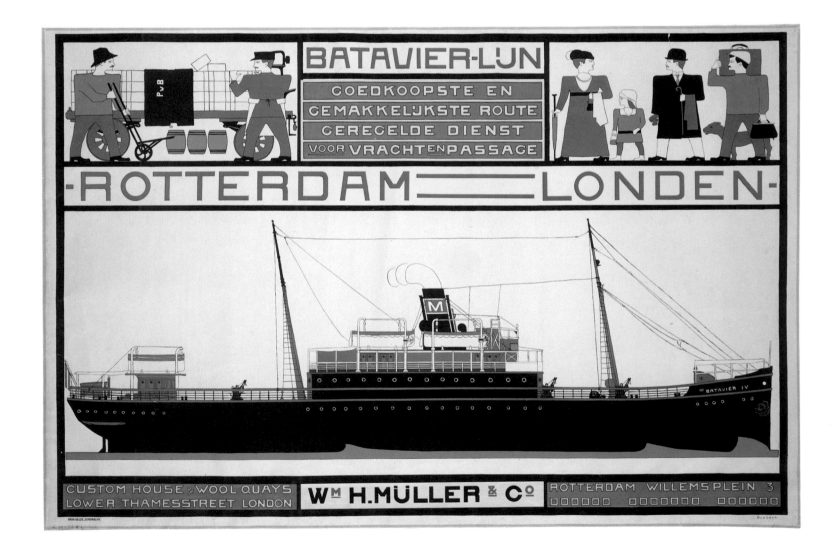

Bart van der Leck, painter, monumental artist and author, received his training at a number of stained-glass ateliers in Utrecht, also from the architect P.J.C. Klaarhamer at the State School for Industrial Art, and finally at the Rijksacademie in Amsterdam. In 1905 he worked with Klaarhamer on illustrations for the *Song of Solomon*; they were reminiscent of Derkinderen's work, which he greatly admired. Van der Leck also designed fabrics for Klaarhamer. In 1912 he signed a contract with the art critic H.P. Bremmer, which brought him into contact with Mrs. Kröller-Müller. In 1914 at the behest of the Müller firm, which owned ore mines in Algeria and Spain as well as a shipping company with a line operating between Harwich and Hook of Holland, Van der Leck made drawings of the mines as preparatory studies for a huge stained-glass window for the firm's office in The Hague. In the same year he was taken on by the company as a colour consultant. He worked together with Berlage, Müller's architect, whose buildings included the St Hubertus Hunting Lodge at Hoenderloo and Holland House in London.

Through his contact with Bremmer, Van der Leck also worked from 1915 for De Nederlanden van 1845 insurance company in The Hague. In 1916 he designed a poster for the Batavia Line of Müller & Co, broke off the relationship with the company, but continued to work now and then for Mrs. Kröller-Müller. He produced abstract, coloured wall surfaces and floor covering for the Hubertus Lodge and designed the spines of dossiers for the museum archive. In 1917 he became part of the De Stijl movement, in close contact with Mondrian and Van Doesburg. He wrote on the position of modern painting in architecture, with which he became increasingly involved. In the area of graphic design he produced posters, including one for his own exhibition in Utrecht (1919) and others for the readings that Mrs. Kröller gave at the Volksuniversiteit.

The manner in which the letters of *De Stijl* magazine's title were divided in pieces was most consistently echoed in Van der Leck's work. In 1919 he designed a poster for the Dutch Oil Factory in Delft, in which the deconstruction of the typography paralleled his preoccupations in his paintings. The round classic letter was reduced in his designs to a more linear form, but – in contrast to Huszár – he respected the diagonal, and his white background displayed a stronger presence than in the more compact forms of Huszár's lettering. Although the design was never printed, Van der Leck continued to use this alphabet from then on, first for his own poster and later in a lighter version for the packaging and advertising of Metz & Co. Store, Amsterdam.

In 1940-41 Van der Leck designed *The Flax* by Hans Christian Andersen, with coloured and segmented areas linked by a light typeface that married well with the illustrations. His letterforms were never constructed on a rigid grid, but condensed from accepted letterforms and then reassembled into an even weave. What was lost in readability was amply compensated for by the strong poetic element gained by his refined, childlike drawn letters.

However, Van der Leck's graphic work was a marginal activity. Aside from painting, his interest lay chiefly in the use of colour for architecture and industrial design.

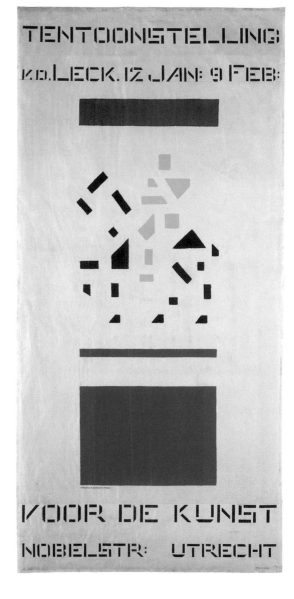

Bart van der Leck Poster for an *Exhibition of Van der Leck*, Voor de Kunst, Utrecht 1920. In 1916 Van der Leck began to paint in a radical new way, using primary colours and fragmented shapes, which he included in the lettering

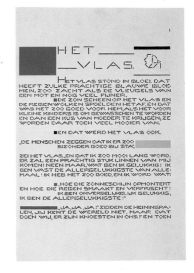

Bart van der Leck Page from *H.C. Andersen, Het Vlas* (The Flax), De Spieghel, Amsterdam 1941. Van de Leck remained true to his mathematical approach to images, designing the book page like a piece of architecture with accents of primary colours

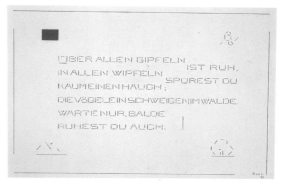

Bart van der Leck Poem, *über allen Gipfeln ist Ruh*, 1932. In Goethe's lithographed lines of poetry, Van der Leck reduces the letterforms to a slender, interrupted construction

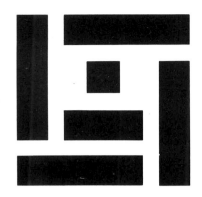

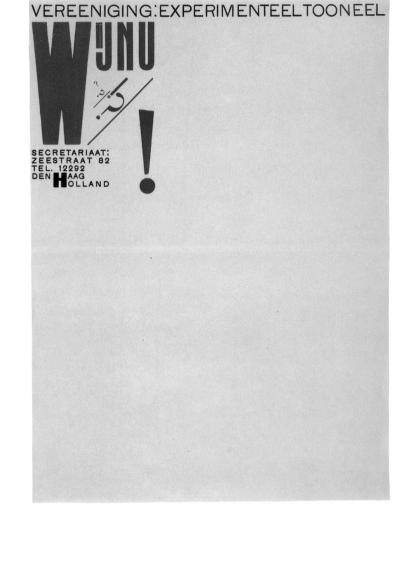

Jan Wils
Trademark for *Wils*,
c. 1917. Piet Zwart
also used this for
Wils' letterhead, his
first typographic
assignment

Piet Zwart
Writing paper for
*WijNu, a society for
experimental drama*,
The Hague 1925.
During its brief
existence the society
screened several
experimental films
in The Hague

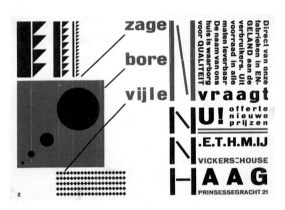

Piet Zwart
Postcard
advertisement for
Vickers House, a
flooring firm, The
Hague 1922. The
words *zagen* (sawing),
boren (drilling) and
vijlen (filing) are
rendered in
typographic material

Piet Zwart
Postcard
advertisement for
Laga, The Hague 1923.
This design for rubber
flooring, constructed
from typesetting
material, is very
much in keeping with
De Stijl compositions

Piet Zwart
Advertisement
10-25-50 KV, Dutch
Cable Factory (NKF)
1925. This
asymmetrical design
is a fine example of
the dynamic and
constructive use of
pure typographic
elements that Zwart
developed in the mid-
1920s

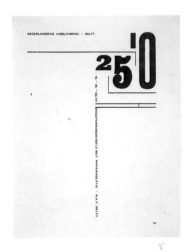

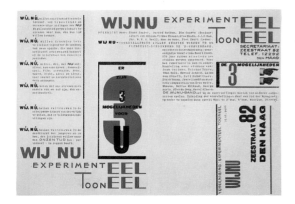

Piet Zwart
Publicity folder for
*WijNu, a society for
experimental drama,*
The Hague 1925

Piet Zwart discovers the printer

Piet Zwart
Full-page
advertisement for
the *Dutch Cable Factory*
(NKF) 1925, which
appeared each month
in the trade journal
Sterkstroom (Power
Charge), creating
much publicity for
the firm's products.
The double 'V' is a
linocut

One of the founders of *De Stijl* was The Hague architect Jan Wils. Piet Zwart, who worked in his office as a draughtsman, trained as a decorative artist in the new art style at the Amsterdam School of Industrial Art. Zwart had made a name for himself with his needlework designs in the manner of the Wiener Werkstätte, and for his interior designs, which were redolent with heavy forms and whimsical decoration. Wils on the other hand was a young man deeply affected by the architecture of Frank Lloyd Wright, which Berlage had introduced to the Netherlands, and under Wils' influence Piet Zwart's work gradually changed. For him the form of the building itself began to prevail over the decoration. In the early 1920s Jan Wils, Vilmos Huszár and Piet Zwart were all members of the architecture and industrial art section of The Hague Kunstkring, an artists' association where new developments were closely followed, particularly those emanating from Germany and Russia, and readings and exhibitions were held.

Designing a letterhead for Wils heralded Zwart's years of typographic activity, despite the fact that he had never before set foot inside a printer's workshop. In an interview in 1968, Zwart explained how he became acquainted with typography: 'I was totally unfamiliar with any aspect of typography. I had done something for Jan Wils, a letterhead, and via him I did something for Vickers House. Those were very straightforward things that I could put together at home with a few lines and indicated by a single word.'

Typical of his advertising cards was the use of heavy, sans-serif lettering set in blocks, the combining of horizontal and vertical text, and eye-catching typeset material couched sometimes in a *De Stijl*-like idiom. Both Huszár and Zwart 'tinkered' in a Wijdeveld manner with letterforms and logos, an influence that Zwart somewhat concealed in the same interview: 'There were also extremes concerning the innovations that had been taking place in typography since the beginning of the century. All those decorative things were made with typographic elements, especially by Wijdeveld. He put together entire pages from copper.' From the two-coloured brochure made for WijNu, an experimental theatre association, it is clear that Zwart was not averse to charging an area with text, lines and bars. While designing pure, typographic advertisements for the Dutch Cable Factory, he developed the skills to create a greater visual tension between the white, unprinted area and the typographic elements used.

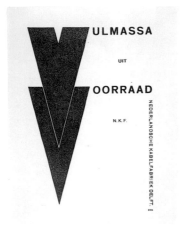

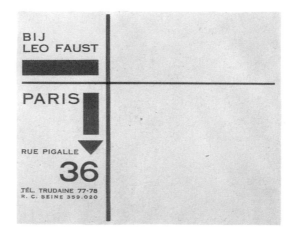

Piet Zwart
Envelope for *Bij Leo
Faust* 1926. For this
restaurant, owned
by a Dutch journalist
living in Paris, Zwart
designed both the
interior and
typographic house
style

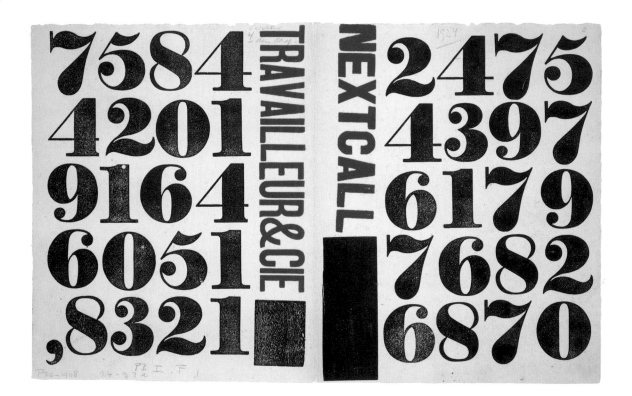

H.N. Werkman
Cover of *The Next Call*,
first issue; Werkman,
Groningen 1923.
Werkman combines
wooden letters with
two simple
Constructivist
printed shapes

H.N. Werkman – poet and printer

H.N. Werkman
Cover and back page
of *The Next Call*, no. 4,
depicting a decorative
and anarchistic
pattern of calendar
numbers; Werkman,
Groningen 1924. The
somewhat ironical
French translation
of Werkman's name
lends an international
touch to the journal

Between September 1923 and November 1926 nine issues of a magazine with the somewhat un-Dutch and mysterious name, *The Next Call*, appeared at irregular intervals. Its circulation, size and number of pages were trifling, the paper was cheap, but its design was original and contrary. Anyone perusing through the original issues now, almost three-quarters of a century later, is still struck by the vitality, sense of freedom and optimism emanating from the pages. The printer and publisher, under the pseudonym Travailleur & Cie, was Hendrik Nicolaas Werkman. He also wrote and designed the pages himself. In the 1920s Werkman ran a large printing firm in Groningen, a city situated 'in a corner where hardly any sound penetrates', as he wrote to the artist Michel Seuphor in Paris. Business was not Werkman's strongest point, and after a series of financial disasters he was forced to install himself in an attic with one single press and a one-man staff.

Here, in the face of economic recession, he printed a large variety of his marvellous 'fripperies', as he himself called them. They were partly executed as one-offs, while some were printed in limited editions. Werkman wrote visual poetry and provocative artistic manifestos, using material from the typecases to assemble semi-abstract, collage-like compositions. He worked with wooden poster letters, copper lines, lead type and blocks. Occasionally he printed in black line and tone, with one other supporting colour, thereby allowing the white area and the texture of the paper to play an important part. Sometimes he experimented with various transparent colours on top of one another.

The Next Call was originally mailed to artist friends in Groningen, but in 1924 its distribution was extended and copies reached Paris, Belgrade and Prague, becoming part of the increasing flood of magazines through which

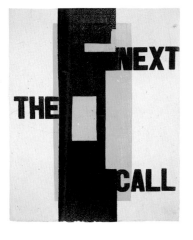

H.N. Werkman
Double-page spread
from *The Next Call*,
no. 4; Werkman,
Groningen 1924. Two
fine examples of
purely visual
compositions of letter
and number forms in
which the
importance of the
individual elements
is no longer relevant

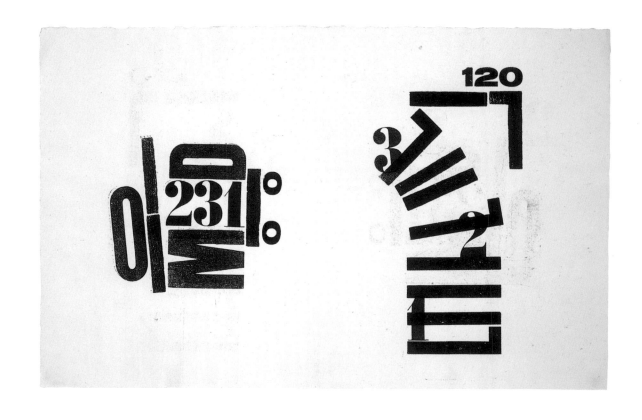

international avant-garde artists remained in touch with each other. Theo
van Doesburg, whose paintings along with those of Van der Leck and Huszár
had been exhibited in the spring of 1922 in Groningen, exchanged *De Stijl* and
Mécano for *The Next Call*. Van Doesburg wrote to Werkman from Paris: 'In my
opinion a modern magazine should be a bonbon filled with dynamite'.

At the time *The Next Call* was more like a firework going off at irregular
intervals. Many years later, historians acknowledged the profound influence
the poetic rebellion of this gentle printer from Groningen had on new
generations of graphic designers.

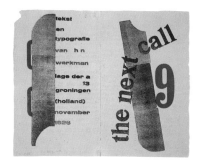

H.N. Werkman
Cover and back cover
of *The Next Call*, no. 9;
Werkman, Groningen
1925. This final issue
of the magazine
illustrates Werkman's
preference for such
simple materials as
rough paper and
plain lettering

H.N. Werkman
Four-page centrefold
from *The Next Call*,
no. 6; Werkman,
Groningen 1924,
giving a tongue-in-
cheek overview of the
'artistic scene' in
provincial Groningen

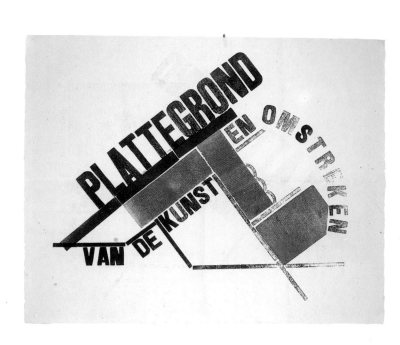

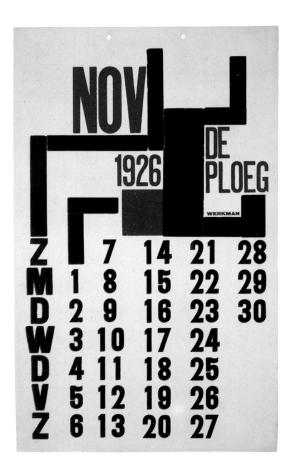

H.N. Werkman
Calendar for *De Ploeg*
artists' group,
Groningen 1926.
Werkman printed the
calendar, creating a
purely typographic
design for the month
of November, while
Ploeg members
illustrated it with
woodcuts

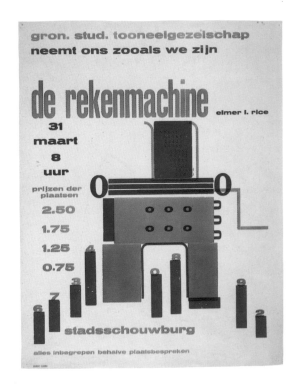

H.N. Werkman
Poster for the play
The Adding Machine
by Elmer L. Rice,
Groningen Student
Theatre Group, 1933

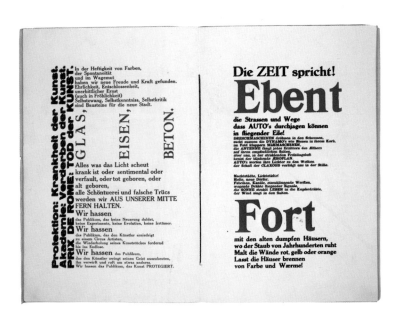

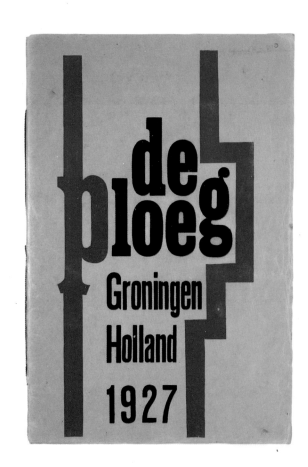

H.N. Werkman
Cover and pages of a
compilation *De Ploeg
Groningen Holland*,
1927, featuring
reproductions of
members' work.
Werkman designed
and printed the
typographic layout,
while Johan Dijkstra
added a six-page
artistic manifesto

Groningen was the home of an artistic group called De Ploeg, to which belonged painters and graphic artists like Jan Wiegers, Johan Dijkstra, Wobbe Alkema and Jan Altink, as well as the printer, Hendrik Werkman. The painters largely worked in an expressionist style, following the example of Die Brücke in Berlin during the pre-First World War years. E.L. Kirchner's work with its garish colours and aggressive forms greatly inspired De Ploeg's adherents, led by Jan Wiegers.

Around the mid-1920s the group was extremely active in exhibiting the work of its members and similar-minded friends from elsewhere in the Netherlands, in organising musical and literary evenings and in publishing folders of graphic work. Werkman printed the posters, invitations, catalogues and illustrated calenders for De Ploeg, and in 1921-22 published *Blad voor Kunst*, the group's art magazine.

A superb sample of typographic art is *De Ploeg Groningen Holland 1927*, an anthology of reproductions of De Ploeg artists' work, accompanied by a manifesto in German by Johan Dijkstra in which he argues fiercely for an artistic freedom 'separate from tradition, academia or social pressures – no crawlers or slaves to the mighty and powerful... No museums here who by their importance trap us in the power of the past. No graveyard for art.' Werkman highlighted important words and sentences in the text by using a different typeface in a contrasting colour, and by setting words vertically and creating gaps in the text, which gave a rough yet nevertheless poetic feel to the design. In Werkman's more formal publications were elements of his individual style, which arose out of the typographic discoveries he made in his own experimental work.

During the 1930s he developed new techniques to convey his poetical visions on paper. He stamped, cut stencils and 'drew' directly onto the paper with the ink roller, including using it on its side. He regularly exhibited his paintings and printed 'fripperies' with De Ploeg in Groningen, but aside from this found little response, apart from an occasional exhibition in Amsterdam or Paris. However, this changed when he met Willem Sandberg in 1938, and the Second World War initiated a late bloom: the numerous, clandestine issues of *De Blauwe Schuit* (The Blue Barge).

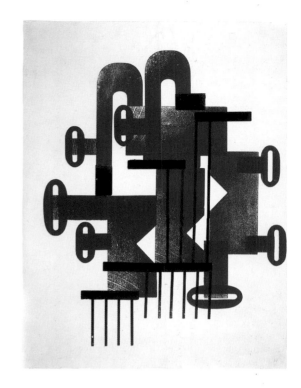

H.N. Werkman
Composition j-o,
1927-1928, one of
Werkman's abstract
'fripperies' using
wooden letters and
other typesetting
elements

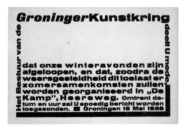

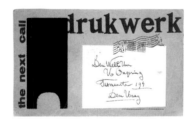

H.N. Werkman
Envelope for mailing
The Next Call,
Werkman, Groningen
1924. Werkman's
fresh and direct style
gives even the
traditional aspects of
an envelope an
expressive graphic
edge

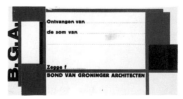

H.N. Werkman
Newsletter of the
Groningen Art Circle,
16 May 1928, in which
Werkman used his
favourite Announce
and Antieke Bold
Italic faces

H.N. Werkman
Receipt for the
*Groningen Association
of Architects*, c.1928, a
colourful alternative
to standard office
stationery

H.Th. Wijdeveld
Poster for an
*Exhibition of ceramics
and carpets of the
decorative artist Theo
A.C. Colenbrander*,
Stedelijk Museum,
Amsterdam 1923.
The poster is a typical
example of Wijdeveld's
decorative filling-in
and his characteristic
construction of
letters from lines and
blocks

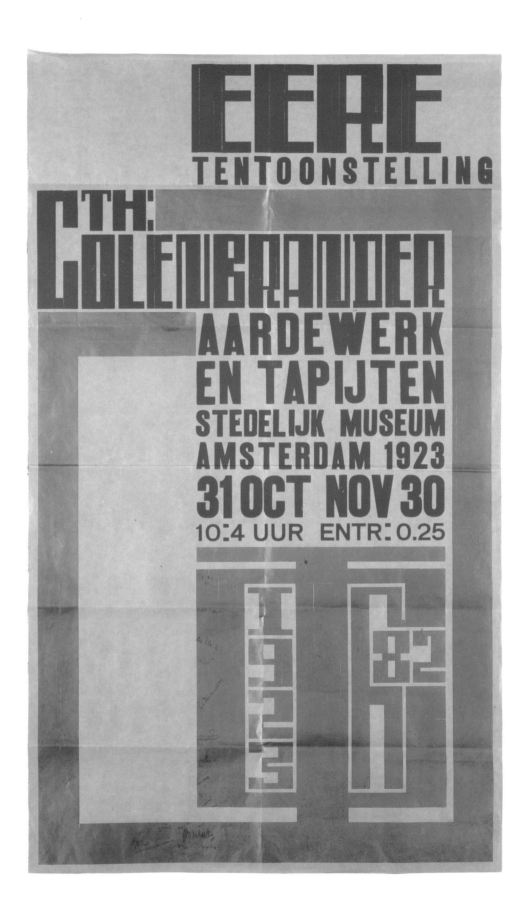

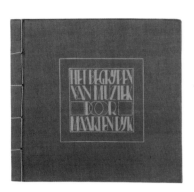

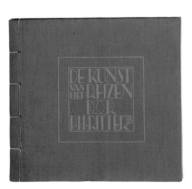

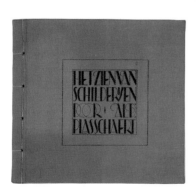

H.Th. Wijdeveld
Covers for four books
from the Pauw series:
*Maarten Dijk, Het
begrijpen van muziek*
(Understanding
Music); *P.H. Ritter Jnr,
De kunst van het reizen*
(The Art of Travelling);
*Albert Plasschaert, Het
zien van schilderijen*
(Looking at Paintings)
and *Albert Vogel,
Voordrachtskunst* (The
Art of Speech-
making): Van Loghum
Slaterus, Arnhem
1919-1920. Wijdeveld
also used the
Japanese method of
binding for his
Wendingen magazines

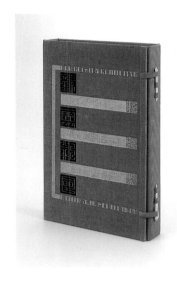

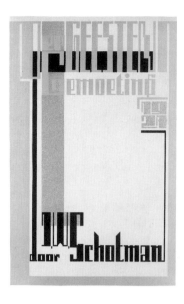

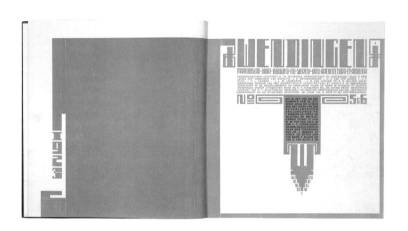

The 'filled-in areas' of H.T. Wijdeveld

Theo Wijdeveld was one of the Netherlands' most colourful architects. His large-scale – often Utopian – projects, such as the Volkstheater, the proposed tower blocks for Amsterdam's Vondelpark, the covered, 20-km deep hole in the ground and his blueprints for futuristic cities are comparable to the projects of Claude Nicolas Ledoux or Max Taut. His work is classified with that of the Amsterdam School, partly due to his work on urban developments for Amsterdam.

Wijdeveld's earliest typography was decorative and similar in style to that of William Morris or Lion Cachet. For example, his cover for the triple issue of the magazine *Architectura* (1917), with its baroque lettering and decorative composition, is without a single straight line. After 1917 his typography was inspired by the work of Lauweriks, who was also a member of *Architectura*'s editorial staff. At this time Wijdeveld's typography was self-consciously 'anti-classical', although he was easily able to deviate from this style.

In the January 1918 issue of his sumptuously produced magazine *Wendingen*, Wijdeveld created complex visuals using typographic elements, which along with the editorial content were the antithesis of Van Doesburg's sober *De Stijl*. Notwithstanding this, a certain tendency towards systematisation and 'filled-in areas' are detected in both publications, recalling the work of Lauweriks, an important yet neglected architect. Lauweriks' systematic designs and layout for his magazine *Ring*, launched in 1908, considerably influenced architects, interior designers and other type-designing outsiders, who until then had hardly felt drawn to what was going on in the printing world. Wijdeveld used simple, architectural shapes, derived from material from the typecase, in an extremely decorative fashion. His concern was more with form than function. He designed posters, alphabets

and book covers, and his typography proves his ability to adopt easily to the wide-ranging use of decorative styles. In the series of covers for, among others, *Het zien van schilderijen* (Looking at Paintings), from the art critic Albert Plasschaert, he used drawn lettering that contrasts with the highly constructed *Wendingen* typography. Nevertheless, lettering designed from lines and blocks became his trademark.

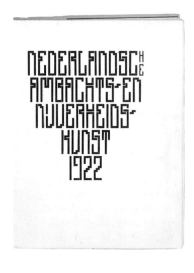

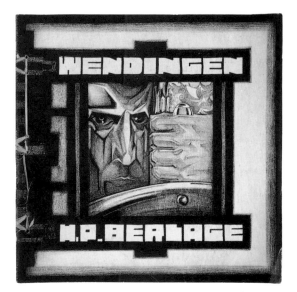

The first issue of *Wendingen* appeared in 1918. The covers were largely executed by artists and commissioned by Wijdeveld, although the inside of the journal still bore his signature. The contents were varied and covered virtually every existing national and international movement of the day in the fine arts, architecture, typography, theatre design and industrial design. The new magazine fulfilled a great need for a journal with a broad range of information, and special issues were also devoted to East-Asian art, Russian icons, Italian art and even aerial photographs of the Netherlands. In total 116 issues appeared, always in the same format and tied with raffia in Japanese fashion. The magazine received much criticism from classic typographers.

Van Royen and De Roos were strongly opposed to Wijdeveld's decorative forms, commenting: 'Really good typography cannot be obtained from bad typesetting surrounded by such an artistic jumble of lines, no more than a gown can make a pulpit orator of a monkey.' But the functionalists were also opposed to this kind of graphic art, calling it: 'artistic', 'anti-social', 'passive' and 'traditional'. Later the critic G.W. Ovink judged Wijdeveld's work for the magazine 'decoration *ad absurdum*' and thought his 'spectacular typeface concoctions' illegible and much forced.

In the introduction to the first issue, Wijdeveld wrote: 'Here are the wanderings through all the various expressions of art, as well as agreeable references to these movements, which are full of forceful power and the precursors of future harmony'. In that sense he was correct. These magazines were a platform for every new trend and have proved a rich source for art historians. They discussed the work of Josef Hoffmann, Frank Lloyd Wright, Gustav Klimt, Hermann Finsterlin, Eileen Gray and Erich Mendelsohn, among others. Covers were designed by the many representatives of new art: members of the Amsterdam School such as Mendes da Costa, Roland Holst, Van Konijnenburg, Toorop, Lauweriks, De Bazel and Lion Cachet; exponents of Expressionism such as Krop, Van de Vecht, Kurvers and De Klerk; and New Constructivism, such as Huszár, Lissitzky, Duiker, Gispen and Van der Vlugt. The handful of covers reproduced here conveys the sheer talent and diversity of the artists involved.

Wijdeveld and Wendingen

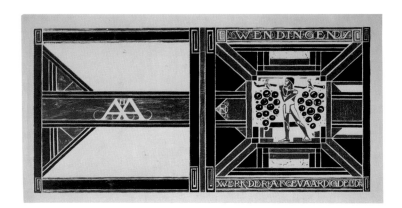

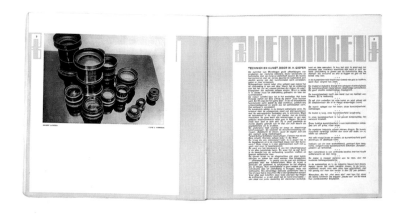

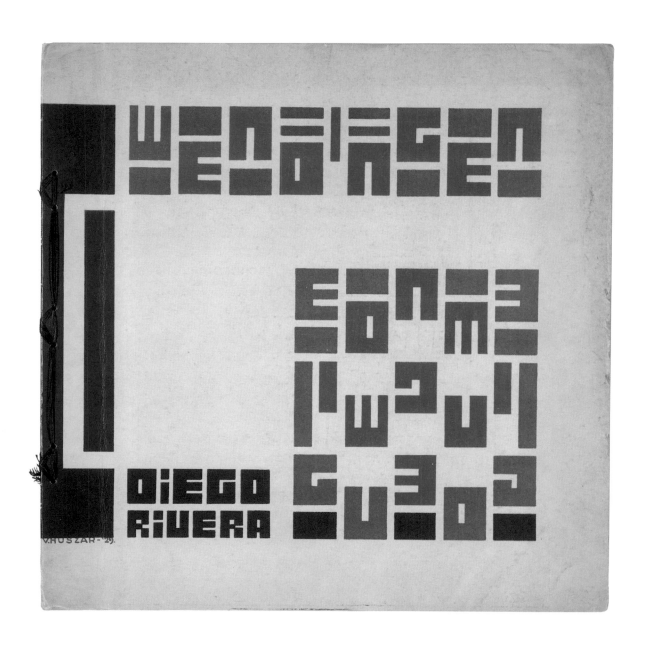

Vilmos Huszár
Cover *Wendingen*, vol. 10, no. 3; C.A. Mees, Santpoort 1929. This issue was devoted to the Social-Realist murals of the Mexican artist Diego Rivera. From the stylised letters of the masthead, Huszár composed an abstract composition

Peter Alma
Cover *Wendingen*, vol. 11, no. 9; C.A. Mees, Santpoort 1930. One of the last issues of the magazine, with a cover that complements its content, featuring the new phenomenon of the 'pictogram'

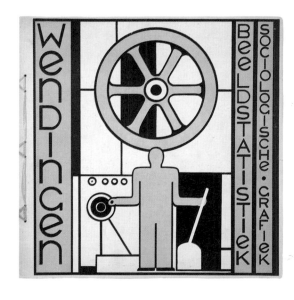

New typography and photomontage

Modernism in art, sculpture and architecture had its counterpart in the applied and graphic arts. The innovation in design that had occurred around the turn of the century was by the 1920s regarded as useless, unhealthy decoration that no longer belonged in an environment of straight lines and abstract, coloured forms. There was a contempt for handiwork as being unproductive and individualistic in the dawning age of rationalism, standardisation and mechanisation.

The more progressive graphic designers considered typography to be bogged down by the blinkered dogmas of unimaginative typeface designers and professional yet bourgeois publishers. In terms that sometimes appeared to be borrowed from Dadaist manifestos or from the social reforming encouragements of Utopian architects, the printed word came under fire. In 1923 El Lissitsky wrote in the journal *Merz*: 'Typographic design is the expression of the pulling and stressing tension of the textual content.' Kurt Schwitters added his comment in 1924: 'Countless rules can be written about typography. The most important is never do it in the same way as someone before you.' He also stated: 'The impersonal printed type is better than the individual signature of an artist', adding, 'simplicity implies clarity, straightforwardness and functional form... Beauty signifies well-balanced proportions'. Schwitters coined the term 'typo-advertising', and the contemporary artist as designer now embarked upon giving shape to these ideas. In 1928 Schwitters set up the Ring Neue Werbegestalter, a circle of 12 graphic designers who, through exhibitions and publications, would champion these ideals and generate commissions. Its Dutch members were Cesar Domela, Piet Zwart and Paul Schuitema.

Similar ideas were being expressed at the Bauhaus. In 1923 in the book *Staatliches Bauhaus Weimar 1919-1923*, László Moholy-Nagy in his essay 'Die neue Typographie' voiced his ideas: 'The nature and purpose of the printed material determines the unrestrained use of any reading direction (not only the horizontal arrangement), any typeface, type size, geometric form, colour, etcetera. With the adaptability, diversity and vitality of the set material, a new typographic language must be created.' He considered the linking of typographic with 'zincographic' techniques, using the objectivity of photography, to be of great importance. In the *Bauhausbücher* series, which he published with Walter Gropius, he demonstrated these principles, particularly in his own book *Malerei-Fotografie-Film* (1925).

It was the typographer Jan Tschichold who, with German thoroughness, set down these views systematically in *Die Neue Typographie*, a book with many examples and prescriptions that for several years was the Bible for aspiring avant-garde typographers. According to Tschichold, designers now wanted to give typographic form to 'a world image that was totally collective and no longer individually specialistic'. Tschichold also devoted a chapter to the relationship between photography and typography. He had no doubt that photography would play an important role in graphic art of the future, and that 'photography would be as symptomatic of our age as the woodcut to the Gothic period'.

His prophesy was confirmed. No fewer than five years later the photograph had become a vital visual element for contemporary graphic designers, who utilized the work of professional photographers or took the pictures themselves. The availability of light, flexible miniature cameras like the Leica often gave the more adept the opportunity to build up their own visual archive.

The general public, including clients, had to overcome a certain resistance in accepting the photograph as image. Among its champions much rhetoric could be heard. Following the arguments of Moholy-Nagy, the photograph was lauded as being 'objective', 'realistic', 'honest' and 'truthful'. Photographs were regarded as elements of a universal visual language. The fact that designers in their advertisements, postage stamps and book covers arranged photographs into suggestive, sometimes propagandist photomontages is not, however, consistent with this idea of 'truth'. As Piet Zwart said in 1934: 'Advertising is at best an assertion, which can be presented through corroborative arguments and suggestion; at worst it is a permissible form of deceit.' Politically speaking, the great examples of the propagandist use of photomontage, El Lissitzky, Alexander Rodchenko and Gustav Klutsis from the Soviet Union, counted on the unconditional sympathy of most of the modern designers. At the exhibition 'Photomontage', which Cesar Domela organised in Berlin in 1931, there were advertisements on view for products of the German capital next to posters preaching 'the construction of socialism under Lenin's banner'.

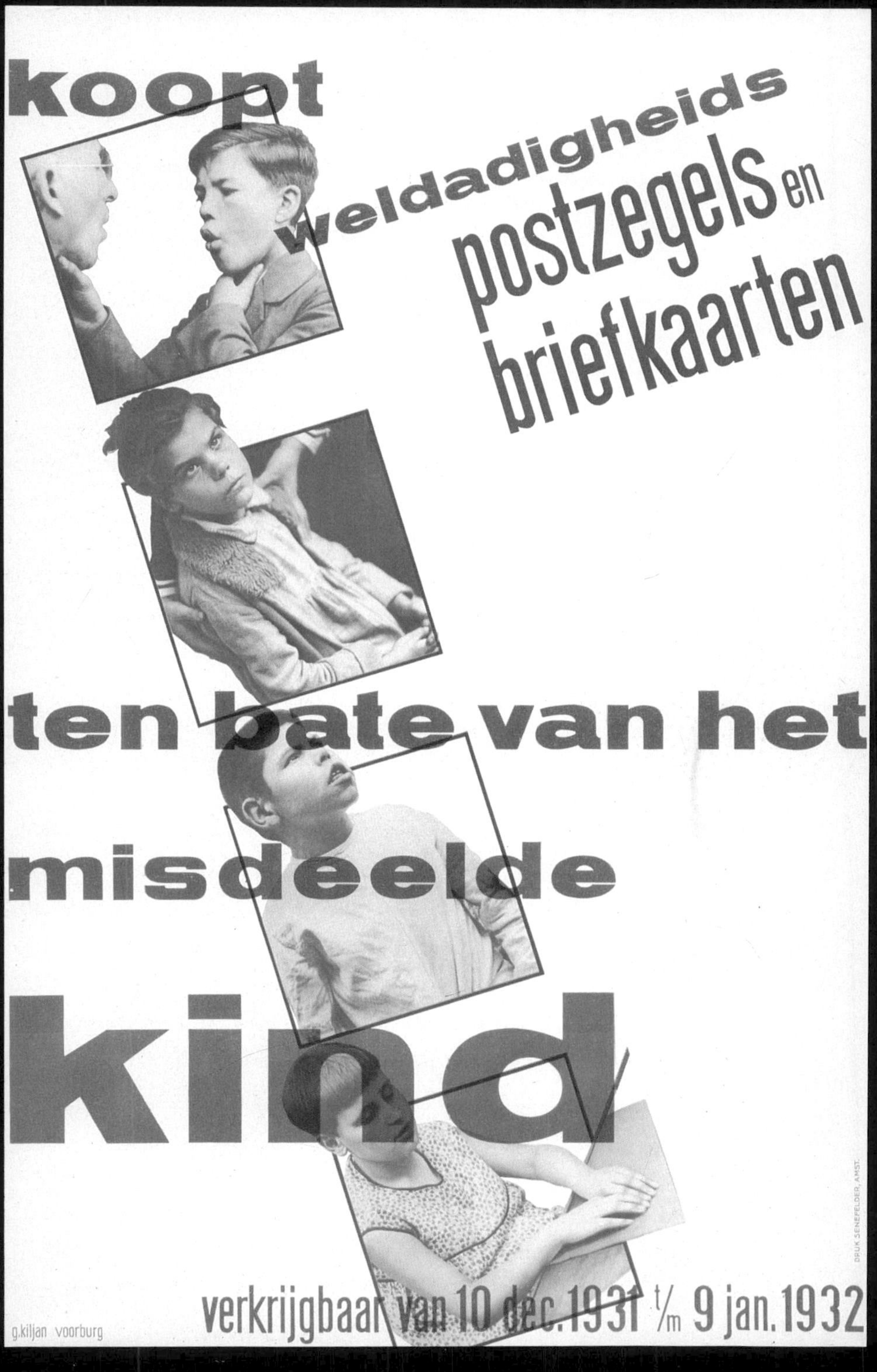
koopt
weldadigheids
postzegels en
briefkaarten
ten bate van het
misdeelde
kind
verkrijgbaar van 10 dec. 1931 t/m 9 jan. 1932
g. kiljan voorburg
DRUK SENEFELDER, AMST.

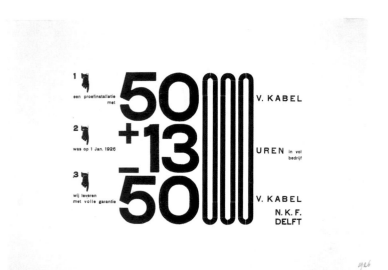

Piet Zwart
Advertisement *50,000*
V Cable..., Dutch Cable
Factory, 1926

Piet Zwart: advertisement design

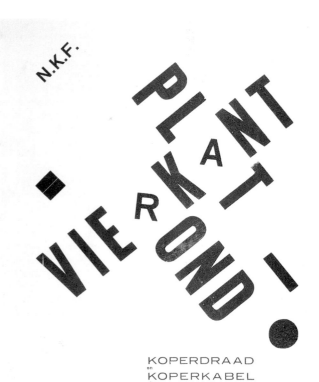

In 1923 Piet Zwart, who was working at the time for the architectural studio of H.P. Berlage, was invited by the Dutch Cable Factory in Delft to design an advertisement three times a month for the trade magazines, *Sterkstroom* (Power Charge) and *Tijdschrift voor Electrotechniek*. He was given carte blanche to write copy in praise of the cable factory's products, and render the visuals in a striking manner. First he drew the advertisements, which meant blocks had to be made – a time-consuming and quite costly business. However at Trio, a printer in The Hague which produced the magazines, he found a group of young typesetters who considered it exciting to set his idiosyncratic and rather complicated sketches by hand.

So it was that between 1923 and 1933 some 300 advertisements were made for the Dutch Cable Factory which, as the general public's reaction confirmed, were eye-catching and frequently humorous. When Zwart began, his idea was nothing more than to capture the reader's attention and in this context he adopted the maxim of Kurt Schwitters, who was designing graphic advertising in Hanover for a living: 'Always do an advertisement differently to anyone else'.

At the beginning the compositions were in the Dadaist mould. Zwart mixed together different typefaces of all sizes and linked these visually with long lines and bars. Occasionally he allowed one single letter to dominate the entire page – a wooden poster letter if this was possible, otherwise it was in linocut. He repeated rhythmically the letterforms, words and even entire lines, and broke up the horizontal text with vertical text.

It is difficult to discern a systematic approach in the designing of these advertisements, even though the emphasis on the diagonal to contrast with the rest was very imaginative. Zwart continually used the advertising copy as his starting point, highlighting a word or form to attract attention and guide the eye to the smaller type. Because they were intended for trade magazines, the texts are informative rather than attention-seeking and by and large bear little resemblance to modern advertising copy. In addition, they were sometimes done tongue-in-cheek. The style of the advertisements, however, gradually became more restrained and fewer elements were used. In the words of Piet Zwart in 1931: 'The new typography is elementary, it negates a preconceived formal design layout, it uses design according to function; it designs a black and white page in such a way that the stresses in the text are expressed: explicitly or in a visual form.'

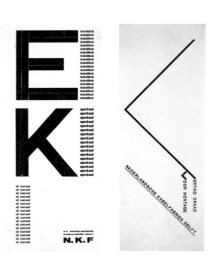

Piet Zwart
Advertisement
*Square Flat Round
Copperwire...*, Dutch
Cable Factory, 1926

Piet Zwart
Advertisement *Electric
copperwire from the
stocks of the Dutch Cable
Factory*, 1926

Piet Zwart
Advertisement
*Tin-plate Wire for
Mounting...*, Dutch
Cable Factory, 1927

Piet Zwart
Advertisement *N226*,
Dutch Cable Factory,
1928. The page is
taken from a
magazine on
electrotechnology
and clearly shows
how the
advertisement
appeared in relation
to the others on the
page

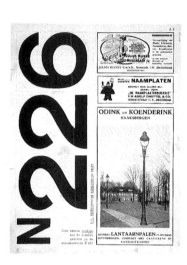

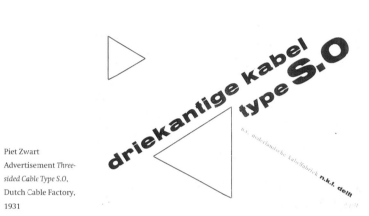

Piet Zwart
Advertisement *Three-
sided Cable Type S.O*,
Dutch Cable Factory,
1931

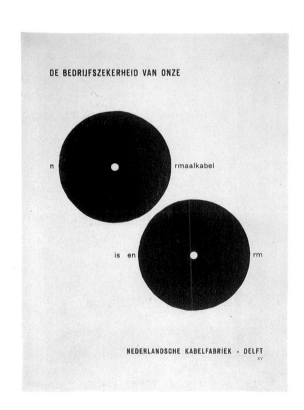

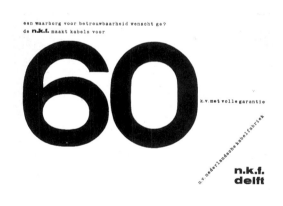

Piet Zwart
Advertisement *60 KV,
Fully Guaranteed*,
Dutch Cable Factory,
1930

Piet Zwart
Advertisement *The
Company's Confidence
in our Standard Cable is
Enormous...*, Dutch
Cable Factory, 1926

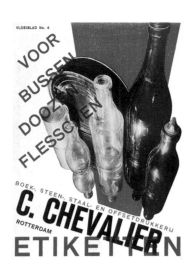

Paul Schuitema
Blotting paper
advertisement,
C. Chevalier Printers,
Rotterdam 1929

Paul Schuitema
Cover of *De Fakkel*
(The Torch), a student
magazine, 1926

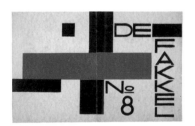

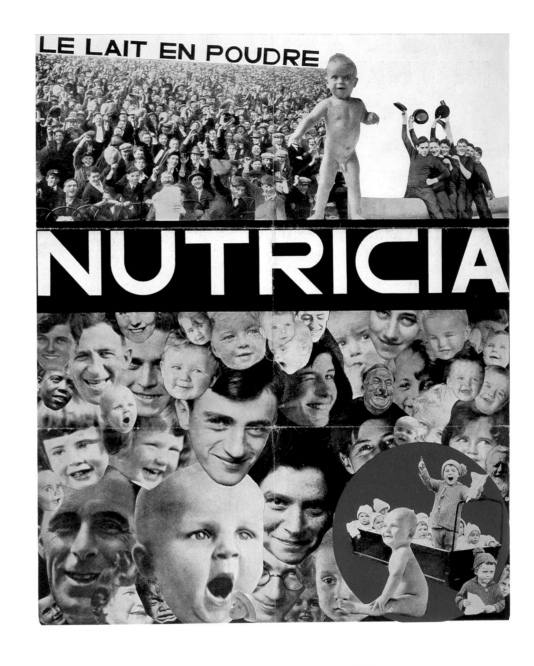

Paul Schuitema
Advertisement leaflet
for *Nutricia Dairy
Products*, Zoetermeer
1930

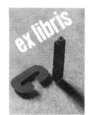

Paul Schuitema
Ex libris, *C. Chevalier
Printers*, Rotterdam
c.1930

Paul Schuitema
Advertisement and
cover for the
architectural
magazine *De 8 en
Opbouw*, nos 23 and 4,
Amsterdam 1932

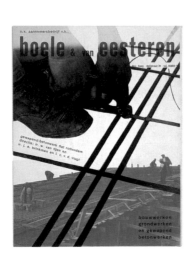

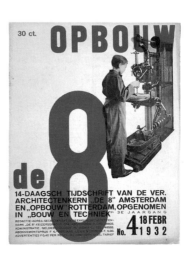

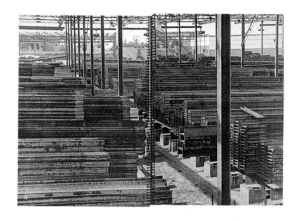

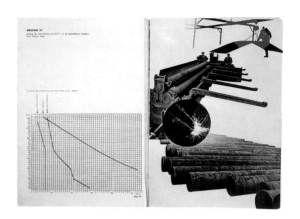

Paul Schuitema and phototypography

Paul Schuitema studied art at the Rotterdam Academy, but in the mid-1920s abandoned painting and drawing and took up graphic design. At first he worked somewhat in the decorative style of Jaap Jongert, but was quickly gripped by the simplicity and clarity of Constructivist principles as conveyed by the cover of *De Fakkel* journal, with its geometric coloured areas and angular lettering. Through his friendship with the photographer Jan Kamman from Schiedam, Schuitema quickly discovered the as-yet barely explored visual power of photography in printing. He began taking pictures as an amateur in 1928 with the emphasis on reproducing unassuming industrial objects, pinpoint sharp, from an unusual angle. His close contacts with the C. Chevalier printing firm gave him an insight into the possibilities and limitations of photomechanical reproduction in letterpress, and of combining photography and typography. He made a number of purely typographic designs such as a cover for the literary journal *De Gemeenschap* (The Community), but he preferred to make use of the photograph's dynamic qualities as a visual element when designing book and magazine covers, brochures, blotting paper and posters.

While the trade press was still discussing the advantages and disadvantages of photography in advertising, Schuitema was developing a powerful form of phototypography that introduced many new aspects: the photocollage, as in his Nutricia baby milk powder advertisement; photomontage, from multiple stills taken from different vantage points; and cinematic picture narratives with shifting perspectives, such as the advertising booklets for the steel welding company De Plaatwellerij and the concrete firm Betondak Arkel. In these, attention was focused not so much on a glossily perfect product, as on a hymn of praise to the stalwart image of a factory at work. Making labour heroic – as in Russian photography – had its repercussions in the Netherlands, even if it was achieved via the indirect route of capitalist enterprise. Although there were few photographic illustrated magazines published in the Netherlands at the time, the photomontage became a feature of modern design throughout the 1930s.

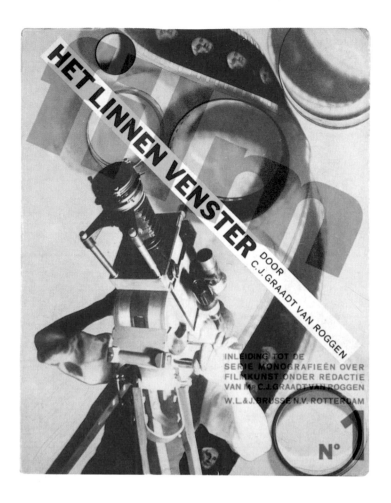

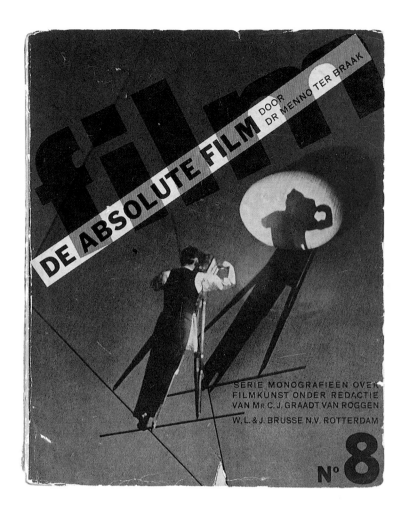

Modern film as a source of inspiration

In 1925 Moholy-Nagy had demonstrated in his book *Malerei, Photographie, Film*, how typography and photography could be drawn together into a cinematic whole, treating the book as a film scenario in word and image. In the Netherlands the medium of film was an important source of inspiration for graphic designers, even though new developments in this field were somewhat late in arriving.

In The Hague in 1926 the experimental theatre association, WijNu, was briefly active screening matinees of avant-garde films such as those of Cavalcanti. As an actively involved WijNu member, Piet Zwart helped organise the International Film Exhibition in 1928 to stimulate interest in the new medium. Together with German film-maker Theo Güsten, he then worked on a film commercial for airmail post for the Dutch post office. His colleagues Paul Schuitema and Gerald Kiljan were also engaged in filming. Around 1930 Kiljan made *Scheveningen*, a documentary on the seaside resort, while Schuitema began shooting his film *Maasbruggen* (Bridges of the Maas).

The Nederlandsche Filmliga, founded in 1927, drew together these activities. It had branches in every large city, where the experimental and art films ignored by the commercial cinemas could be screened: chiefly French, German and Russian avant-garde films and (also Dutch) documentaries. Russian directors such as Eisenstein and Pudovkin visited the Netherlands and their revolutionary work made a lasting impression. Until 1933 there was much interest in Filmliga's activities, and its attendant advertising in the form of posters, brochures and the *Filmliga* magazine strongly reflected the vigour and realism of the new cinema. Film montage, double images and diagonal camera angles, made familiar in the documentaries of Dziga Vertov, were echoed in the photomontages of Schuitema and Zwart.

Between 1931 and 1933 the publishing firm Brusse brought out a series of books entitled *Monografieën over Filmkunst* (Monographs on Cinematography), edited by C.J. Graadt van Roggen. In each of the ten volumes, a prominent writer or film critic dealt with a certain aspect of the cinema, including 'The Talking Film', 'Russian Film-making' and 'The Comic Film'. Zwart designed the typography for the series, using red and blue photomontages for the covers together with certain recurring elements, such as the word 'film' in large type and the title and author's name in a diagonal, light bar. The photomontages were composed of fragments from existing film clips and the designer's own photographs, which overlapped and cut into one another. The books were lavishly illustrated with film stills, and by positioning pieces of film diagonally and placing film sequences one under another, Zwart conveyed the essential aspect of the medium – movement – on the printed page.

Piet Zwart
Cover of *C.J. Graadt
van Roggen, Het linnen
venster* (The Linen
Window), 1931, the
first of a series of film
monographs; W.L. &
J. Brusse, Rotterdam

Piet Zwart
Cover of *Menno ter
Braak, De absolute film*,
W.L. & J. Brusse,
Rotterdam 1931.
The shadow of a film
operator, suspended
in space, falls onto an
oval shape. It is the
most Surrealist cover
Piet Zwart created for
the series

Piet Zwart
Poster and
programme for
an *Internationale
Tentoonstelling
op Filmgebied*
(International film
exhibition), The
Hague 1928. Using
the letters ITF as
starting point, Zwart
designed a graphic
house style for all the
exhibition's publicity

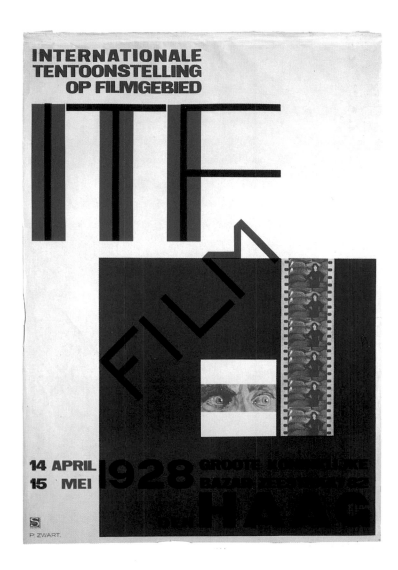

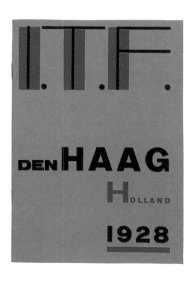

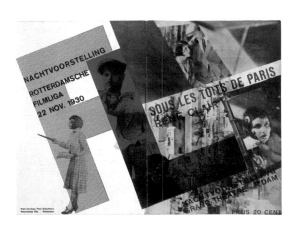

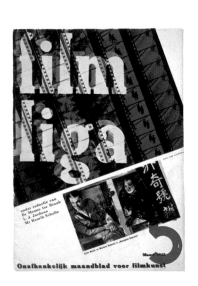

Paul Schuitema
Leaflet for the
Rotterdam Filmliga,
1930. On 22
November 1930 in
the Grand Theatre,
Rotterdam, the film
society screened a
late-night showing
of *Sous les toits de Paris*
by René Clair

Paul Schuitema
Cover of *Filmliga, an
independent magazine
on the art of film
making*, March issue,
1932. Diagonal
photomontages were
a recurring element
in photography, here
combined with letters
that have been
photographically
doubled to symbolise
the focusing of the
lens of a film
projector

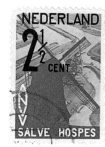 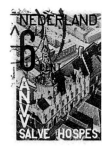

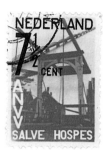 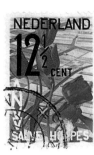

Despite the problems that the Dutch Postal, Telegraph and Telephone Service (PTT) continued to bear with Van Royen's unyielding attitude concerning design, between 1920 and 1940 he gave the company an individual identity that is evident to this day. While he was not in the front line of developments in visual art and design, he nevertheless introduced new forms to the PTT. He commissioned Van der Vlugt to design a phonebox that later gained international recognition. At the end of the 1920s he gave various commissions to Zwart, including the design of invitations, programmes and menus for the International Radio Communications conference in The Hague. Zwart initially used only lower case letters, but there was much objection to this. He then changed the format to upper case, which was subsequently accepted and highly commended. For the Post and Telegraph departments he designed brochures, leaflets and booklets. In 1931 he was commissioned to design an airmail stamp and two special stamps for trade and industry. His use of photography in the design was new for a postage stamp.

Zwart's associates, Gerard Kiljan and Paul Schuitema, also designed 'photographic' stamps. Kiljan produced the annual child welfare stamps of 1931 in aid of handicapped children. Unfortunately, the general public thought the theme was too realistically depicted and the work was much criticised. Schuitema made a series of stamps for the tourist board in which the photograph filled the entire picture plane, with the typography reproduced across it.

Within the organisation these functional objects were regarded as 'incidental', but the art critic A.M. Hammacher, himself working for the PTT at the time, wrote that they were part of a new modernist approach to design, not individual whim. He went on to cite the new functionalist architecture of the Van Nelle coffee factory in Rotterdam by Brinkman and Van der Vlugt, and the work of Le Corbusier and the Bauhaus. But even he supposed that, 'the result will be already entirely outdated within a few years'. After 1932 Van Royen retracted his policy towards postage stamps and once more requested that they be traditionally engraved. However, for advertising and public information, the 'functional' style held sway alongside a more illustrative design style revived in the 1930s.

The Dutch PTT and New Functionalism

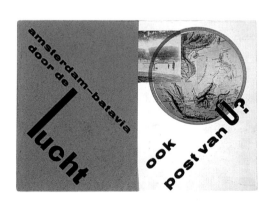

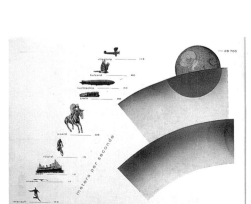 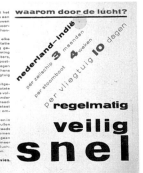

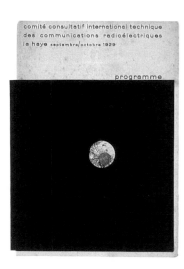

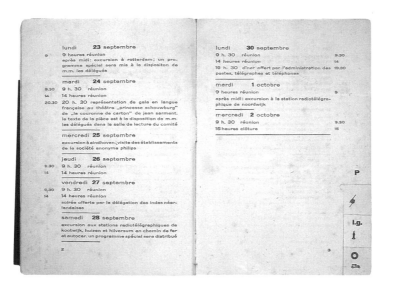

Piet Zwart
Cover and spread
from the programme
for the *Conference on
Radio-electronic
Communications*, PTT
(Post Office), The
Hague 1929.
For a while Zwart
considered capitals to
be unnecessary and
uneconomical, so
that all the printed
material for the
conference was in
lower case

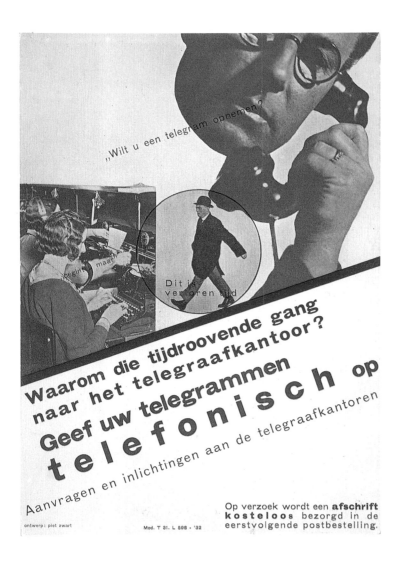

Piet Zwart
Advertisement sign
*Send your Telegrams by
Telephone*, PTT (Post
Office), The Hague
1932. Photomontage
in red and blue

Piet Zwart
Information leaflet
Via Scheveningen Radio
on the sending of
telexes via the
Scheveningen radio
signal; PTT (Dutch
Telephone Service),
The Hague 1929.
Shown here is a
photogram of a roll of
perforated telex
paper

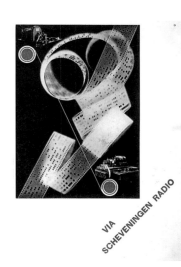

Vilmos Huszár
Page from a brochure
on *Internal telephone
systems*, PTT (Post
Office), The Hague
1931

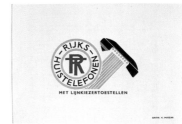

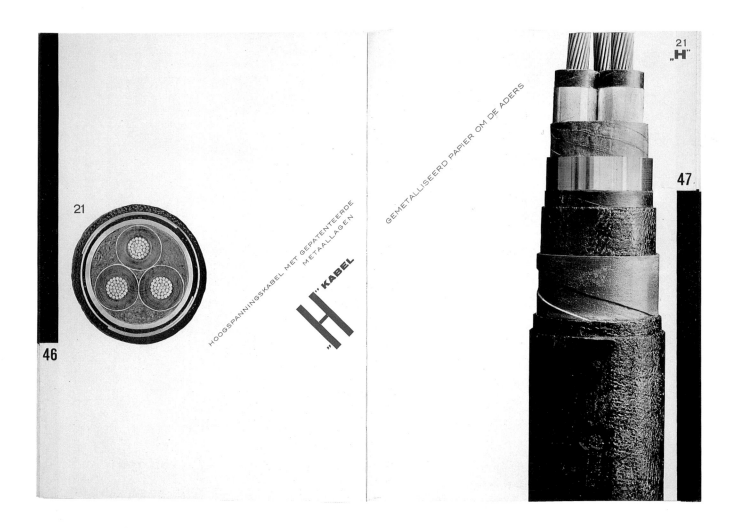

The Dutch Cable Factory in Delft

Piet Zwart
Four pages from a catalogue for the *Dutch Cable Factory*, Delft 1928. This was the first time close-up photography was assigned an immediately recognisable function. The German Jan Tschichold, however, who set the pace for the new typography, thought the black vertical bars to be somewhat 'formal'

Piet Zwart
Two pages from the English version of a catalogue for the *Dutch Cable Factory*, Delft 1929. The diagonal was an essential ingredient in drawing attention to and breaking up the direction of the type

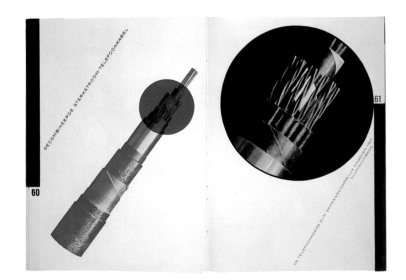

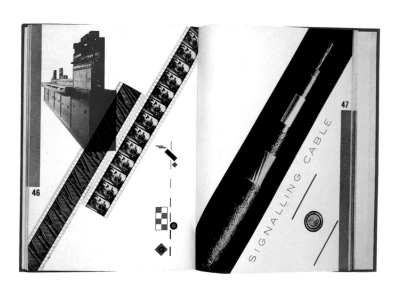

The contact that Zwart had established through Berlage with the Dutch Cable Factory blossomed into an intense collaboration. Zwart's interest in industry and technology helped, as it was something of an exception for an industrial artist.

Commissioned in 1926 to design the firm's illustrated catalogue for various types of high-tension and telephone cable, Zwart decided against technical drawings and instead chose a new medium: photography. He hired a professional photographer to take close-ups of cable samples, cross-sections of thick cables and cable ends, which lay exposed layer for layer. The shots were then reproduced two-thirds of the actual cable size on the catalogue page (the pages were the then uncommon DIN A4 size).

Zwart planned the catalogue as a visual story that unfolds across each subsequent double page, with the photographic images and accompanying text alternating between horizontal-vertical and diagonal layouts. The aim appeared to be to capture the harsh and fleeting images typical of scenes from Russian film documentaries of the time. This is borne out by the introductory panoramic pictures and photomontages of buildings, the 'tilting' of the camera and the zoom effects, which unite the left and right pages.

The typographic experience Zwart gained with the Dutch Cable Factory advertisements is expressed in the zigzag vigour of the lines of text used throughout, effectively exploiting the white of the page, while the visual material – the photographs of cables – was largely static. In a second booklet designed for Delft Cables five years later, things were radically different. Similar to Schuitema's *De Plaatwellerij* advertising booklet, Zwart emphasised the industrial process that was captured step by step in pictures, and in which the machine operator played a role. In his search for more control over visual material, Zwart, like Schuitema earlier, chose photography and had mastered the techniques. The cinematic quality of his framed shots was heightened by using alternating wide and narrow pages in the booklet, which means that, when one leafs through it, a part of the preceding or following page remains visible, creating fantastic visual effects of clashing photographic fragments. The booklet's dynamic content contrasts strangely with its stark blue cover and the light, condensed silver type, which Zwart obviously wanted to associate visually with wire.

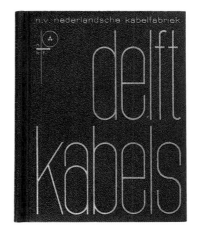

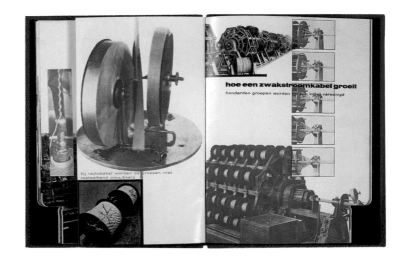

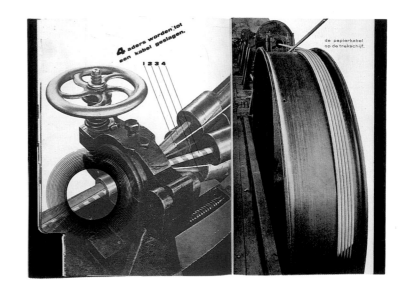

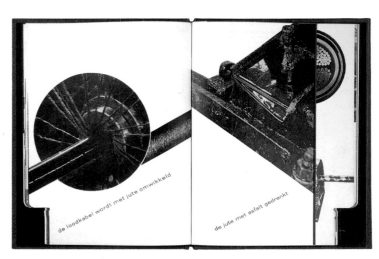

Piet Zwart
Cover and pages from an advertising brochure *Delft Cables*, Delft 1933. Zwart had previously hired a photographer for catalogue pictures, but this time he took them himself, creating dynamic images of every aspect of the company

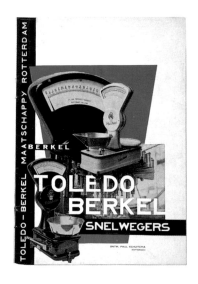

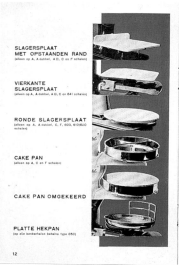

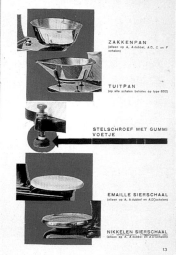

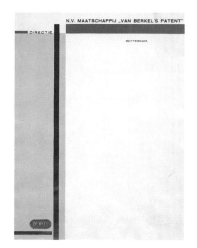

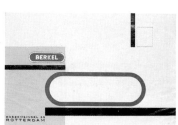

Van Berkel's Patent Company, Rotterdam

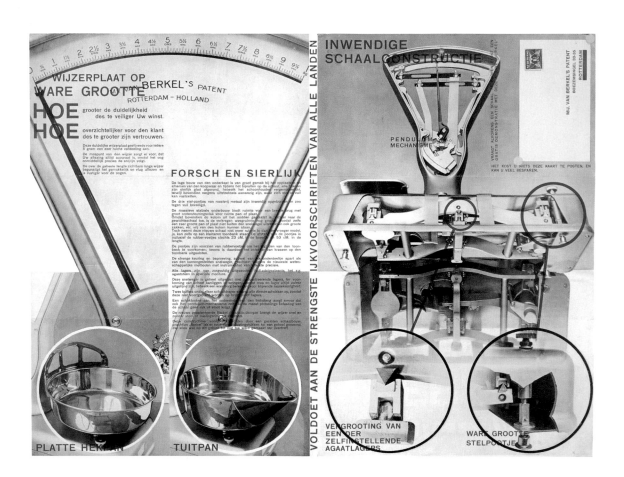

In a reading of around 1930 on the principles of modern advertising, Zwart said: 'These principles compel the designers to go directly after their goal. Prettifying is unfamiliar to them. Their designs are just as businesslike as the organisation they are advertising. This fact is recognised by the managements of some of the largest factories in the Netherlands, among others, by the Dutch Cable Factory in Delft and Van Berkel's Patent in Rotterdam'.

What the Dutch Cable Factory was to Piet Zwart, the NV Maatschappij Van Berkel's Patent in Rotterdam was to Paul Schuitema: a company that gave him a free hand to experiment with new techniques and materials in the designing of their commercial advertising. The firm produced weighing scales and butchers' cutting machines, and it seemed that the gleaming metal and the technical aspect of these products had magical powers of attraction for designers of the day.

From 1926 to 1928 Schuitema worked with the Schiedam photographer, Jan Kamman, who had been one of the first to investigate the potential of modern photography and apply it practically on the principle that 'with modern photography you can see the beauty of crystal, lamps, flowers and machine. This is achieved by means of the technical refinement of the material.' Schuitema designed his Van Berkel advertisements based on a similar philosophy of pinpoint-sharp and highly detailed photographs.

A good example is the brochure *Toledo Berkel Snelwegers* (for Van Berkel). Schuitema preferred to use cut-out, photographic forms standing out sharply against red tinted areas. On the cover, sets of different-sized weighing scales were fused into one eye-catching photomontage. On the inside pages the products were dealt with individually. The copy was set as usual in sans-serif, with the main texts in upper case and reversed-out to heighten the effect on the cover. Where necessary Schuitema drew the letters with a compass and ruler, for as he wrote in 1929: 'Letters: the printer's material...They should be neutral and extremely legible... Our letters should be composed from the most simple basic forms.' In this brochure he was less inclined to use diagonals, but showed a preference for strong colour with black and white contrasts and – whenever the design required it – a caricature drawing. Photography gave him the opportunity to make dramatic, life-size reproductions of objects, and to enlarge the details, which were given lively symbols like circles and arrows.

Schuitema's purely typographic compositions were austere. Van Berkel's writing paper in three colours, with horizontal and vertical bars and a pithy logo, is a good example of his simple typographic style. The basic elements are systematically arranged, can be used in various combinations and together form a recognisable house style.

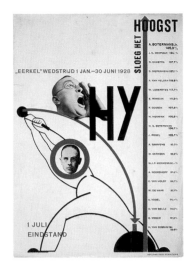

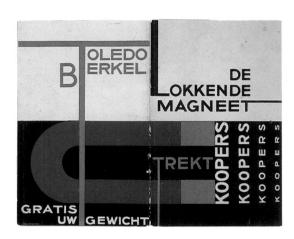

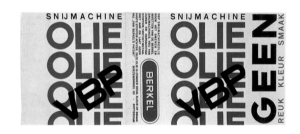

Paul Schuitema
Advertisement *He Hit
the Highest*, Berkel's
Patent, Rotterdam
1928

Paul Schuitema
Cover of the brochure
The Enticing Magnet,
Berkel's Patent,
Rotterdam c.1927

Paul Schuitema
Label for *Van Berkel
Cutting Machine Oil*,
Berkel's Patent,
Rotterdam c.1930

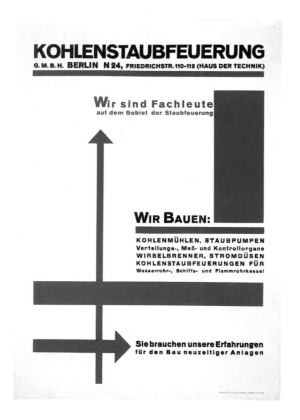

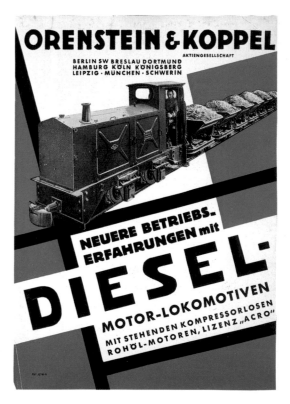

Cesar Domela
German brochure
advertising the
burning of powder
coal as fuel. Executed
in severe horizontal
and vertical lettering

Cesar Domela
Brochure for *Diesel engine trains*, Ornstein & Koppel AG, Berlin c.1930. The diagonal photographic compositions were typical of the new dynamic typography in advertising

Cesar Domela
Cover of *Marianne Raschig, Hand und Persönlichkeit* (Hand and Personality); Gebr. Enoch Verlag, Hamburg 1931

Cesar Domela and photomontage in Berlin

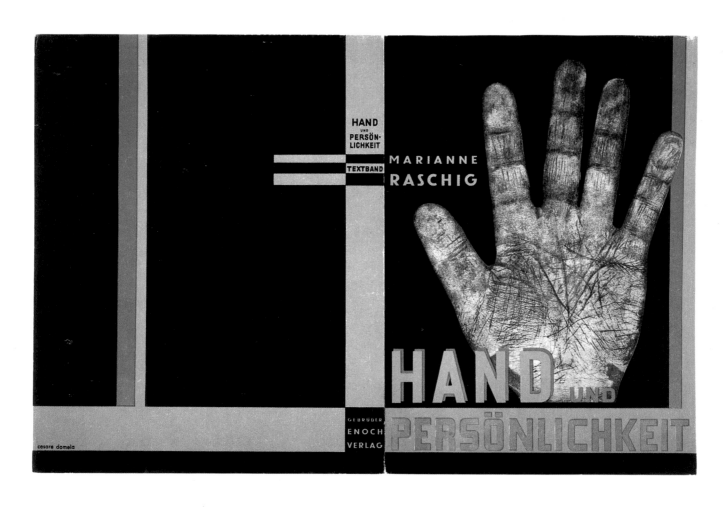

In 1924 Theo van Doesburg reproduced a woodcut by the Dutch painter Cesar Domela in his journal *De Stijl*. Commenting on this, Van Doesburg wrote that the work was evidence 'of a serious study in a Cubistic and Constructivist direction' and called Domela 'a young artist of fine calibre'.

Domela, born in 1900, the son of the great socialist leader Ferdinand Domela Nieuwenhuis, had left the Netherlands following his father's death in 1919 and was painting in Ascona in a Cubist style. He made friends with Raoul Hausmann in Berlin and Henry Laurens in Paris, and when he met Mondrian and Van Doesburg in Paris in 1924 his paintings fitted in readily with the precepts of the De Stijl artists, whom he was allowed to join as the youngest member of the group. Like the others he dreamed of the future integration of the visual arts and architecture. After a short stay in Amsterdam, Domela moved in 1927 with his young wife, Ruth Derenberg, to Berlin. The city was a stimulating artistic centre where he quickly made friends with avant-garde artists like Hans Richter, F. Vordemberge and Kurt Schwitters, but it was as difficult to make a living there with Constructivist paintings as in Amsterdam or Paris. Like his contemporaries, Domela discovered that in advertising and book design he might realise some of his visual principles. He had gained some typographic experience in Amsterdam with his friend Arthur Müller-Lehning, when Moholy-Nagy designed the layout for Müller-Lehning's *International Revue i10* magazine, but chiefly he mastered the techniques of graphic art on his own, as Zwart and Schuitema had done before him. His first typographic experiments were convincing enough for Schwitters to invite him to join his group, the Ring Neue Werbegestalter.

After 1928 Domela was no longer satisfied with the restrictions of the flat canvas and turned to making wooden reliefs, which became his trademark. In his graphic work he no longer considered lettering and lines dynamic enough. He soon discovered the visual power of photography, particularly that of photomontage, and this was the technique he used for his book covers, advertisements and brochures, proclaiming in his youthful enthusiasm that it was the most outstanding contemporary medium for graphic communication. He proclaimed in a reading given to the Berlin Typographic Association: 'Nowadays photography is one of the most important communication means, in view of the fact that the image, more so than the printed word, is internationally understood... It was not invented, as is often maintained, but arose out of a necessity of the time, which new opportunities for expression and combinations of materials required.' This reading marked the opening of the large 'Photomontage' exhibition, which he organised in spring 1931 at the Staatliche Kunstbibliothek, Berlin.

That Domela was forced against his ideals to work on commissions for capitalist industry was a dilemma he shared with other kindred spirits. As an antidote to this he also designed covers for left-wing publishers like De Baanbreker-Servire in The Hague.

The assumption of power by the Nazis in 1933 forced Domela to leave Germany. In Paris he established the first silkscreen printing studio for advertising and designed posters and magazine covers, but in 1936 he returned again to painting.

Cesar Domela
Cover of *Michail Sjolochov, De stille Don* (The Quiet Don), Servire – De Baanbreker, The Hague 1931. For this popular Russian book Domela used the typical Russian device of creating a photomontage from various photographic images

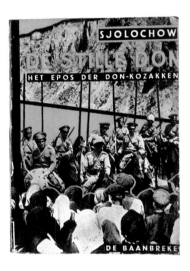

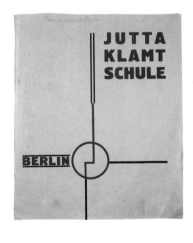

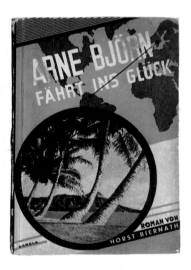

Cesar Domela
Cover of a prospectus for the progressive *Juute Klamt Dance School*, Berlin c.1928. The design ties in with both Domela's De Stijl paintings and the principles of the new typography

Cesar Domela
Cover of *Horst Biernath, Arne Björn fährt ins Glück*, one of the last commercial photomontages executed by Domela before moving to Paris; Zeitschriftenverlag, Berlin 1933

Functionalism and decoration

Jacob Jongert
Poster for *Van Nelle*
coffee and tea;
Rotterdam, c.1930

Functionalism in architecture and design as well as abstraction in the visual arts continued to make themselves felt in the 1930s, but there came a turning point. Economic crisis and a threatening world political situation evoked the opposite – occasionally even frivolous – response, fuelled also by the late effect of the 1925 Art Deco exhibition in Paris. The international emergence of realism in painting went hand-in-hand with a huge demand for illustrative design. The idealised image of the machine lost momentum and many preferred a decorative style to the aesthetics of functionalism.

Gerard Kiljan regarded the new functionalism as only one of many ways of designing, and by the late 1930s even Piet Zwart was using illustrative drawings in his work. On the other hand, a demand for functionalism remained in architecture and typography. In the 1930s industry discovered that the tubular chair and widespread use of prefabricated buildings helped to realise an ideal of light and airy living conditions. Economic efficiency also played an important role, as revealed in such company posters as those for the Gispen firm of lamp manufacturers. Artists, who in the 1920s were still geared to decoration and embellishment, after 1930 moved to using a more austere design style: for example, Jacob Jongert in his posters and packaging for Van Nelle. Whereas approaches to design in the 1920s were divided between distinct schools of thought, with the journal *Wendingen* on the one hand and the New Functionalism on the other, in the next decade these divisions became less clear and many methods of working were combined. Straight lines and round forms were used together, while the 'kidney' shape, mainly derived from the reliefs of Swiss artist Hans Arp, remained popular in graphic and industrial design until the 1950s.

In 1939, a special graphics edition of the progressive architectural journal *De 8 en Opbouw* was published under the title *Grafies-nummer*. In this issue the youthful Dick Elffers and Wim Brusse seemed to deny everything they had been taught. Elffers expresses the thought that 'designers and illustrators who had been trained in the spirit of Bauhaus Dessau or in similar-minded schools and studios' – he was one himself – 'are partly attempting to disengage themselves from this influence. Limitations in technique and composition (photography and so-called synthetic drawing) seem to be an obstacle to development'. Elffers compared the situation to 'changes which the "new buildings" are showing here and there'; and undoubtedly referred to the new baroque elements that architect Sybold van Ravesteyn – once a champion of New Functionalism – was introducing in his buildings to the dismay of his modernist colleagues. The architect wrote at the time: 'In the Paris of Le Corbusier even the modern man or woman seeks the attractiveness of a Rococo restaurant with its animated quietness.'

Elffers argued for 'a vigorous art bringing new symbols with it', and illustrated this with examples of book and magazine covers in which the drawn illustration was assigned a greater role in the design than the photograph. A certain Surrealist influence – extreme perspectives and suspended symbolic shapes – was also unmistakable. Brusse pointed out even more emphatically the limitations of photography: 'Isms and New Functionalism lent renewed character to photography, though not without this leading here and there to it being overestimated...Photography is denied the possibility of giving expression to the imagination that lives in the mind over and above reality. Photography is doomed to remain on the surface.' Young designers were required, he added: 'to visualise from a powerful inner realm of ideas'.

The older generation like Kiljan, Schuitema, Cahn and Zwart were angry and amused by turns: 'In what sense can a technique be a hindrance to development? We are of the opinion that the cause of any possible hindrance must lie with its user'. Despite the decorative elements in their own work they spoke somewhat haughtily of Brusse's 'strange conclusions' and thought it 'amazing that a young person had never experienced the visual power of photography'.

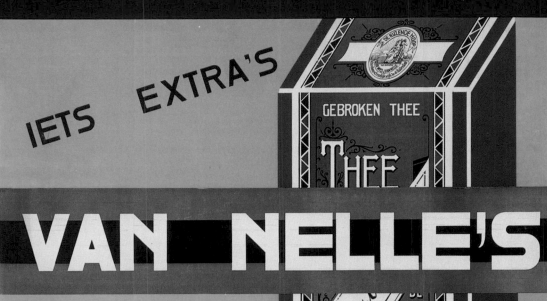
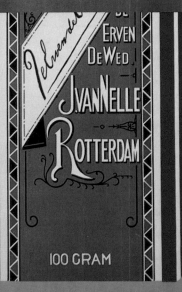

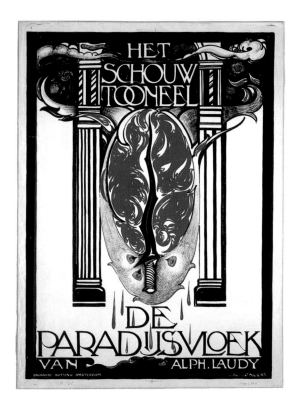

Jacob Jongert and Rotterdam

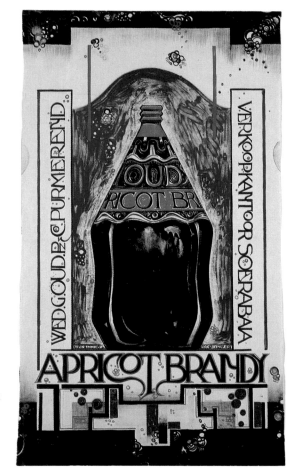

Jacob Jongert
Poster for *Alphonse
Laudy, The Curse of
Paradise*, Het
Schouwtooneel, 1919.
The monumental and
decorative approach
clearly betray the
influence of Jongert's
mentor and friend,
R.N. Roland Holst

Jacob Jongert
Poster for *Apricot
brandy*, Wed. G. Oud
Pz and Co, Purmerend
1920. Jongert
composed numerous
decorative labels and
flyers for the wine
merchants

As a graphic designer Jacob Jongert served industry for a large part of his working life. Proceeding from an idealism based on fruitful cooperation between artist and industry in bringing good and functional design to everyday life, he believed that advertising should remain unfettered and not dependent on official prescriptives.

Jongert began his training at Quellinus, a school for industrial arts and drawing, and later attended the Rijksacademie, Amsterdam. He became friendly with Roland Holst and helped him with his monumental murals for the Dutch General Diamond Cutters' Association. During this time he learnt what the freedom of the artist meant within a given framework – what applied art, in fact, was. Inspired by De Roos, Jongert devoted himself to graphic techniques and began designing advertisements for industry. In this he was influenced by a visit to the Werkbund exhibition of 1914 in Cologne. His advertising posters and labels designed for Oud, a wine and spirit merchants, were characterised by stylised decorative forms and an individual way with typography. He developed a house style for the firm, including its brochures for which he used the shape of De Bazel's bottles. Through the VANK he also received commissions from other companies, not only for the design of advertisements but until 1919 also for murals, book covers, wallpaper and carpeting.

At the time Jongert was still working in what was labelled the 'new art' style, influenced by Roland Holst's work. In 1918 he was appointed lecturer at the Rotterdam Academy, teaching applied arts, and demonstrating that good design should both be beautiful and serve its purpose. From 1919 he designed the graphics for the Rotterdam coffee, tea and tobacco factory of De Erven de Wed. J. van Nelle, and also created layouts for the annual Utrecht Trade Fair.

Jongert's work, which began on a decorative and traditional note, later became more functional; adapting to the demands of the age. At the Rotterdam Academy his colleagues were Kiljan and Zwart, whose work he considered too stark and dogmatic. For him, an artistic and personal approach remained the most important starting point for design, even in his more constructed posters and packaging for Van Nelle. He also developed an instantly recognisable house colour and type for the Van Nelle products. In the 1930s Jongert used photomontage, as in his brochure for Beverol car oil. He was also the co-founder of the R33 artists' group, which championed personal expression in graphic design, and it was here that he met the young Dick Elffers.

Two other Rotterdam designers were Machiel Wilmink and N.P. de Koo. Wilmink was on the editorial staff of *De Reclame* magazine and was in charge of Studio M.W., where modern advertising design was regarded as a collaborative effort between copywriter, illustrator, typographer and photographer. The work, however, varied considerably in quality. De Koo was primarily an industrial artist who designed furniture and interiors, but also did graphic work, especially for the PTT. He drew all his designs in a clear, quasi-technical style incorporating an inventive use of colour.

Jacob Jongert
Advertisement for
Van Nelle's Prisma tea,
Rotterdam 1928.
During the 1920s,
Jongert, as chief of
the company's
advertising
department, switched
to a more spare and
functional design
style chiefly executed
in primary colours

N.P. de Koo
Information leaflet
for *Rotterdam: Outline
of the Housing
Programme*,
Rotterdam City
Council, 1924. De Koo,
like Jongert after him,
preferred hand-
drawn, sans-serif
letters, which formed
decorative blocks of
text

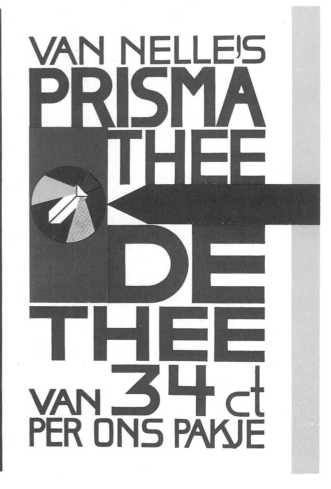

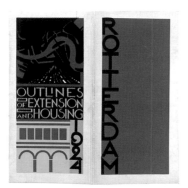

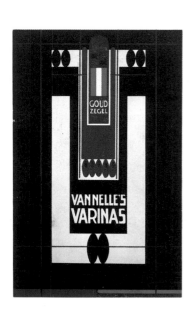

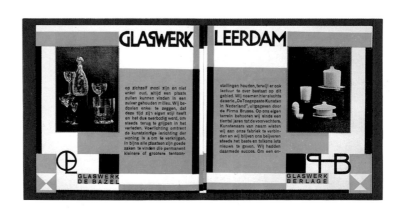

Jacob Jongert
Advertisement for
Van Nelle Varinas,
Rotterdam 1923.
In 1919 Jongert
began designing
advertisements and
packaging for the tea,
coffee and tobacco
products of De Erven
De Wed. J. Van Nelle

Machiel Wilmink
Pages from an
advertising book for
Leerdam glass, with
illustrations by
De Bazel and
Berlage/Zwart,
Leerdam 1923-1924

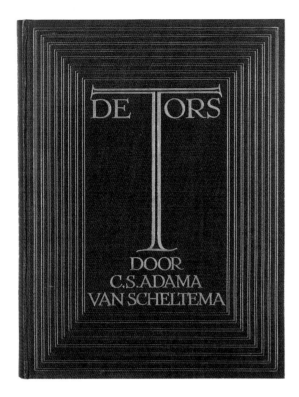

W.L. and J. Brusse Publishers

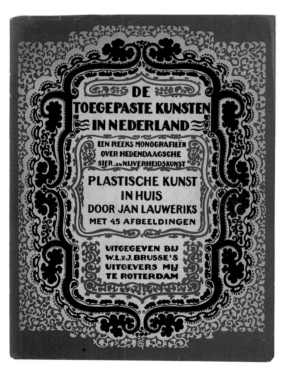

S.H. de Roos
Cover of *C.S. Adama
van Scheltema, De Tors –
zeven zangen* (The Tors
– Seven Songs), W.L.
and J. Brusse,
Rotterdam 1924. For
the cover blocking
and text De Roos used
his Erasmus, a book
type brought out a
year earlier by the
Amsterdam Type
Foundry as a follow-
up to the heavier
Hollandsche
Mediaeval

R. Gerbrands
Cover of *Jan Lauweriks,
Plastische kunst in huis*
(Plastic Art in House),
one of a 24-part series
on Dutch applied
arts; W.L. and
J. Brusse, Rotterdam
1924

The idealistic views of the Brusse brothers' publishing house, founded in 1903 by Willy and Johan Christiaan Brusse, were very important to graphic design in the Netherlands. Its prime concerns were that the books should be given to artists to design, and that great care was applied to their production in terms of paper quality, type and illustration. Many of the Brusse brothers' publications were printed by G.J. Thieme of Nijmegen and also by Flakkeesche of Middelharnis.

The Brusse brothers placed artistic concern over and above business matters. In a Rotterdam address book of 1905 the company is listed as a 'publisher in the field of literature, the sciences and essays on contemporary subjects, etcetera'. On the other hand, they also published the popular *Boefje* (Rascal) series of crime novels written by a third brother and journalist, M.J. Brusse. The company's interest in a broad area of industrial art was demonstrated in a series of 24 booklets, *De Toegepaste Kunst in Nederland* (Applied Art in the Netherlands) by A.A.M. Stols with covers designed by R. Gerbrands, which were issued between 1923 and 1935, and in the VANK's Yearbooks published from 1919 to 1932. Stols devoted a section of his series to the making of beautiful books and praised Brusse's goals as a publisher. The company also devoted much attention to social politics in literature, and published among others the work of the socialist poet Henriëtte Roland Holst and Adama van Scheltema. Within Brusse itself the socialist ideal was upheld: directors and personnel were treated on equal terms and there was an openness to innovation in many fields.

Their series on architecture, *Moderne Bouwkunst in Nederland*, with essays and readings from, and about, Berlage, used for the first time the new type Hollandsche Mediaeval by De Roos. De Roos himself was hired as a consultant and was particularly responsible for embossing the poet Boutens's translations of classical Greek literature in gold. Modern art and film were covered in the series *Monografieën over Filmkunst*, designed by Piet Zwart. Following the Second World War, Brusse published the ideal home magazine *Goed Wonen* (Good Living). Many artists worked for Brusse including De Roos, Lauweriks, Vilmos Huszár, Piet Zwart, Wim Brusse and Jan van Krimpen, and the publishers were active for more than 50 years in stimulating new and classical styles in graphic design.

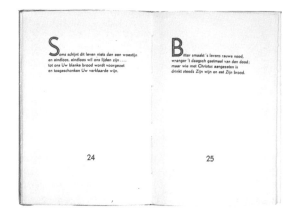

Piet Zwart
Cover of *Constant van
Wessem, De komische
film* (The Comic Film),
one of a series of
monographs on the
art of film-making;
W.L. and J. Brusse,
Rotterdam 1931.
Piet Zwart combined
Charlie Chaplin's
attributes with a
double self-portrait

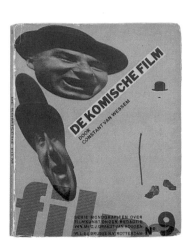

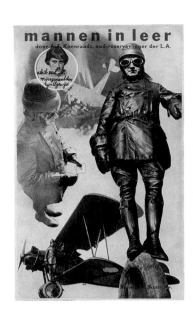

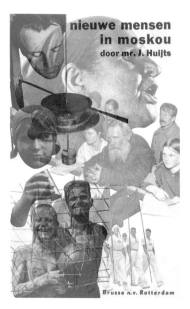

Wim Brusse
Cover of *A.J.
Koenraads, Mannen in
leer* (Men in Leather),
a typical collage of
photographs taken
from a variety of
angles; W.L. and
J. Brusse, Rotterdam
1935

Wim Brusse
Cover of *Johan Huijts,
Nieuwe mensen in
Moskou* (New People
in Moscow), W.L. and
J. Brusse, Rotterdam
1935. Brusse used
blue and brown in
this photomontage
in the same way that
Piet Zwart used red
and blue to illustrate
the series of film
monographs

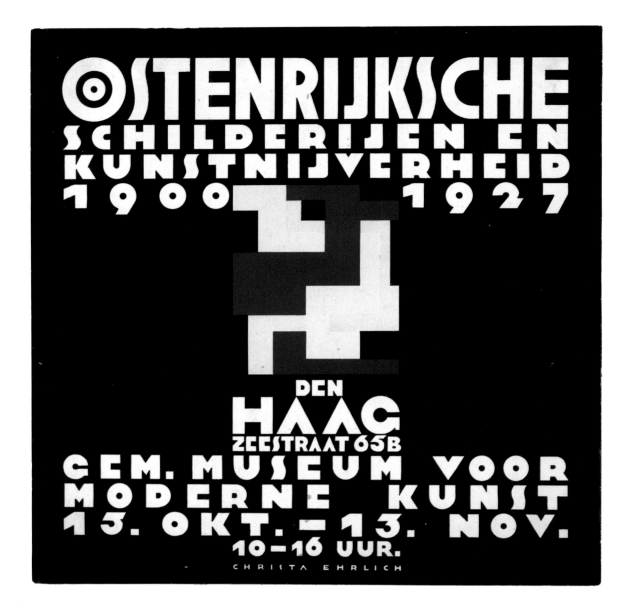

Christa Ehrlich
Poster for an
*Exhibition of Austrian
paintings and crafts*,
Gemeentemuseum,
The Hague 1927.
A pupil of Josef
Hoffmann, Ehrlich
arrived in the
Netherlands from
Vienna in 1927, and
became known as a
designer of modern
cutlery and
silverware for Begeer
in Voorschoten

Raoul Hynckes
Poster for an
*Exhibition on art works
by Dutch living masters*,
Stedelijk Museum,
Amsterdam 1932. In
contrast to what one
would expect from
his Magic Realist
paintings, Hynckes'
illustrations show a
light touch and a
clear, Cubist-inspired
style

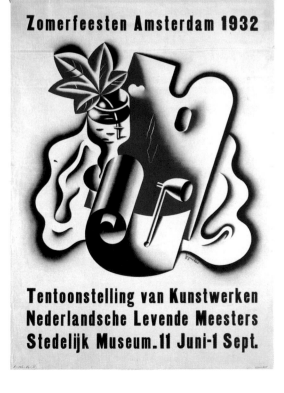

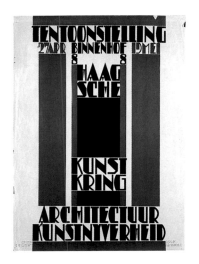

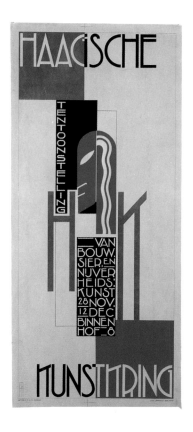

Posters: from decorative to functional

C. Mus Jnr
Poster for an
*Exhibition on applied
art in architecture,*
The Hague Art Circle,
1929. The drawn
letters are in keeping
with Wijdeveld and
the Amsterdam
School

P.A.H. Hofman
Poster for an
*Exhibition on building,
decorative and
industrial design,*
The Hague Art Circle,
1931. Hofman
designed numerous
posters and book
covers using a blend
of functional and
decorative styles

In spite of the clamorous champions of phototypography, who indulged themselves in such small-scale type matter as leaflets and brochures produced with letterpress, several established designers – particularly poster designers – remained involved with traditional design. Russian artist/designers had demonstrated that in theory there were few technical restrictions to the use of photography for lithographic posters, but the drawn poster was still preferred by some. Posters for such cultural events as art exhibitions remained couched in the decorative tradition; it was years before photography made a respectable impression in that quarter.

The tradition of extravagant decoration *à la* Roland Holst was followed by Wijdeveld's baroque games with typographic elements, which was widely imitated. The drawn letter, often geometrically distorted, was the building stone for architectonic type compositions using bars and architraves, to which simple symbolic representations were sometimes attached. This can be seen in the work of P.A.H. Hofman in The Hague and other designers of, and for, the city's Kunstkring or artists' society. One design of this period by the Austrian, Christa Ehrlich, who later made a name for herself as a designer of modern silverware for the firm of Begeer, shows a much freer approach to modernism, with an abstract-geometric composition in the centre and an elegant Austrian way of positioning the typography. A poster from Hynckes also reveals that developments in painting found their counterpart in graphic art, both in the choice of motifs and in the fragmented construction, where echoes from the Cubism of Braque and Léger resound.

The manufacturer and industrial designer, W.H. Gispen, was originally under the spell of the decorative embellishments of the Amsterdam School and of Wijdeveld's geometric in-filling. In his 1926 poster Gispen aligned

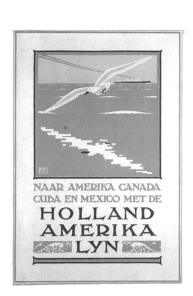

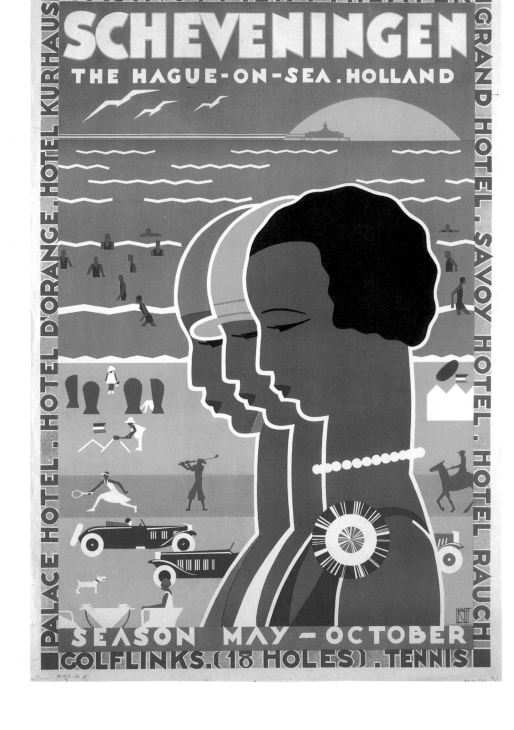

L.C. Kalff
Poster advertising
Go to America, Canada,
Cuba and Mexico with
the Holland-America
line, Rotterdam 1929

L.C. Kalff
Poster advertising
the *Seaside resort of*
Scheveningen,
The Hague 1931

him stylistically with the bright colours, blocked letters and stylised figures that N.P. de Koo used for a small graphic design for the city of Rotterdam, and which also characterised Schuitema's earlier work. A few years later he converted to the New Functionalism and designed steel tubular furniture. In his graphic work he followed the current trend and utilised photography, such as in his posters for Giso Lamps.

De Koo was different. In his VANK posters or in those for the Phoenix brewery in Amersfoort, he set about his work in the same way as for the PTT, relying on his own solidly constructed sans-serif capitals, combined with pithily drawn and distinctive images. It was a style that Vilmos had employed in his Miss Blanche cigarette advertisements and which was later to be pursued by Jacob Jongert.

Louis Kalff also had an industrial background as a lighting consultant for Philips. He drew posters in an eclectic fashion, sometimes with an eye on English taste as in his poster for the Holland America line, or leaning towards Ludwig Hohlwein's advertisement for Philips, but always with an unexpected decorative treatment of Art Deco elements. Good examples are provided by his brochures and posters for Scheveningen Zeebad, the developed part of Scheveningen's coastline.

From the numerous posters produced for shipping and tourism at the end of the 1920s, it is clear that foreign poster artists had made a big impression in the Netherlands, particularly the work of the Frenchman A.M. Cassandre. His powerful and simplified forms, visual inventions and dramatic expressions of force and speed were often translated for Dutch use.

N.P. de Koo
Poster for an open-air exhibition on the *Dutch East and West Indies*, Arnhem 1928

W.H. Gispen
Poster for the *Rotterdam-South America line*, Rotterdam 1926

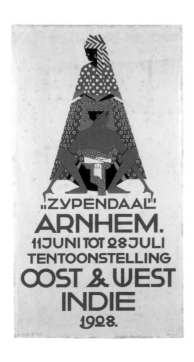

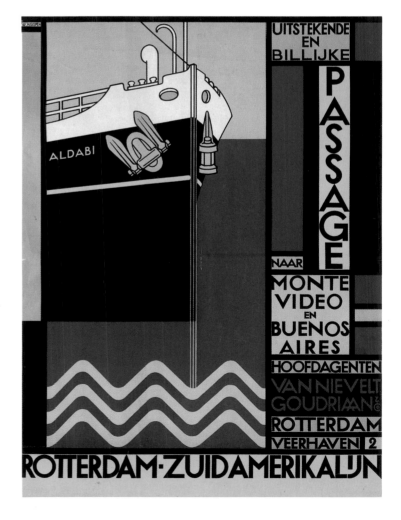

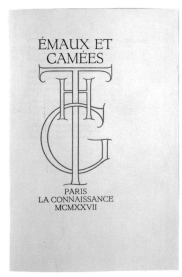

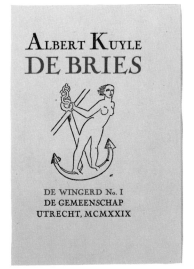

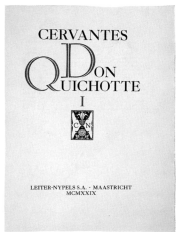

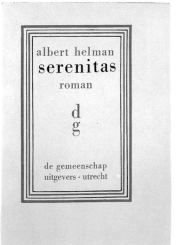

Charles Nypels
Title page for
*Théophile Gauthier,
Emaux et Camées*, a
poetry anthology in
the series *La tulipe
rose*: La Connaissance,
Paris 1927. De Roos
drew the monogram
and his Erasmus book
type was used

Charles Nypels
Title page for *Albert
Kuyle, De Bries* (The
Breeze) for the
Wingerd series;
De Gemeenschap,
Utrecht 1929. The
drawing is by Jozef
Cantré and the type is
the French-inspired
Gravure 11 from the
Amsterdam Type
Foundry

Charles Nypels
Title page for
*Cervantes, Don Quichotte
ou l'ingénieux Hidalgo
Don Quichotte de la
Mancha in four volumes*,
Leiter-Nypels,
Maastricht 1929-
1931. De Roos drew
the initials of this
asymmetrical title
page

Charles Nypels
Title page for *Albert
Helman, Serenitas,*
De Gemeenschap,
Utrecht 1930. The
Bodoni typeface, used
only in lower case, is
an interesting
example of Nypels'
unconventional
typography

Charles Nypels, master printer

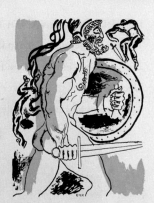

Charles Nypels
Spread from the
poetry anthology
*Anton van Duinkerken,
Het Wereldorgel*
(The World Organ),
De Gemeenschap,
Utrecht 1931.
The oblong format is
somewhat curious;
Charles Eyck
produced the
drawings

There was a great tradition in printing, not only in the west but also in the south of the Netherlands. Charles Nypels came from a long line of Maastricht printers and he continued in the tradition. He trained at the Amsterdam Type Foundry of Sjoerd de Roos, which signified for Nypels the beginning of a fruitful career in which he could take his place among the most important Dutch typographers, such as Van Royen, Stols and Van Krimpen. He admired the classical tradition in which they worked, interpreted within a modern context, with close attention to book cover and title pages, restrained and carefully thought-out contents, functional initials, spare decoration and appropriate illustrations. For the latter Nypels employed mainly woodcuts from, among others, Joseph Cantré. The choice of paper for each edition played an extremely important role, while the typefaces were classic but still of the period, such as Hollandsche Mediaeval, Grotius, Erasmus Mediaeval and Gravure. Later Nypels occasionally used the more modern Nobel.

Nypels' company, Leiter-Nypels, was in fact a commercial printer but he was himself largely interested in fine books. Throughout his life he was a risk-taker who experimented idiosyncratically with established forms. His first editions appeared in 1920 and in subsequent decades it was clear how his work had changed, becoming freer and more fresh-looking with the incorporation of new ideas. His contact with the editor and staff of De Gemeenschap, a Utrecht magazine and publishing house (later to become Het Spectrum), for whom from 1925 he worked as a typographic consultant, enabled him to produce such varied popular series as *Schijnwerpers* (Spotlights), *De Bongerd* (The Orchard), *Windroos* (Wood Anemone), *Wat leeft en groeit* (What Lives and Grows) and a number of almanacs. Nypels was no modernist, and remained within a distinct typographic tradition. However, in 1935 he translated into Dutch *Typografische Gestaltung* by Jan Tschichold, a champion of modern typography, and it was published in 1938 by Duwaer in Amsterdam. Throughout his life Nypels nurtured a passion for French and Dutch literature and in 1945, together with Leeflang and Van Wees, he founded the De Roos foundation for publishing fine books.

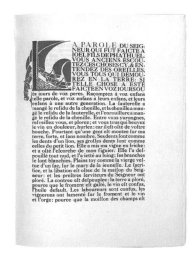

Charles Nypels Decorative vignette from *La prophétie de Ioël* (The Prophet Joel, book of the Old Testament), which is set in Plantin and is an early example of Nypels' typographic style. The colourful woodcuts are by Henri Jonas; Leiter-Nypels, Maastricht 1923

Charles Nypels Christmas greeting *Lucas 11, 1-14*, set in Plantin, with woodcuts by Jozef Cantré, who illustrated numerous publications for De Gemeenschap; De Gemeenschap, Utrecht 1927

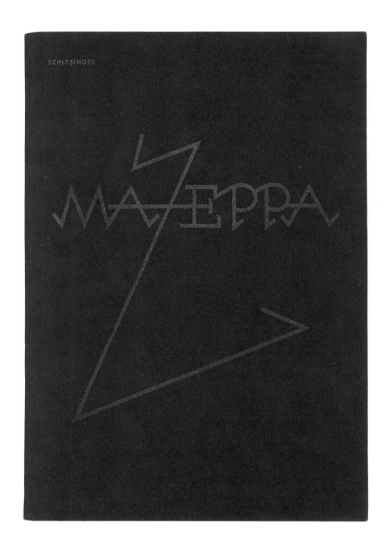

Stefan Schlesinger

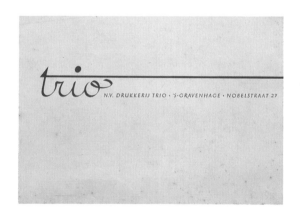

Stefan Schlesinger's work brought a graceful, Central European touch to Dutch graphic advertising around 1930. After abandoning his architectural studies in Vienna, Schlesinger worked in the Vienna studio of the well-known poster artist, Julius Klinger. His mentor's decorative ideas and playful letterforms, and echoes of the Wiener Werkstätte, can be found in Schlesinger's earlier work for Metz & Co, the Amsterdam furniture store, which dates from the time he moved with his Dutch wife to the city in 1925.

Schlesinger liked letterforms that represented the personality of their creator, such as those by E.R. Weiss, Lucian Bernhard and Imre Reiner. Subsequently, his attention shifted from drawn illustration to mechanical forms and he designed a great deal of lettering for packaging for Talens, the ink manufacturing firm, and for boxes of writing paper for the Van Gelder paper company. For Trio Printers in The Hague, where his brother-in-law was director, he designed an elegant calligraphic logo, writing paper and calendars as well as various advertising print. He specialised in book covers and embossing, and designed *ex-libris* plates which were cherished collectable items in the 1930s. 'To reinforce the love of beautiful letterforms', as he himself put it, he produced a number of type reference books for designers and painters of lettering and advertising signs. It was typical of Schlesinger that in so doing he attempted to advocate a closer link between the letterform itself and the message of the text.

Schlesinger developed his best-known house style for the packaging, posters, advertisements and film commercials of Van Houten, the chocolate manufacturers. His fine, stylised design for the company logo was used unaltered for decades. For the body texts he developed an elegant, sans-serif letter very similar to the Optima of Hermann Zapf, designed 20 years later.

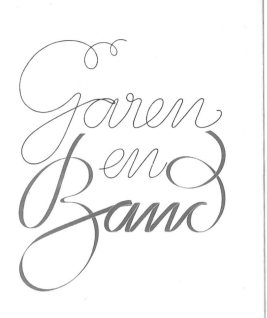

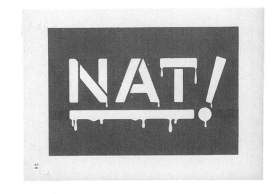

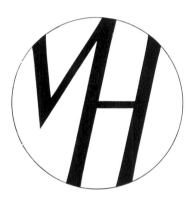

Stefan Schlesinger
Two examples of type
'Garen en band'
(Thread and ribbon)
and 'Nat' (Wet) from
*Examples of Modern
Lettering for Decorative
Painters*, Nunspeet
1939

Stefan Schlesinger
Logo for *Van Houten*
chocolate
manufacturers,
Weesp, c.1936

Stefan Schlesinger
Invitation card for an
*Exhibition of
Schlesinger's work*, Trio
Printers, The Hague
1932. The printing
firm showed the work
of graphic designers
such as Huszár and
Zwart in its new
exhibition space. The
logos of Schlesinger
and Trio feature
prominently on the
invitation

6

At the end of the 1930s the Amsterdam Type Foundry, for whom Schlesinger
had already designed brochures, commissioned him to design an eye-catching
commercial type, Hidalgo. On the outbreak of the Second World War,
Schlesinger also embarked upon the design for a script type for commercial
advertising. The bulbous shapes of the letters appeared to have been written
with a flat nib and were not interrelated. Schlesinger had completed the
lower case and certain capitals when he was transported by the Nazis in 1942.
After the war, Dick Dooijes completed the alphabet. The type appeared in
1948 in a standard and semi-bold version called Rondo.

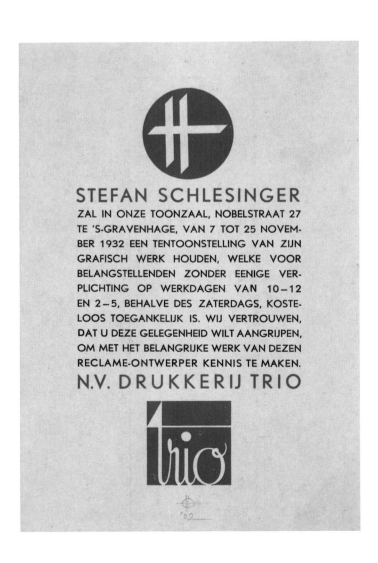

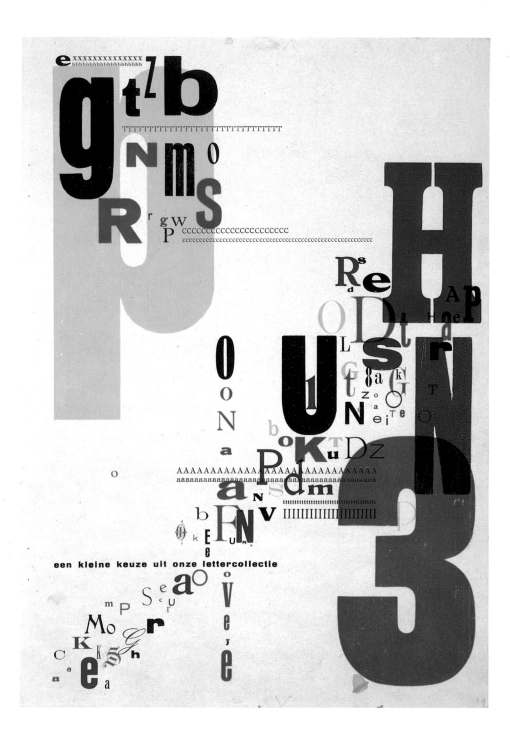

Trio Printers

Piet Zwart
Blotting paper for *Trio Printers*, The Hague, c.1925

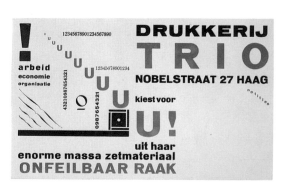

Piet Zwart
Cover and page from
*Trio Printers' advertising
book*, The Hague 1931.
While Zwart worked
for Trio for many
years, the firm was
somewhat taken
aback by his
extravagant approach
to the brief, and the
commission never
progressed any
further than a few
sample proofs

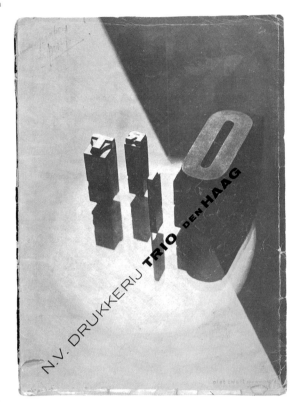

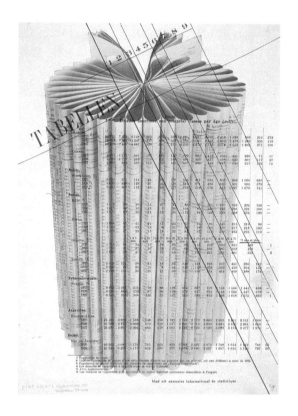

Printers as well as publishers have had a stimulating effect on graphic design developments in the Netherlands. As we have seen, this was invariably due to the interest and background of an enthusiastic director. In The Hague, F. Kerdijk, director of Trio Printers from 1923 to 1948, invited artists to design type materials or to exhibit their work in one of the firm's spaces set up in 1930 for the purpose.

Trio, initially known as the South Holland Book and Commercial Printers, was founded in 1894 by three participants of a failed typographic strike of that year. They ensured that the company was set up as a cooperative so that staff shared in the profits, owned three-quarters of the firm and from 1924 participated in policy-making. Kerdijk was similarly motivated and also had an instinct for the new trends of the day, admiring the work of Piet Zwart. He recognised that increasing numbers of clients were moving with the times as far as graphic design was concerned, and he commissioned artists to design advertising, calendars, type sample sheets and writing paper for the firm in all manner of graphic styles. Kerdijk was the brother-in-law of Stefan Schlesinger, who worked for Trio and was no doubt influential.

Designers for Trio included V. Huszár, Pam G. Rueter, Tine Baanders and Piet Zwart. In 1926 Trio commissioned the latter to make an extensive sample of types, which appeared in 1931 only in proof form. Despite the limited edition of proofs, Zwart's cover for the type samples, with its arresting photograph of emboldened T R I O letters, the colourful image of the firm's available typefaces and the sheet with examples of tables, eventually became famous. Trio did much printing for the publisher A.A.M. Stols, such as his *Halcyon* magazine, and from 1941 Stols himself was a consultant for Trio for several years and a member of its board of managers. In the difficult economic climate of the 1930s the number of special editions remained relatively small compared to the output of standard printing. During the Second World War, Trio was also involved in much clandestine printing.

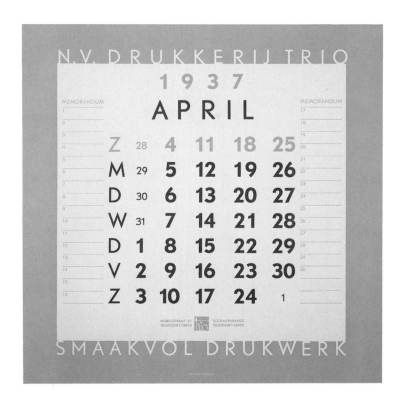

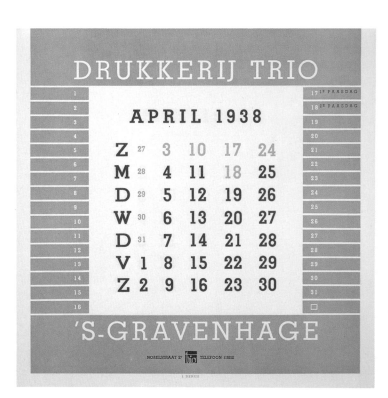

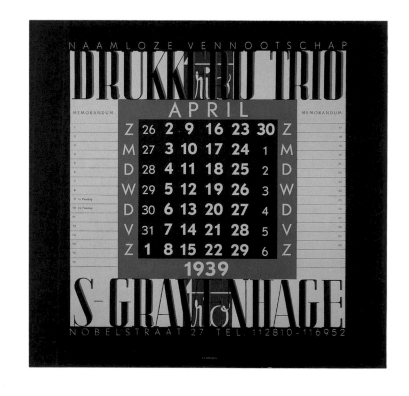

Stefan Schlesinger
Calendar for *Trio
Printers*, 1937

Job Denijs
Calendar for *Trio
Printers*, 1938

Tine Baanders
Calendar for *Trio
Printers*, 1939. Three
calendars from three
different designers in
which the functional
typography acts as a
visually unifying
element

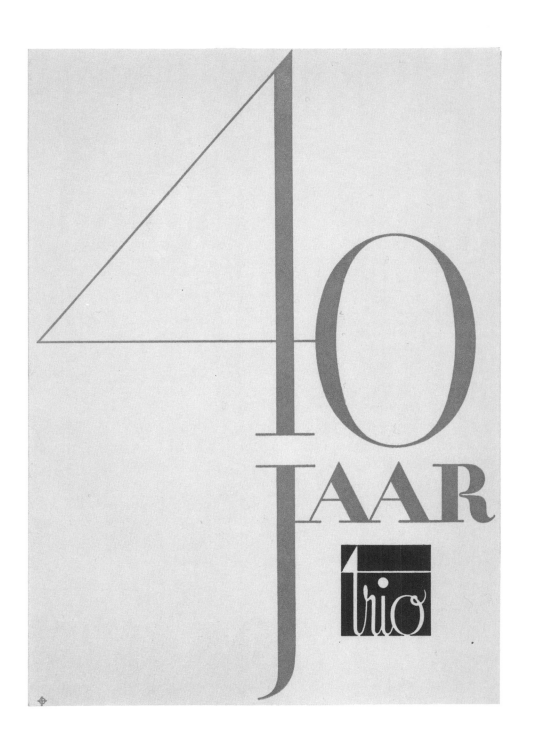

Stefan Schlesinger
Folder *40 years Trio*,
The Hague 1938

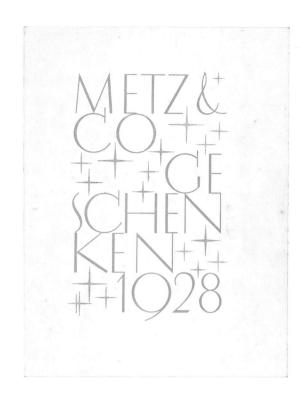

Contemporary graphics for Metz & Co

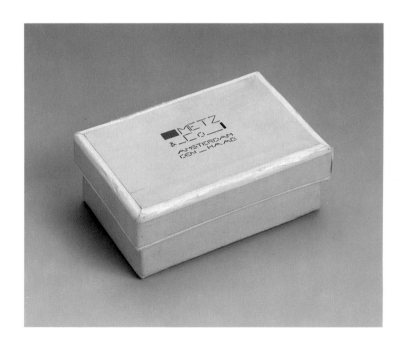

Stefan Schlesinger
Cover of a Christmas
season catalogue for
Metz & Co, Amsterdam
1928. Schlesinger's
designs from the
1920s are
distinguished by a
decorative, Austrian-
inspired calligraphy

Bart van der Leck
Lettering for a
jewellery box for *Metz
& Co*, Amsterdam and
The Hague c.1935.
Since 1929 Van der
Leck had designed
carpets and soft
furnishings for the
store and advised on
colour schemes for
interiors

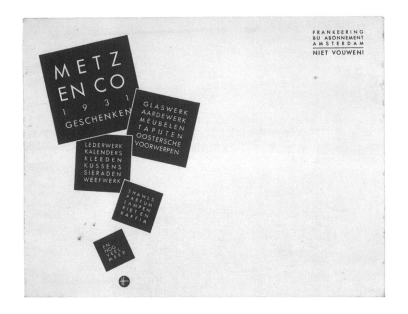

Anyone wanting up-to-the-minute interior décor in the 1930s patronised one of the branches of Metz & Co for the stark, modern designs of the Thonet brothers or Gerrit Rietveld, glass from Leerdam and colourful fabrics designed by Sonia Delaunay or produced by the fabric manufacturer Weverij De Ploeg.

Metz & Co had been under the far-sighted management of J. de Leeuw since 1900. It was he who imported the internationally renowned Liberty fabrics from London. In the 1920s he also introduced stylish, deluxe furniture from Paris and Vienna. At the same time he was gradually taking on more and more Dutch industrial artists, such as Paul Bromberg, Elmar Berkovich and Willem Penaat. They advised clients personally on interior schemes and at the same time designed exclusive furniture that was partly produced in Metz's own studio.

De Leeuw's introduction to Rietveld and the painter Bart van der Leck around 1930 brought renewed vigour to the store. In 1934 Penaat, Rietveld and Van der Leck turned the Metz branch in The Hague into a hypermodern showroom. This meant that clients could not only shop at Metz for Penaat's solidly designed furniture, but also find there matching interiors for the most avant-garde houses. In general, however, Van der Leck's abstract and geometric carpets and floor coverings, and the zigzag and tubular chairs of Rietveld and architect J.J.P. Oud were purchased in small numbers by a public wary of experimental design.

In any event De Leeuw enjoyed the publicity and expected stylish products from graphic designers. From 1926 Stefan Schlesinger designed the firm's spring and autumn catalogues, letterhead and advertisements; his elegant and original calligraphic style suited the business attitudes of the 1930s. In the mid-1930s young graphic designers such as Dick Elffers and Cas Oorthuys followed with more spartan designs. Bart van der Leck designed superb bags and boxes in his inimitable style of fragmented letterforms and areas of primary colours, which properly reflected Metz & Co's combination of exclusivity and the avant-garde.

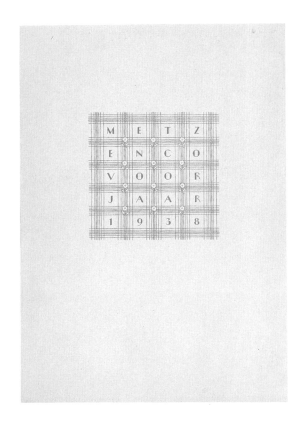

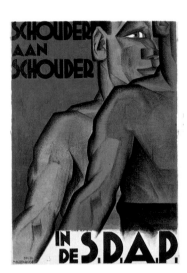

Meyer Bleekrode
Poster *Shoulder to
Shoulder with the SDAP*,
Amsterdam 1930

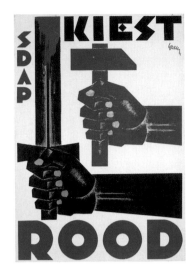

Walter (surname
unknown)
Poster *Choose Red*,
SDAP (Labour Party),
Amsterdam 1929

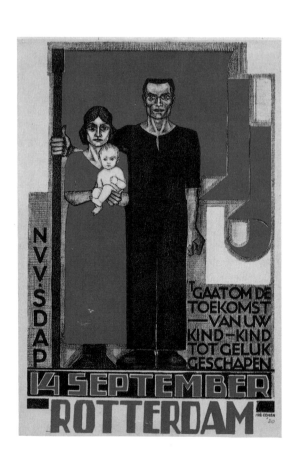

Fré Cohen
Poster *The Concern is
for your Child's Future*,
SDAP (Labour Party),
Amsterdam 1930

Posters for the social struggle

In the posters for left-wing political parties, trade unions or leftist splinter groups the legacy of the political cartoon – as drawn by painters such as Piet van der Hem and Jan Sluijters and illustrators Albert Hahn, Louis Ramaekers and L.J. Jordaan – was easily recognisable. Posters of the 1920s often depicted the traditional symbols of the left, such as the hen, the red banner, the red morning sky and the young, idealistic worker's family gazing into the future. This is well captured in a poster by the Amsterdam graphic artist Fré Cohen, which incidentally is striking for its stark stylisation. She was particularly active as a designer for the Amsterdam City Council and often employed decorative elements that were strongly aligned to the architectural details of the Amsterdam School.

Around 1930 the posters of the workers' movement became more forbidding, with echoes of German Expressionism and Cubism in their design. Posters that 'cried out' replaced decorative symbolism, as can be seen in the dour heads depicted by painter Meyer Bleekrode, while the illustrator Walter chose succinct, readily identifiable symbols.

Political posters displayed the first use of photography in the medium. It is noteworthy, too, that the human figure provided the most convincing image. Schuitema's poster, *Transport workers*, is a fine example of this: the head of a young worker faces the masses that form his body in a new form of symbolism conveyed by the new technique of photomontage. The poster by Cas Oorthuys and Jo Voskuil for *D.O.O.D. – De Olympiade onder dictatuur* (The Olympics under a Dictator), to herald an information and art exhibition directed against the staging of the Berlin Olympic Games in 1936 by Hitler, is satirical and aggressive, influenced by John Heartfield's montages for *Arbeiter Internationale Zeitung*.

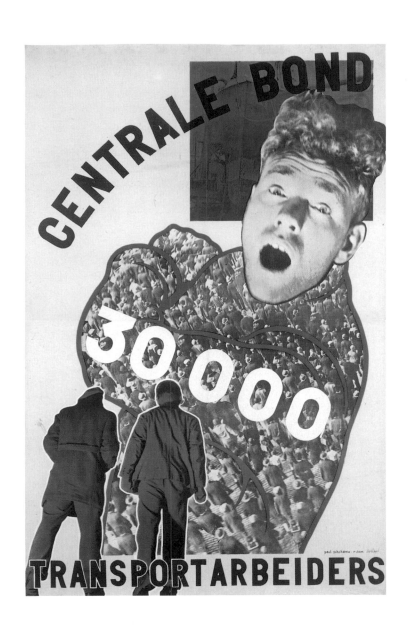

Paul Schuitema
Poster for the *Central
Transport Workers'
Union*, Amsterdam
1930

Cas Oorthuys,
Jo Voskuil
Exhibition poster
*The Olympics under a
Dictator*, De Geelvinck
Building, Amsterdam
1936

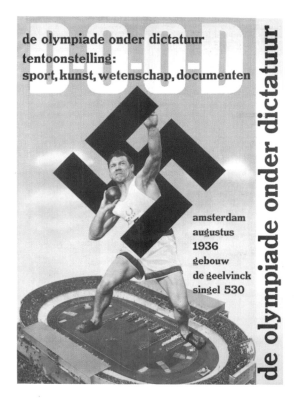

Depression, emigration and occupation

H.N. Werkman
Cover of the *Turkish
Calendar 1942*,
De Blauwe Schuit,
Groningen 1941

The 1930s convey a confused picture of art, architecture and graphic design. Modernism appeared to have lost its momentum and Dutch art critics spoke scornfully about 'isms' as a defeated phase, when around 1930 neo-Realism and Magical Realism in painting began to gain currency. In Stalin's Russia all artistic revival came to an abrupt end in 1932, even though the ominous significance of this barely penetrated the Netherlands. When Hitler seized power in 1933, there was no longer room in Germany for artists who did not conform to the reactionary and racist cultural policies of the Third Reich.

The huge exodus began and the Netherlands offered a modest refuge for emigrant artists, graphic designers and photographers, all of whom helped determine the overall image of graphic art in the Netherlands. Occasionally, their contribution was short-lived, as was the case with Moholy-Nagy and Paul Urban, although Hajo Rose and Friedrich Vordemberge-Gildewart stayed longer. Those that remained – Gerd Arntz, Helmut Salden and Otto Treumann – eventually played an important role in Dutch graphic design.

The contrast between old and new ideas increased, coming to a head in political controversy. Designers and photographers took an ever stronger political stand against economic recession, unemployment, Nazi Germany's racial politics, the emergence of anti-democratic parties and the Spanish Civil War. They contributed in their own manner with pamphlets, posters and reports, visible in exhibitions such as 'D.O.O.D.' and 'Foto 37' in Amsterdam.

There were glaring contrasts in art education. Against the classic academic viewpoint, which hardly altered with the appointment of the German monumental Expressionist artist Campendonk as director of the Amsterdam Rijksacademie, Bauhaus ideas were given a new lease of life in the Netherlands by Paul Citroen's New Art School and the Institute for Industrial Art Education run by Mart Stam, both in Amsterdam. While such fine artists as Carel Willink and Raoul Hynckes depicted a mood of crisis and disaster in their paintings, in 1938 Amsterdam's Stedelijk Museum held, for the first and last time before the war, an exhibition of abstract art represented by the likes of Mondrian, Arp, El Lissitzky and Paul Klee.

The curator and graphic designer, Willem Sandberg, was the Stedelijk's central figure. He helped sustain an interest in contemporary and innovative art, architecture and design in the Netherlands. Even architects of the new International Style were in an increasingly defensive position against historicist movements advocating a return to rustic brick and Beaux-Arts styles for official public buildings – supposedly to impress the public.

The war and occupation effectively strangled all innovation due to the German attempt to 'Nazify' Dutch culture. Designers were still able to eke out a living with fairly innocent activities such as government exhibitions, but with the setting up of the Kultuurkamer, or Chamber of Culture, and the carrying out of racist policies a choice had to be made: for or against. Many went against the regime and several, such as H.N. Werkman, J.F. van Royen and Paul Guermonprez, paid with their lives for their resistance and clandestine work.

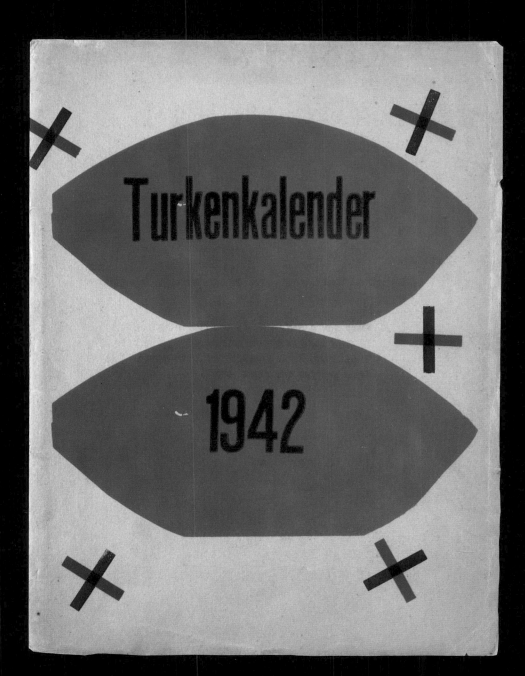

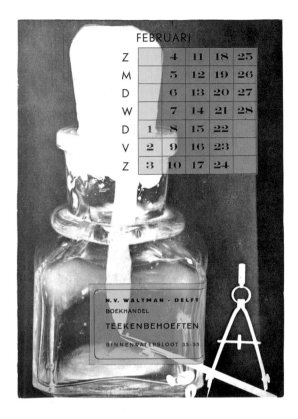

In the graphic arts not everyone complied with the strict functional rules taught by the masters Zwart, Schuitema and Kiljan. Dick Elffers was a student of Zwart, Jongert and Kiljan at the Rotterdam Academy and later assisted both Schuitema and Zwart. For a period after 1929 Elffers adopted the type-photo-line approach of his masters in an original and free manner, but in the 1930s he saw the limitations of a purely functional approach. In 1937 he spoke of the importance of an individual artistic vision and what he viewed as the equal standing of photography to all other graphic techniques, such as drawing and painting: 'The artist is free to use any technique providing the subject matter requires it.'

As a youth Elffers had worked as a painter and decorator and attended painting classes at the Rotterdam Academy. He professed to no fixed style, but was artistically wilful and went his own way. He used photography for a calendar for the Technische Boekhandel & Drukkerij J. Waltman Jr, a book and printing firm in Delft, but also drew illustrations. On the cover of a graphic issue of the functionalist architectural magazine *De 8 en Opbouw* in 1939, compiled by Elffers and Wim Brusse, Elffers drew two clowns, thereby putting the visual cat amongst the pigeons. One reader's reaction summed up the view of the majority: 'Let us hope these young persons are not *the* young persons, as this does not elicit many expectations.'

Henny Cahn came from the same background in typo-photography as Elffers. He was taught by Kiljan and Schuitema in the advertising department of The Hague Academy and over the years remained true to their principles, while using a range of technical and graphic possibilities and original variations. While his work shows similarities here and there to that of his masters, he clearly distinguished himself in the composition and impact of the message. And while Cahn was not a follower of Elffers' freer ideas, he often used small illustrative drawings in his designs, as well as using lower case or capitals. He too favoured the then-popular script letter. Like Kiljan, Cahn's designs were frequently very instructive and easily captured the working and ease of advertised appliances, such as electric clocks, flashing light signals for calling someone in a company, or the domestic telephone. In his advertisement for crispbakes, he lists in a business-like manner the ingredients used, which at the time was not obligatory. His compositions were built up in layers and spatially well thought out. Considered a constructivist, his treatment of space came literally to the fore in his store-window displays and exhibition designs.

Dick Elffers and Henny Cahn

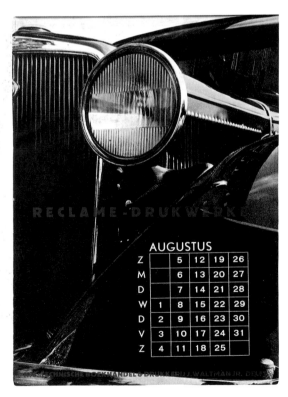

Dick Elffers
Pages (February and August) from a calendar for *W.V. Waltman Printers and Booksellers*, Delft 1934. The calendar features two new and distinctive photographic elements: the photogram and close-ups of modern technology

Henny Cahn
Advertising card for
*Jan Wempe, fruit and
vegetable suppliers,*
The Hague c.1935

Dick Elffers
Lettering for the
packaging of *Simons'
Healthfood Biscuits,*
Rotterdam c.1935

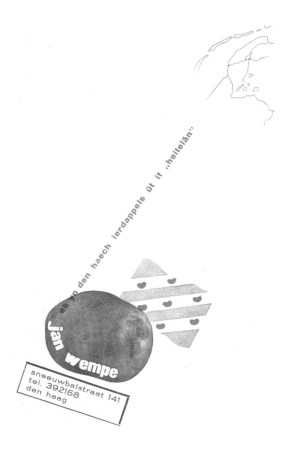

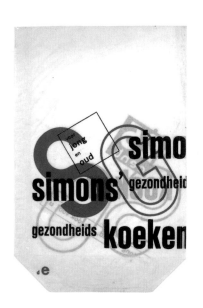

Henny Cahn
Brochure for *Electric
clocks and telephones:*
PTT (Post Office),
The Hague c.1935

Henny Cahn
Advertisement card
for *Lüschen's
'Wholemeal Sports'
Crispbakes,* The Hague
c.1935

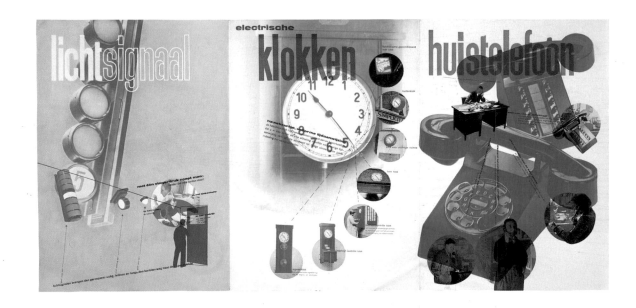

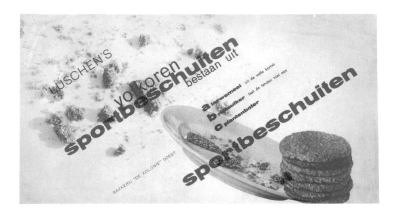

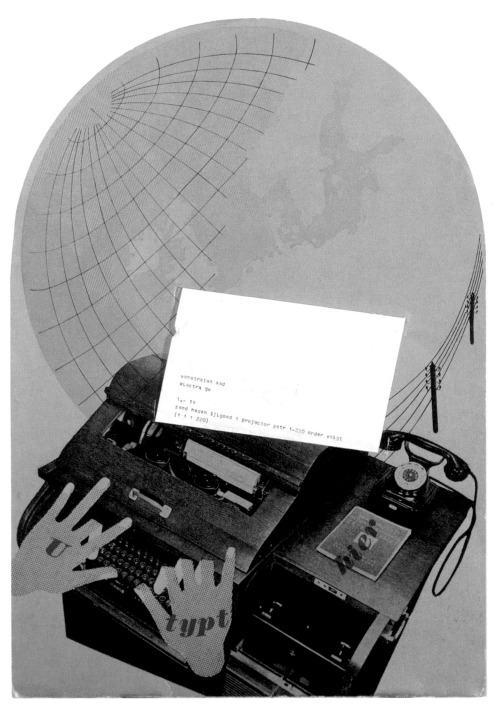

Henny Cahn
Telex booklet 'You
Type Here', PTT (Post
Office), The Hague,
c.1938. The centre
pages contain a strip
of paper with 'typed'
advertising copy

N.P. de Koo
Postbox flyer 'Mail for
the Dutch East Indies',
PTT (Post Office),
The Hague 1937

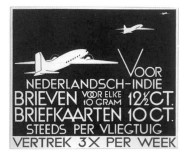

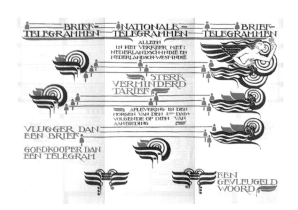

Willem Arondeus
Leaflet listing
Telegram rates, PTT
(Post Office),
The Hague 1937

Wim Brusse
Staff diary 1939, PTT
(Post Office), The
Hague 1938. The date
has been punched out
of the diary's cover

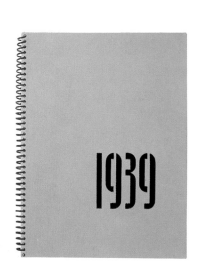

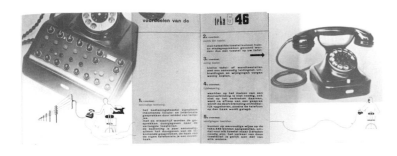

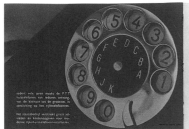

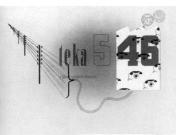

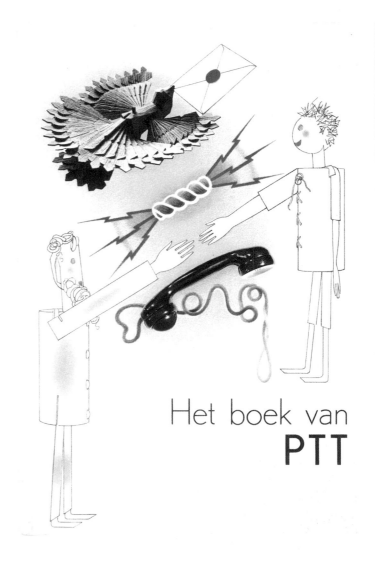

Het boek van
PTT

Henny Cahn
Brochure for *Teka
telephones*, PTT (Post
Office), The Hague
1938

Piet Zwart
Cover and pages for
The PTT Book, PTT (Post
Office), The Hague
1938

The PTT in the 1930s

Over the years, various designers worked for the PTT and employed the new functionalist style, mainly for public information brochures. Henny Cahn executed various designs for the telephone department in which he developed a treatment of space using graphic means. He designed such small items as a circular flyer on transparent paper for the telegraph department; and for a Teka booklet promoting an internal telephone system with 'small, automatic workings', he punched holes so that the reader could look inside. He made a three-dimensional design, again for the telegraph department, with an actual telex message emerging from a photograph of a telex. Huszár worked for the same department and designed a brochure on PTT training for drivers, and for Radio Scheveningen he designed a letterhead and envelopes. In the same period William Sandberg was commissioned by Van Royen to design the window displays of the PTT building on Zeestraat in The Hague, which conveyed information about services to the public.

In the early 1930s Zwart began work on *The PTT Book*, providing an overall view of the company, which was not published until 1938. It was a feast of a book, combining typography, illustration and photomontage. The linear appearance of Zwart's inter-war style made way here for an enjoyable and extremely personal vision of design.

N.P. de Koo, who as interior designer had advised Van Royen on numerous aesthetic matters, was responsible for the stark typography of many announcements, advertising, brochures and post office signage. During these years designers were already producing a PTT annual diary, and one eye-catching example was Wim Brusse's, who used cut-out lettering for the diary cover. In sharp contrast was Willem Arondeus's 1937 brochure for telegram rates. It was decorative and used classic typography – a style that Van Royen

probably preferred, but one which by this time had already become outdated and old-fashioned. In 1928 the first PTT Press and Publicity Service was established, and advertising design for the company was placed increasingly in its hands. Van Royen remained to keep a watchful eye, but left much of the growing amount of printed material to be dealt with by others.

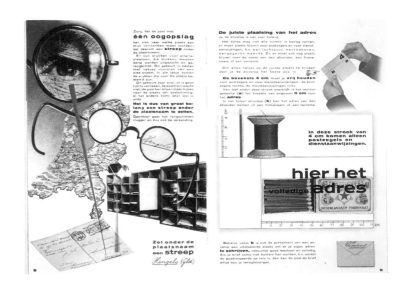

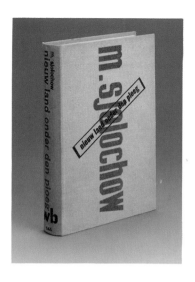

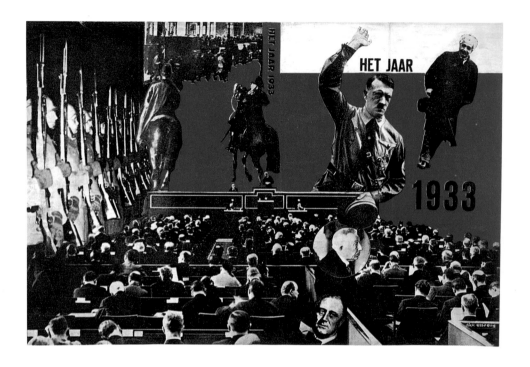

Graphics and politics

Through the 1930s, the increasing political polarities in Europe, unemployment and the general state of crisis was reflected in politically orientated printed matter. Young left-wing Dutch designers, in thrall to Bauhaus ideals and Russian Constructivism, offered their services. They produced posters, brochures and book covers, in which they combined a simple, arresting typography with penetrating photographs of the daily social reality and evocative, often caricatural photomontages. Foreign examples were John Heartfield's satirical photomontages for the *Arbeiter Illustrierte Zeitung*, which appeared in Berlin until 1933 and afterwards in Prague; the *USSR im Bau* magazine with photographs and layout by El Lissitzky and Rodchenko; and the succinct Russian posters that had been exhibited in the summer of 1931 in Amsterdam's Stedelijk Museum.

Cas Oorthuys and Mark Kolthoff, following the German example of *Der Arbeiterfotograf*, also began working in 1931 as worker-photographers for anti-fascist brochures and journals such as *Links Front*, *AFweerfront*, and *Links Richten* from the revolutionary writers' collective of the same name. These were activities with a short life. Together with Jo Voskuil, Oorthuys subsequently founded the OV20 advertising agency, which produced commercial work as well as political pamphlets, posters and brochures. Book covers for translated Russian literature by Michail Sjolochov and Ilja Ehrenburg were designed in robust, elementary typography.

Collaboration between like-minded graphic designers and photographers such as the Oorthuys-Voskuil duo, was especially noticeable in the second half of the 1930s. There was Jan Bons and Carel Blazer, Wim Brusse and Fred van Dordrecht, Carel Blazer and Wim Brusse, Eve Besnyö and Hajo Rose. Increasingly they looked beyond national boundaries to highlight the plight

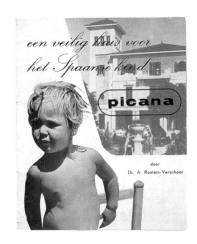

Wim Brusse
Cover of the brochure
*A Secure House for the
Spanish Child*, Comité
Hulp aan China,
Amsterdam 1937.
The photographs
were taken by
Fred van Dordrecht

Cas Oorthuys
Pages from a booklet
aimed at combating
unemployment and
recession in the
Netherlands; Dutch
Communist Party,
Amsterdam 1935.

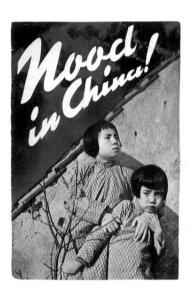 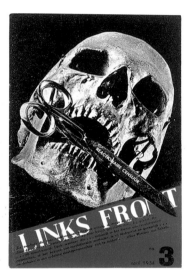

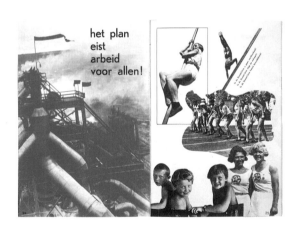

of victims of the Spanish Civil War and of the famine in Asia caused by the Sino-Japanese war. The ties forged at that time prepared designers to confront the Second World War, and led to new theories that had less to do with social and political struggles than with optimism and reconstruction.

Eva Besnyö and Cas
Oorthuys
Cover of the brochure
China in Need!,
Amsterdam 1938

Cas Oorthuys
Cover of the
magazine *Links Front*,
Amsterdam April
1934. One of five
issues edited by Jef
Last, Nico Rost and
Joris Ivens. The
illustration depicts
the opposition being
'gagged' by the censor

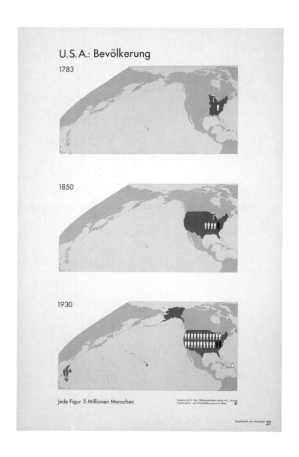

Otto Neurath, Gert Arntz and the Viennese Method

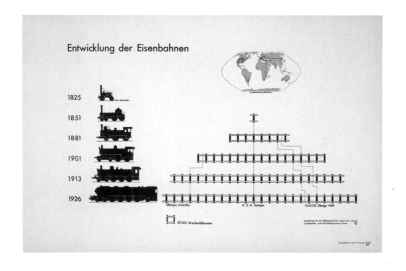

The Viennese sociologist and philosopher, Otto Neurath, was a man of brilliant ideas. He also possessed the willpower to turn his ideas into action, and moreover had a shrewd eye for competent staff. One notion was his 'pictograms': his so-called Viennese Method of illustrating statistics by appealing visual means, intended for use in education, trade, commerce and human communications (largely in books and exhibition panels).

During the time he was curator of the Viennese Gesellschafts und Wirtschaftsmuseum, he found in the Rhinelander Gerd Arntz the precise graphic translator for his ideas. From 1929 Arntz designed simple yet succinct graphic symbols for pictograms. These were executed in linocut, then printed on a platen press so that they could be systematically arranged into series. A pictogram had to be legible, distinctive and artless while conveying the correct information on a large or small scale.

Between 1931 and 1934 pictograms were introduced in Moscow, where Arntz trained graphic designers in the Viennese Method at Isostat, the economic information and propaganda institute.

Owing to the tense political situation in Germany and Austria, Neurath and Arntz emigrated to The Hague in 1934 where they continued their work under Mundaneum Den Haag – Stichting voor Beeldpedagogie, a foundation set up for the purpose. Arntz expanded the number of graphic symbols so that by 1940 the total basic reserve was 1,140 different items. In the pre-war years many exhibition panels and illustrations for encyclopedias and books were designed, for instance for Neurath's own book *Modern Man in the Making / De moderne mensch ontstaat.* Another of Neurath's ideas was the use of symbols to create an international visual language, called the International Picture Language, which would facilitate communication between peoples,

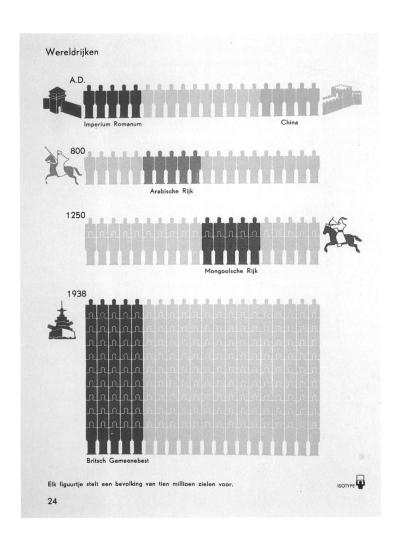

Wereldrijken

A.D.

Imperium Romanum   China

800

Arabische Rijk

1250

Mongoolsche Rijk

1938

Britsch Gemeenebest

Elk figuurtje stelt een bevolking van tien millioen zielen voor.

ISOTYPE

24

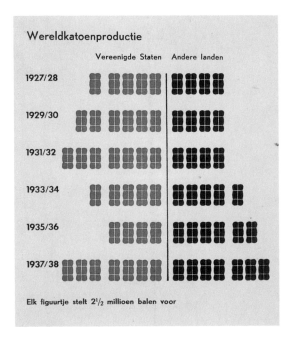

Wereldkatoenproductie

	Vereenigde Staten	Andere landen
1927/28		
1929/30		
1931/32		
1933/34		
1935/36		
1937/38		

Elk figuurtje stelt 2$\frac{1}{2}$ millioen balen voor

despite language barriers. After the German invasion of the Netherlands, Neurath escaped to England where he founded the Isctype Institute with Marie Reidemeister. Arntz remained in the Netherlands and continued his work at the newly established Dutch Foundation for Statistics, which flourished in the post-war period of reconstruction. Pictograms became well known and over the years the simple characters created by Arntz's hand took on a life of their own. They were increasingly appropriated by others, and were used in an adapted form for the design of traffic signs and the routing of such international travel centres as airports and railway stations.

Gerd Arntz
Pictograms for *World Empires, from Otto Neurath, De moderne mensch ontstaat* (Modern Man in the Making). Noord-Hollandsche Uitgevers Maatschappij, Amsterdam 1940. Grouping and colour coding contribute to the overall clarity of these pictograms

Gerd Arntz
Pictograms for *World Cotton Products, from Otto Neurath, De moderne mensch ontstaat* (Modern Man in the Making), one of the many clear symbols Arntz developed for industrial products

Gerd Arntz
Illustration *Uniform and Uniformity, from Otto Neurath, De moderne mensch ontstaat* (Modern Man in the Making), an example of stylistic forms and colours for illustrations

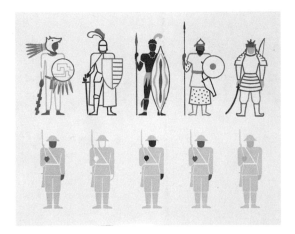

N.P. de Koo
Information booklet
*International Chamber
of Commerce Rotterdam*,
Rotterdam 1929.
A fine example of a
pictogram, although
incorrect according to
the standards set by
Otto Neurath because
variations in size are
not denumerable

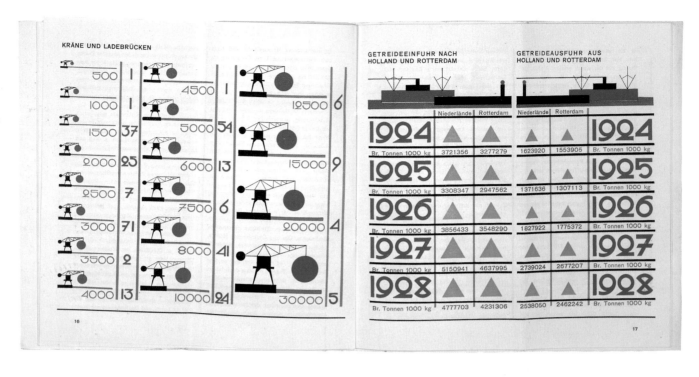

Pictograms for everyone

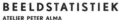
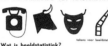

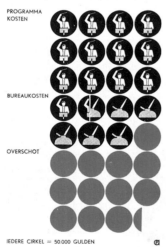

Peter Alma
Brochure *Peter Alma
Pictogram Studio*,
Amsterdam 1935

Peter Alma
Pictograms depicting
an *Overview of
Expenditure* from the
AVRO's annual report,
1935, AVRO Radio,
Amsterdam 1936

Peter Alma
Pictograms on *Annual
Meat consumption in
Amsterdam per Head of
Population*, Stedelijk
Museum, Amsterdam
1937

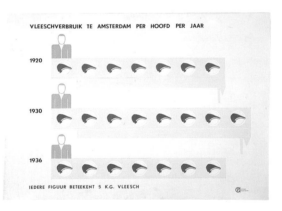

Neurath was convinced that pictograms would become a universal means of conveying information, and tried to familiarise designers from various countries with the system. For instance El Lissitzky from the Soviet Union, Jan Tschichold from Germany, Augustin Tschinkel from Czechoslovakia and Rudolf Modley from the United States all used and applauded the modern hieroglyphics of Neurath and Arntz.

Willem Sandberg, who wanted to be a painter but in 1927 studied psychology in Vienna, came into contact with pictograms early on and was inspired by the social implications of the method. Back in the Netherlands as a freelance designer he made his first pictograms for the exhibition 'Employment for the Disabled' at the Stedelijk Museum. He published a brochure about the method in 1929 in which he wrote: 'It attempts to link exact science with inspirational art and to unite the clear simplicity of both.' Sandberg employed an individual, playful style of pictogram in his public information exhibitions for government institutions and for trade fair stands.

Piet Zwart was fleetingly interested in the phenomenon of the pictogram and in 1930 made a series of three-dimensional panels for a PTT exhibition in Antwerp after receiving written information on the principles of the method from Neurath. The Dutch artist and graphic designer Peter Alma was undergoing part of his practical training as an illustrator in Vienna and dedicated an issue of the *Wendingen* magazine to pictograms. He worked in Moscow, was head of a branch of Isostat in Charkow, and on his return to Amsterdam in 1935 set up his own studio for pictograms, where he produced exhibition panels for the city and worked on commercial commissions.

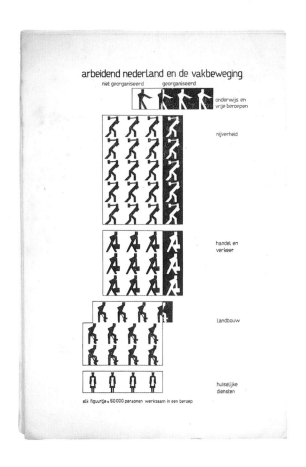

Willem Sandberg Pictograms representing *Working Netherlands and the Trade Unions from The Past in Egyptian Reliefs: The Present in Statistical Images*, Sandberg, Amsterdam 1929. Sandberg created a personal and expressive graphic style for his visual statistics

Willem Sandberg *Museumstatistics* from *W. Sandberg and H.L.C. Jaffé, Contemporary Art in the Stedelijk*, Stedelijk Museum / Meulenhoff, Amsterdam 1962. Sandberg composed visually playful statistics using type

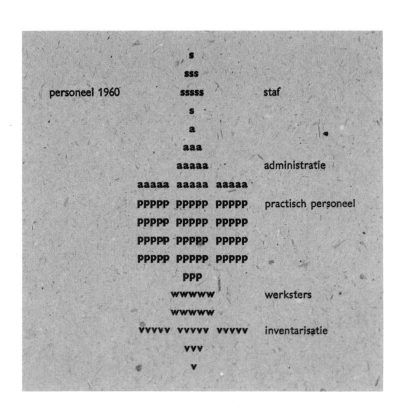

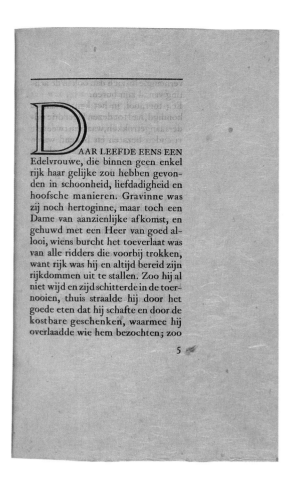

Publishing by and for emigrants

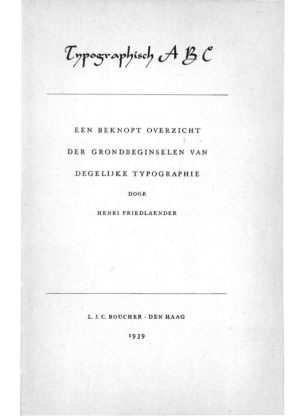

Henri Friedlaender
Page from *Jacques de Baisieux, Het zijden harnas* (The Silk Armour), the first of the *Folemprise* series of books; L.J.C. Boucher, The Hague 1932

Henri Friedlaender
Title page from *Henri Friedlaender, Typographisch ABC*, L.J.C. Boucher, The Hague 1939. The text is based on the typographic courses Friedlaender gave for typesetting apprentices from Mouton, a printing firm in The Hague

Many left-wing writers and publishers fled Germany after the Nazis seized power in 1933. Many emigrated to the United States, but a number of them – in the hope that Hitler was a temporary phenomenon – moved to neighbouring countries such as France and the Netherlands, where they hoped to continue their work. In Amsterdam the publishing houses of Querido and Allert de Lange offered accommodation to the German-language Exil department, run by Fritz Landshoff and Hermann Kesten respectively from the famous Berlin publishers Kiepenheuer. For book designs, mostly covers, two graphic artists of a very different nature were hired: Henri Friedlaender and Paul Urban.

Henri Friedlaender, born in Lyons, worked as a typographic consultant for Mouton Printers in The Hague. He designed the typography and covers for fine editions of L.J.C. Boucher in The Hague and after 1933 for Amsterdam's Exil editions. His covers were based purely on letterforms. Titles were generally either drawn by hand or done in a combination of hand-drawn and printed letters. In contrast to Paul Urban, Friedlaender's starting point was the classic letterform, to which he added a punchy, personal touch.

Paul Ludwig Urban, originally from Munich where he trained in graphic art at the Kunstgewerbeschule, worked from 1927 in Berlin as a book designer and illustrator for the socialist Universum-Bücherei für Alle, the communist Neue Deutsche Verlag and the Büchergilde Gutenberg. Together with John Heartfield he was one of the founders of the Association Revolutionärer Bildender Künstler Deutschlands, and drew political cartoons, designed lettering for banners and photomontages for leaflets and political magazines. The somewhat rough and, for the Netherlands, quite unusual lettering he designed for this kind of work can be seen in his numerous book covers for Allert de Lange from 1933 to 1937. The lettering was intended to give the impression of being quickly set down with a brush. The dynamic photomontages Urban had frequently used in Berlin were rarely to be found in his Amsterdam book covers. He preferred to combine his lettering with a large, drawn form. Just how accurate his sporadic illustrations were is revealed in *Geschichten aus sieben Ghettos* by Egon Erwin Kisch, alternately sober, clownish and nostalgic.

Another emigrant was Helmut Salden, who taught photography at the Folkwangschule in Essen and after the Spanish Civil War came to the Netherlands with the help of the writer Marsman. Through contact with another writer, Menno ter Braak, he received his first commissions designing covers for the literary magazine *De Vrije Bladen* (The Free Journals), followed by covers for Ter Braak's translations of the work of Hermann Rauschning and hardback covers and jackets for publisher A.A.M. Stols. After the war he was much in demand for classic calligraphic cover designs.

Paul Urban
Cover for *Max Brod,
Novellen aus Böhmen*,
Allert de Lange,
Amsterdam 1936. The
letters, drawn with a
brush, are reminiscent
of those found on
banners and
pamphlets of the
Weimar Republic

Henri Friedlaender
Cover of *Heinrich
Mann, De Hass –
Deutsche Zeitgeschichte*,
Querido, Amsterdam
1933. Despite the
classic letterform,
this is an unusually
vehement cover for
this expatriate
publisher

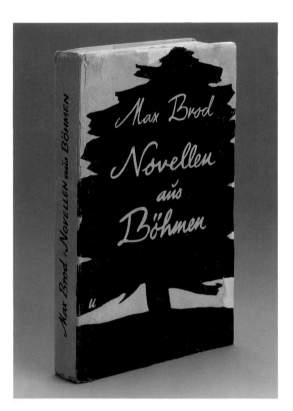

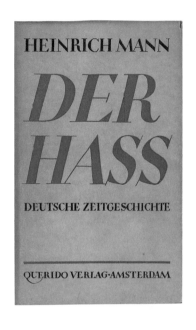

Paul Urban
Cover and
illustrations for *Egon
Erwin Kisch, Geschichten
aus sieben Ghettos*
(Stories from Seven
Ghettos), Allert de
Lange, Amsterdam
1934

Helmut Salden
Cover of *Hermann
Rauschning, De
nihilistische revolutie*,
Leopold, The Hague
1939. The book's
translator Menno ter
Braak wrote: 'He
[Salden] aims to strike
a balance between the
demands made by
marketing... and the
cover as a symbol of a
book's content'

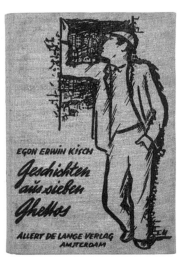

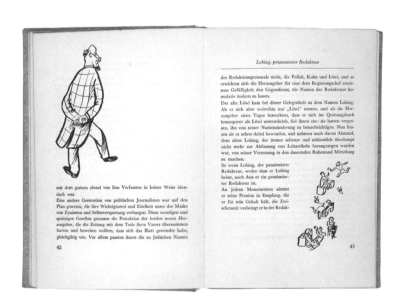

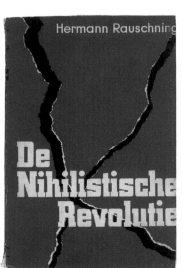

ABCDEFGHIJKLMNOPQRSTUV

abcdefghijklmnopqrstuvwxyz12345

ABCDEFGHIJKLMNOPQRSTUY

abcdef ghijklmnopqrstuvwxyz12345

Typography in the 1930s and 1940s

Both the Amsterdam Type Foundry as well as its rival the Joh. Enschedé printing firm in Haarlem, followed the initial successes of their type designers De Roos and Van Krimpen by regularly introducing new typefaces. The foundry mainly looked to expand its assortment of modern advertising typefaces, often imitating popular foreign examples. The many new sans-serif faces that appeared in Germany and England, such as Kabel by Rudolf Koch (1927), Gill Sans by Eric Gill (1928) and Futura by Paul Renner (1928) required a Dutch equivalent. Thus under De Roos' guidance the sans-serif Nobel series, which appears to be an adaptation of Berthold Grotesque of 1928, was born. Certain variations, such as Nobel Open Initials, were developed by De Roos himself. Between 1932 and 1934 he designed Egmont, the third-largest type family, distinguished by its broad capitals, long, lower-case ascenders and thin serifs. In one calligraphic movement the descenders and ascenders could be joined. Egmont became popular for book typography and the more sophisticated commercial printing. Interesting too was Libra, a modern uncial from 1938 that appeared to be written with a broad, flat pen.

Stefan Schlesinger designed Hidalgo, a bold advertising type suitable for punchy copy slogans and in the large sizes of six to 40 *augustijn* usable as wooden type for posters. It was very fashionable in the 1930s. He also designed the greater part of the script type Rondo, which was completed by Dick Dooijes after the war.

Jan van Krimpen concentrated on book type and designed consecutively Romanée (1929), with a decorative upper case series, and Romulus (1931), with special italics in slanting Roman – the latter according to a theory by the English typographer Stanley Morison. Romulus existed as part of a plan to create a complete family of type 'which would embrace everything that can be reasonably necessary for the printing of books'(Jan van Krimpen). The Dubbele Augustijn Open Kapitalen (1928) was largely intended for the title pages of books. Among grammar school pupils Krimpen's gracious Antigone Grieks (1928), used for the schools' edition of Homer, was well known. The 16th-century official style of Italian calligraphers such as Ludovico Vicentino degli Arrighi inspired Cancelleresca Bastarda (1937), an italic type with many additional calligraphic variations and ligatures. The type matched Romulus as an 'authentic' italic. In collaboration with the British Monotype Corporation, Van Dijck appeared in 1938, a Roman and italic type named after the 17th-century typecutter Christoffel van Dijck. Earlier Van Krimpen, at the request of the printer Oliver Simon of London's Curwen Press, had designed the decorative Curwen Press Initials.

Jan van Krimpen
Title page of a poetry
anthology *Charles
Péguy, La tapisserie de
Notre Dame*, A.A.
Balkema, Amsterdam
1946. The typeface is
(Double Augustijn)
Open Capitals (1928),
which is set by hand
and complements
Romaneé, as well as
being specifically
used for book titles.
Van Krimpen also
drew a Greek
variation

Jan van Krimpen
Curwen Press Initials,
1929. Van Krimpen
composed these
elegant initials
exclusively for
London's Curwen
Press

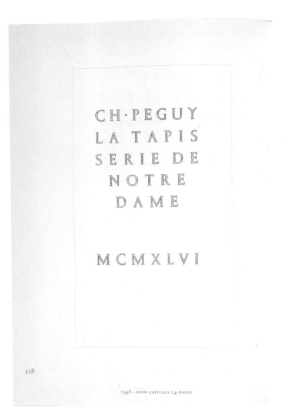

CH·PEGUY
LA TAPIS
SERIE DE
NOTRE
DAME

MCMXLVI

118

1946 · OPEN CAPITALS 24-POINT

Stefan Schlesinger
*Figaro type sample
sheet*, Amsterdam
Type Foundry, 1940.
Schlesinger designed
this advertising letter
in 1938, including
capitals and number
tables, which is based
on 19th-century
wooden letters.
The name Figaro was
already used by
Monotype so the type
was quickly renamed
Hidalgo

André van der Vossen
The *Woodcut Letter*,
introduced by
Enschedé in 1926,
is used here for *Jan
Walch, De vreeselijke
avonturen van
Scholastica* (The
Terrible Adventures
of Scholastica),
C.A.J. van Dishoeck,
Hilversum 1933. The
initial was carved by
M.C. Escher

S.H. de Roos
New Year greeting for
*Amsterdam Type
Foundry*, 1938. The
foundry introduced
an eye-catching new
letter with this card,
Libre – a modern
uncial, based on 5th-
century script, which
did not have separate
upper-case and lower-
case letters

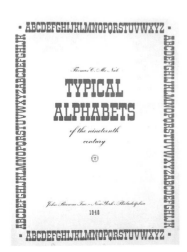

het geluk
dezer wereld
moge ook
het uwe zijn in
1939

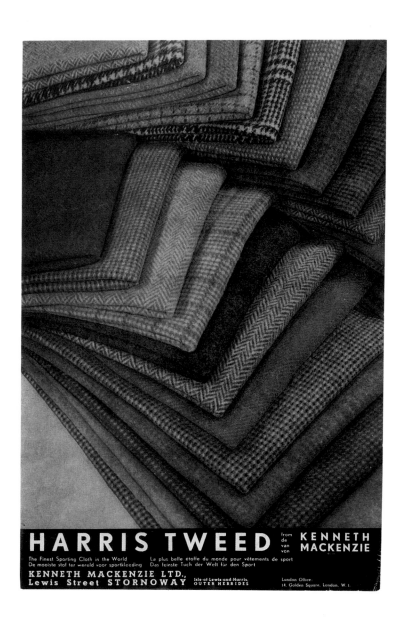

HARRIS TWEED

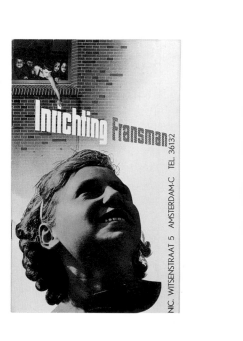

László Moholy-Nagy
and Paul Hartland
Full-page
advertisement for
Harris Tweed from the
trade magazine
International Textiles,
Amsterdam 1934.
During his short stay
in the Netherlands,
Moholy-Nagy,
together with
Hartland, ran the
magazine's art studio
in Amsterdam and
there dabbled in
colour photography

Hajo Rose
Brochure for
Inrichting Fransman,
a furniture company,
Amsterdam c.1938

From Bauhaus to New Art School

Hajo Rose
Leaflet and invitation
for a *Grand Ball
organised by the Society
of Friends of the New Art
School*, Amsterdam
1938. The invitation
was printed on old
newspapers and the
leaflet was in the
form of a necktie

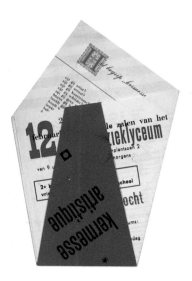

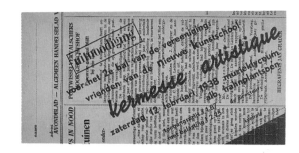

Owing to national socialist policies in Dessau, in August 1932 the Bauhaus was transferred to Berlin-Steglitz. Less than a year later, when Hitler had come to power, it was forced to close its doors. It had existed, like the Weimar Republic, for 14 years. Numerous teachers, students, and ex-students had already left Germany and some stayed for shorter or longer periods in the Netherlands as immigrants, such as the painters Josef Albers and Johannes Itten, the ceramicists Franz and Marguerite Wildenhain, the architect Lotte Beese and the designers and photographers Andreas Feininger, Heinz Allner, Paul Urban, Hajo Rose and Paul Guermonprez. The last two worked together in Amsterdam as graphic designers under the name Coop 2.

Bauhaus teacher László Moholy-Nagy who, from 1927 to 1929, was a distinguished assistant on Arthur Müller-Lehning's avant-garde magazine *Internationale Revue i 10* (he designed the logo and standard typography) remained in the Netherlands from 1933 to 1934. There he gave readings for Filmliga, exhibited at the Stedelijk Museum and in Amsterdam experimented with colour photography when designing advertisements for the magazine *International Textiles*. The painter Friedrich Vordemberge-Gildewart fled Germany in 1938 and earned his living with typographic designs for the Amsterdam printers, Duwaer.

Just as Moholy-Nagy took charge of the New Bauhaus in Chicago, in 1933 ex-Bauhaus student Paul Citroen set up the New Art School in Amsterdam to promote Bauhaus principles. Citroen taught in the style of Johannes Itten's Vorkurs (Basic Course), greatly emphasising the study of materials and forms. Lessons were given in rented premises or in artists' studios. The applied arts were an important component in the training: graphic design, photography, fashion and interior design were taught by Hajo Rose, Paul Guermonprez, Helen Ernst and Alexander Bodon. The precepts of New Photography and the New Typography as practised by Moholy-Nagy, Herbert Bayer and Jan Tschichold can be identified in the work of the school's teachers and students. Among its students were Otto Treumann, Violette Cornelius and Jan Bons.

Citroen and Guermonprez also taught at The Hague Academy from 1935, enabling Bauhaus principles – already introduced by their colleagues G. Kiljan and Paul Schuitema – to gain an even stronger foothold. The same was also true at the Amsterdam Institute of Industrial Art Education, where architect Mart Stam became director in 1939 and Johan Niegemann head of interior design. Both had gained a reputation as visiting lecturers at the Bauhaus. War and occupation, however, brought such ideals to an end.

Hajo Rose
Information brochure
on the *New Art School*,
Amsterdam c.1938

Hajo Rose
Brochure *Gymnastics
and Eurhythmics*, Else
Süss-Gutheim,
Amsterdam c.1938

Lotte Stam-Beese
Stamped binding for
the magazine *Beter
wonen 1913-1938*
(Better Living 1913-
1938), edited by L. van
der Wal; Arbeiderspers,
Amsterdam 1939

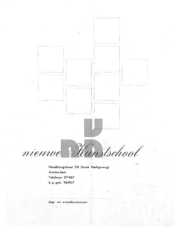

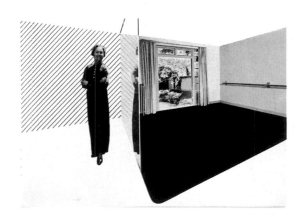

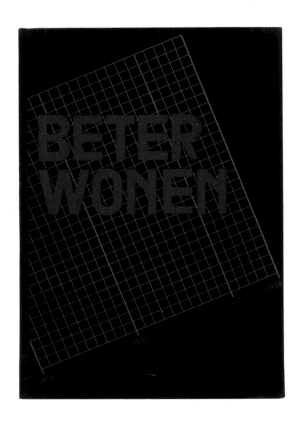

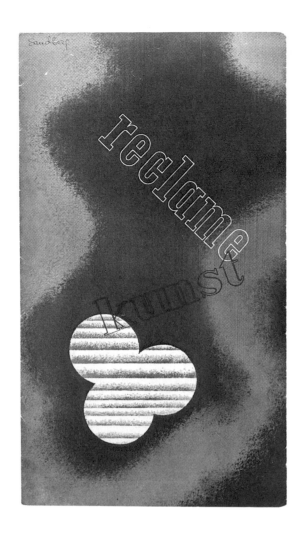

William Sandberg
Brochure for an
*Exhibition on
advertising art*,
Stedelijk Museum,
Amsterdam 1935.
This was a
comprehensive
exhibition held in the
museum where VANK
members also
showed work

Willem Sandberg
Brochure for *Spin
Printers*, Amsterdam
1937. Sandberg also
designed writing
paper and
photographic
calendars for the
printing firm

Willem Sandberg
Brochure for a
performance
Impressions, Ballet Jooss,
Stadsschouwburg,
Amsterdam c.1938.
A stylised perspective
is combined with
diagonally arranged
text

Sandberg, the early years

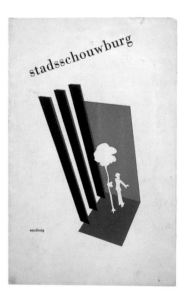

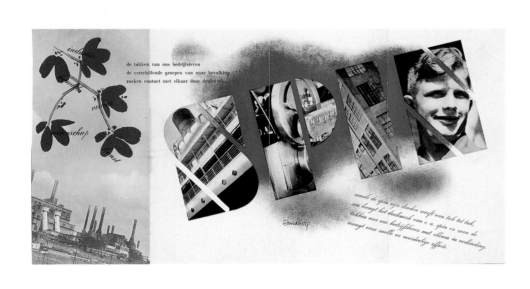

Following a childhood spent in Assen, close to the Asser woods, and after
attending drawing, painting and philosophy classes under L.A. Roessingh,
Willem Sandberg arrived at the Amsterdam Rijksacademie in 1919, where he
remained for only six months. During this time he became familiar with
Marxism through the writer, Herman Gorter, and owing to his fragile health,
with the Mazdaznan movement and its doctrine based on natural cures. In
these circles he also met Johannes Itten, then a lecturer at Weimar's Bauhaus.
In 1922 Sandberg studied at the Academie de la Grande Chaumière in Paris,
and it was here that he decided to abandon art and involve himself with the
Mazdaznan doctrine. He continued in this vein until 1926, and the following
year attended lectures in Vienna given by the psychologists Buhler and Adler.
He came into contact with Otto Neurath's pictograms, and shortly after
became acquainted with Naum Gabo and Walter Gropius in Germany.

Returning to Amsterdam, Sandberg worked increasingly in graphic
design, not only in the area of the pictogram but also producing book covers,
brochures, programmes for the Amsterdam Stadsschouwburg (Concert Hall)
and calendars for Spin Printers. He organised exhibitions at the behest of
such government bodies as the National Insurance Institute, the Economic
Information Service and the PTT. He worked for the annual Trade Fair and
for Nijgh & van Ditmar Publishers. At the same time Sandberg was studying
psychology in Utrecht. In 1932 he joined the crafts and industrial art
association VANK and played an active role within it and later with GKf
(a similar association). He became involved with the Stedelijk Museum, which
organised annual exhibitions of work by VANK members. Typical of these
were a Moholy-Nagy show, 'The Chair', 'Photo 37', 'Abstract Art',
'International Posters' and 'Advertising Art'.

The latter show was held in November 1935 and originated from a
collaboration between VANK and the Advertising Association. Sixty-nine
designers submitted work, including Alma, Cohen, Huszár, De Koo, Sandberg,
Wilmink, Schuitema, Kiljan and Zwart. The last three gave a joint reading
entitled 'Typography and advertising, design and advertising, photography
and advertising'. In a brochure designed by Sandberg, the interior designer
and architect, Paul Bromberg, gave his curious vision of art and advertising,
in which it appears that much advertising was still regarded as well-meaning
and positive: 'The combination of art and advertising appears to be a
compromise for both parties. Art is after all identified with a hazy,
unassailable apparition; a dreamlike state isolated from every reality, while
advertising on the contrary must present reality in a compressed form.'
Bromberg felt that for too long 19th-century thinking had held sway over art
and craft and the masses. He added: 'Then New Functionalism was introduced
by artists as collective advertising...New Functionalism is a specially
prepared, extra powerful essence of reality. This outstanding advertisement
by artists also demonstrates that they are pre-eminently suited for the
advertising sector. Their intuition, their originality, their imagination and
their fanaticism cannot be surpassed.' In 1937 Sandberg became director of
the Stedelijk Museum.

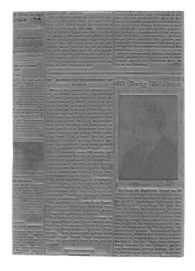

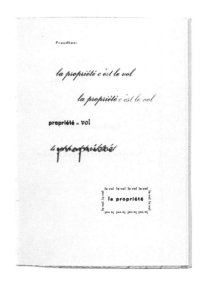

Willem Sandberg
Cover and page from
'lectura sub aqua' -
experimenta
typografica, Duwaer,
Amsterdam 1944

Willem Sandberg
Ex libris for the
Library of the Stedelijk
Museum, Amsterdam
1940. A purely
typographic design,
produced a year after
Sandberg had met
Werkman

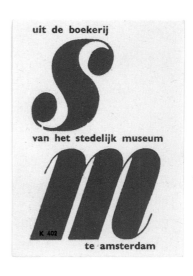

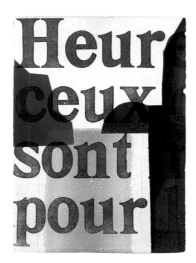

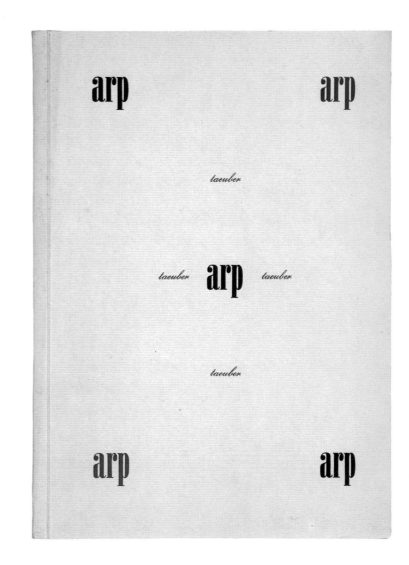

Clandestine and illegal presses

H.N. Werkman
Cover of *Gebed*
(Prayer), De Blauwe
Schuit, Groningen
1941

Friedrich
Vordemberge-
Gildewart
Cover and typography
from *Hans Arp, Rire de
Coquille*, Vordemberge-
Gildewart,
Amsterdam 1944.
Poems illustrated by
Sophie Taeuber-Arp
and printed by Frans
Duwaer

Jan Bons
Cover and title page
for *Kafka*, Bons,
Amsterdam 1943.
The book, in a limited
edition of 30,
comprised seven
short stories from
*Beschreibung eines
Kampfes* (Description
of a Fight), illustrated
with seven
lithographs and a pen
drawing by Bons. It
was printed by Frans
Duwaer

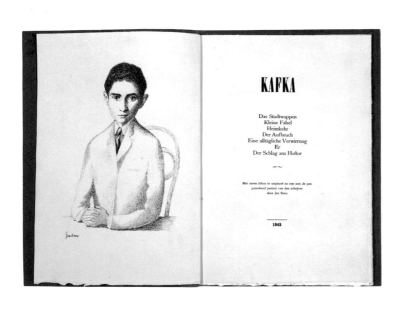

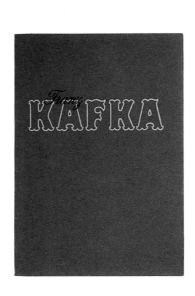

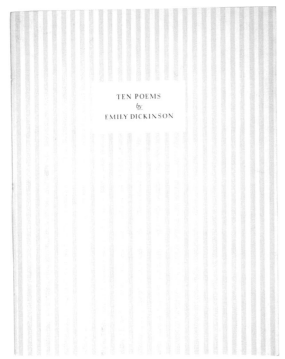

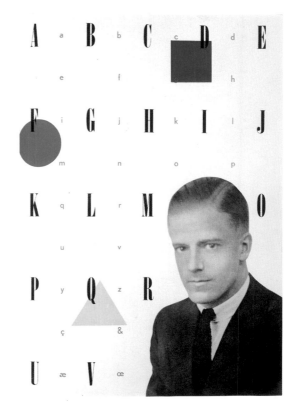

After the German invasion of the Netherlands in May 1940, the occupiers strengthened their grip by degrees on Dutch culture. Jews were discriminated against, and in 1942 a Chamber of Culture was established and the activities of artists, and press and publishers were severely censured.

Slowly an illegal press came into being: stencilled flyers evolved into a network of newspapers and weeklies that gave news outside the 'official' line and urged resistance. Increasingly, from 1942 books and booklets were also secretly printed, mainly in limited editions. As well as poetry anthologies with poignantly appropriate verses, outstanding poetry was often written and illustrated under pseudonyms. Short stories, plays and novels were published in special, sometimes even luxury form, despite a paper shortage.

The Amsterdam publisher A.A. Balkema, with his Five Pounds Press, was very prolific at this time. He commissioned Jan van Krimpen to design numerous fine editions, and in 1944 also published the more progressive *experimenta typografica* by William Sandberg. Just as productive was De Bezige Bij publishers run by C. van Blommestein and Geert Lubberhuizen, which apart from books also published many illegal illustrated broadsheets, with the proceeds benefiting the Dutch Resistance Movement.

Throughout the country clandestine publishers were active: the Mansarde Press in The Hague run by publisher Bert Bakker, illustrator Cees Bantzinger and printer Fokke Tamminga; *De Blauwe Schuit* in Groningen owned by the printer Werkman and F.R.A. Henkels; the *Molenpers* of Jan Vermeulen in Leiden and the Bayard Press of F.G. Kroonder in Bussum. A.A.M. Stols also published many fine underground editions. The typography employed generally followed the rules of traditional book design and was printed with patriotic intent in such typefaces as Hollandsche Mediaeval,

Erasmus, Lutetia, Egmont and Romulus. Some exceptions were Werkman's quirky fripperies such as the Turkenkalender, Sandberg's *experimenta typografica* and Vordemberge-Gildewart's interpretation of Hans Arp's poems. Printers responsible for such work included Trio and ANDO in The Hague, J. Enschedé in Haarlem, Meijer in Wormerveer, Hendriks in Utrecht, Boosten & Stols in Maastricht and J.F. Duwaer and Sons in Amsterdam. Shortly before the end of the war, the printer H.N. Werkman became a victim of Nazi reprisals, as did Frans Duwaer before him, who had not only printed magnificent books, but more importantly thousands of fake identity cards. After the liberation, the first exhibition in the Amsterdam Stedelijk Museum was devoted to 'The Free Book in an Unfree Time'.

Freestyle images and austere design

The years following World War Two were marked by economic reconstruction and an attempt to regain the political and social climate of the pre-war period. The cultural situation too was largely a reflection of this. The National Institute, founded in 1945 and disbanded a year later, endeavoured to impart nationalist feelings in youth through folk songs and dance. New ideas were regarded as dangerous for the spiritual health of the nation.

In marked contrast to this were Sandberg and similarly minded friends who wished to stimulate new opportunities in the development of art and design. In the graphic arts the pre-war avant-garde line was continued, especially by those designers, such as Sandberg, Treumann, Bons and Elffers, who knew each other from the New Art School or had worked for the Resistance Movement.

This circle was involved in the founding in 1945 of the Association of Practitioners of the Applied Arts (GKf), as a successor to VANK. It was divided into branches, including one that embraced graphic artists. In 1948 the Association of Advertising Designers and Illustrators (VRI) was also founded, and both these institutions promoted fundamental discussions on working practices and the ethics of the profession. The two associations reflected a division in spirit and ideas that has remained current up until the present day. Like VANK, the GKf was important to members in obtaining commissions, establishing rates of pay, resolving business disputes and organising exhibitions. The association created new initiatives, such as the collaboration with the Employers Organisation of Printers over publishing Christmas issues of *Printers Weekly*, or the positioning of a noticeboard for the 'well-designed' poster in Amsterdam. In 1947 the publishers' association CPNB reintroduced the pre-war selection for the '50 best-designed books'. In graphic design a great diversity of styles continued to exist, on the one hand the illustrative mode of Bons, Wijnberg, Wernars, Elffers and Treumann, and on the other the more stark typographic and compositional styles of Sandberg, Brusse, Jongejans, Wissing and Crouwel. Much design work in the post-war period was commissioned by Dutch cultural bodies, and later there was an increasing demand from industry. Immediately after the war the annual Trade Fair posters were again produced by graphic designers.

Sandberg devoted a great deal of attention to design at the Stedelijk Museum, which contributed further to its development. As well as this The Hague Academy, where Schuitema and Kiljan were still teaching, and the Amsterdam Institute for Industrial Art Education (later to become the Rietveld), where Mart Stam was director until 1948, guaranteed continuity with the pre-war period.

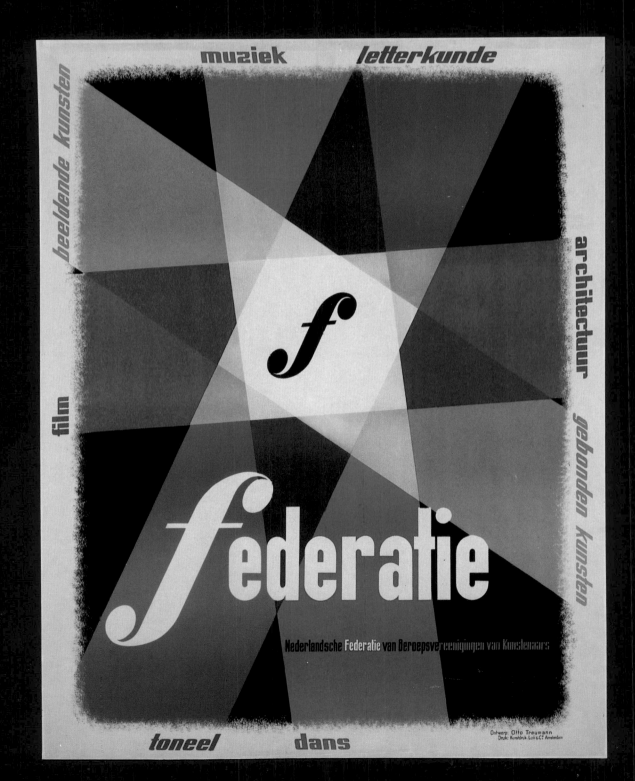

Sandberg, typographer and museum director

With his inspirational personality and his exceptional position as museum director and designer, Willem Sandberg contributed greatly to Dutch graphic design after the war. His own work was largely typographic. He designed using a variety of typefaces, primary colours and simple paper types such as rough packing paper or cardboard. He used illustration or photographs only rarely and when necessary – for instance in exhibition catalogues. His work fell outside the traditional and for this reason Sandberg has been an example for new generations of designers.

During the war he began his 'experimenta typografica', divided into 19 parts, in which he used new ways to highlight and enliven texts. For the first time torn figures and letters appear, which were to characterise Sandberg's later work.

H.N. Werkman, the Russian Constructivists and Piet Zwart, for whom Sandberg designed the booklet *Keywords*, all influenced him. Sandberg's graphic work reflected his life: straightforward and very socially involved. For him design was solely the means of conveying a message, it had no purpose in itself. His vision was focused on the present and on the future, which was reflected in his work and in the policies he followed at the Stedelijk Museum. He did not limit the institution to fine art but – inspired by Alfred Barr of the Museum of Modern Art, New York – introduced photography, film and industrial design to the museum. For him these were not separate areas, but closely interwoven by a kindred mentality. In the field of graphic design Sandberg, between 1945 and 1950, organised many exhibitions, for instance on the work of H.N. Werkman, 'Swiss posters', 'Livres illustrées', 'Foto '48', 'The Swiss book' and 'The poster: image of the age'.

His vision was expressed in two issues of *Kwadraat* (Quadrate) magazine, published by Steendrukkerij de Jong (well-known lithographic printers), *Nu* and *Nu2*. He said: 'We can try to escape the reality, to escape into the past, or to get to know the present, to investigate and capture it; the future starts now – are we going with it?' On the cover of *avantgardecahier 1*, which Sandberg designed, is the title *open oog* (open eye): looking, literally and figuratively, had great meaning for Sandberg. For him a letter was a symbol, and this was expressed very clearly on the cover he designed for the Christmas issue of *Printers Weekly* (1966).

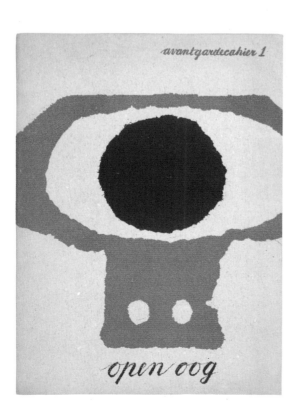

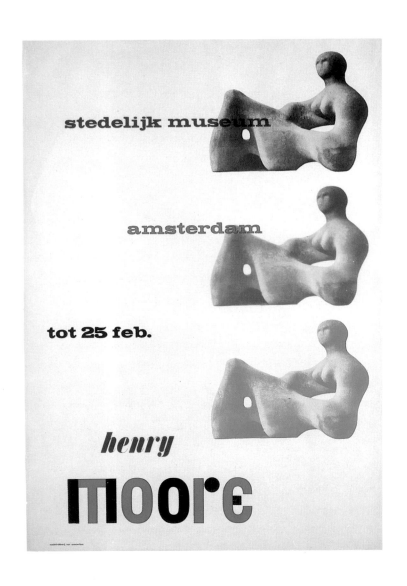

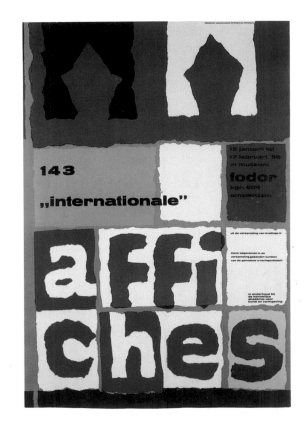

Willem Sandberg
Exhibition poster for
Henry Moore Sculpture,
Stedelijk Museum,
Amsterdam 1950

Willem Sandberg
Information folder
for *ICTYA: the
International Center for
the Typographic Arts*,
New York 1961

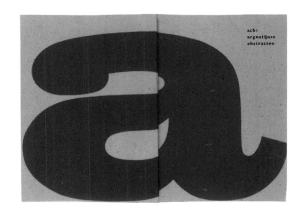

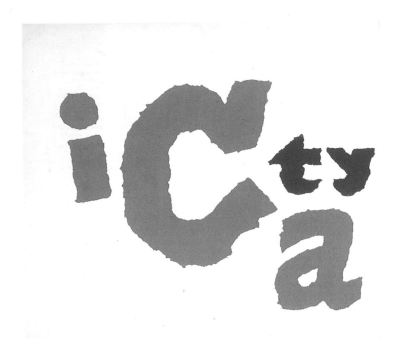

Willem Sandberg
Exhibition poster *143
International Posters*,
Museum Fodor,
Amsterdam 1958

Willem Sandberg
Front and back cover
of a catalogue *Eight
Argentinean Abstract
Artists*, Stedelijk
Museum, Amsterdam
1953

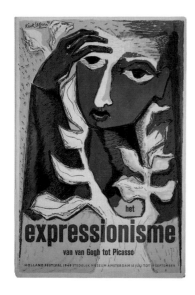

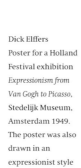

Dick Elffers
Poster for a Holland
Festival exhibition
*Expressionism from
Van Gogh to Picasso*,
Stedelijk Museum,
Amsterdam 1949.
The poster was also
drawn in an
expressionist style

Jan Bons
Poster for an
exhibition on
architect *Gerrit
Rietveld*, Stedelijk
Museum, Amsterdam
1959

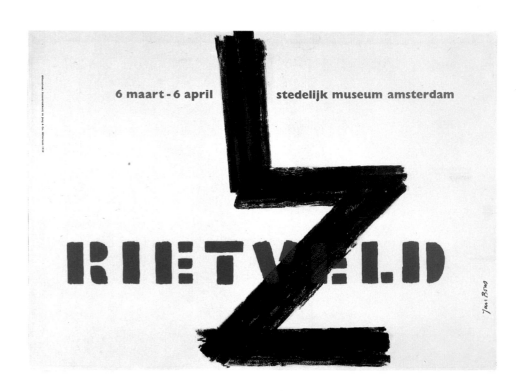

Posters for the Stedelijk Museum

Charles Jongejans
Exhibition poster
*Foreign Industrial
Design*, Stedelijk
Museum, Amsterdam
1956. It features
photographs of
industrial products,
some shown as
fragments

Wim Strijbosch
Poster *Graphics*,
Stedelijk Museum,
Amsterdam 1960

Jan Bons
Exhibition poster
Commissions, Stedelijk
Museum, Amsterdam
1956. Work was
shown from the
Society of Practising
Monumental Artists

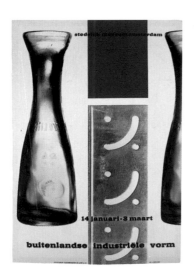

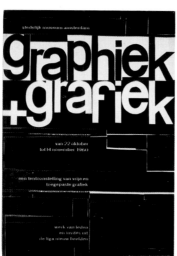

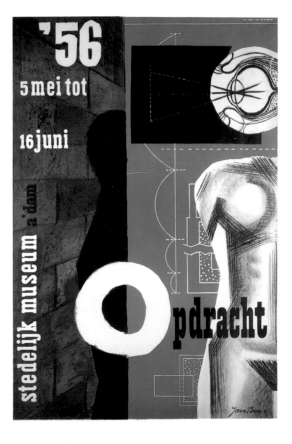

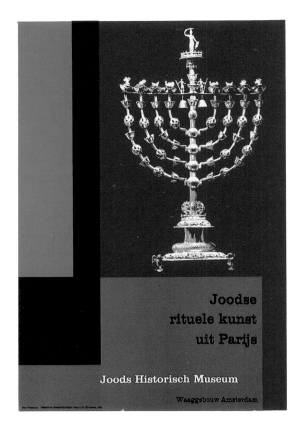

Otto Treumann
Exhibition poster
*Jewish Ritual Art from
Paris*, Jewish
Historical Museum,
Amsterdam 1958

The war had kept the Netherlands isolated for five years from artistic developments taking place in the rest of the world, and in the country itself there had been little opportunity for new cultural ideas to develop. While some dreamed of a new society in which democracy, prosperity and social progress held sway and cultural life would gain a potent impulse, others hoped for a reinstatement of traditional values.

Sandberg regarded 'his' Stedelijk Museum as a means of breaking through the Netherlands' cultural isolation and raising the issue of the social role of the arts. With his varied exhibition agenda he cemented links with the Dutch avant-garde artists of the first quarter of the century and reinstated their contribution to history. At the same time he introduced the public to events abroad and to radical developments in the recent art of their own country. This agenda carried the Stedelijk Museum to the centre of the international art world and brought with it vehement controversy.

Just as in the 1930s, Sandberg's interest was largely focused on architecture, interior and industrial design, photography and graphic art. The quickly changing exhibitions, with their stream of folders, catalogues and posters, gave Sandberg the opportunity to commission an entire succession of older and younger designers. Alongside Sandberg's own and quite distinct typographic posters, the work of numerous illustrators found a place, including the expressive posters of Dick Elffers and Mart Kempers, and Jan Bons' monumental works. Charles Jongejans and Otto Treumann worked with photography, thereby creating a link with the 1930s – although now colour photography added another visual element to their designs. The example of such Amsterdam museums as the Stedelijk, Museum Fodor and the Amsterdam Historical Museum in having all their printed matter designed, ultimately had an important influence on graphic design. Museums elsewhere in the Netherlands also acquired a better eye for the function and the individual form of printed material to accompany their exhibitions. Type material became a visual metaphor for policies that ranged from the conservative to the progressive, and acted as a visual guide for clients from industry and other public services.

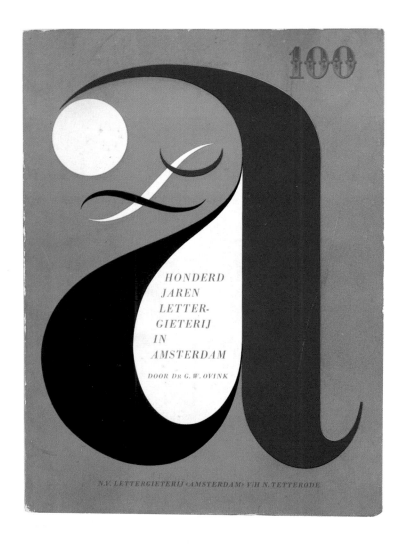

Dick Elffers

The pre-war experimental approach demonstrated by Dick Elffers as a painter and graphic designer remained typical of his work after 1945. In his graphic work Elffers revealed his origins as a draughtsman and painter. He employed photography for commemorative works, for promotional publications for companies, on covers and in posters only to highlight the text. On the cover of *Vrije Katheder* (1945), however, and later in his posters for exhibitions at the Rijksmuseum, he used a photographed object to convey information.

After 1946 the decorative aspect of his paintings and graphic work gradually disappeared – partly due to disillusionment caused by the war – and was replaced by a more expressive manner of working. Elffers knew about Flemish Expressionism and was a great admirer of Henri Matisse. Immediately after the war Sandberg mounted exhibitions of French and German Expressionism, and Elffers designed for one of these shows the poster entitled *Expressionism from Van Gogh to Picasso*. The attempt at a new modern form was gradually developed in his posters, which in the immediate post-war years were still closely linked to his heavy Expressionist paintings. Elffers moved to brighter colours and a changing combination of illustration, decoration and free or formal, mainly hand-drawn typography. Figuration was increasingly stylised or omitted entirely, under the influence of the 'primitive images that you see on the wall of my home, and which I received at the time [1960] – somewhat more rigid forms, more simple, more immediate'. There remained in his work influential traces of French and German painting, of Picasso and also of Rouault, Matisse, Marc, Beckmann and later of Poliakoff, Bissière and Bazaine.

Elffer's own posters were made into booklets, which presented him with new, unexpected opportunities. His posters were 'street paintings', as he

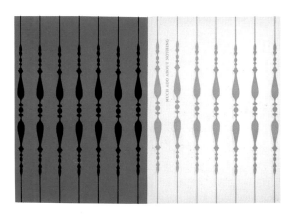

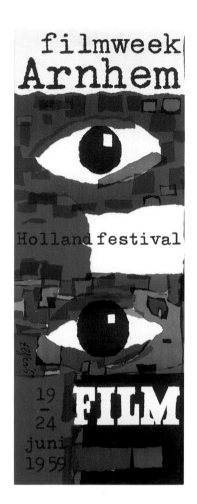

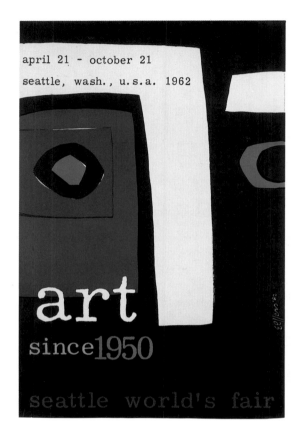

called them, always cheerful, striking in colour and form and beautifully composed. He experimented with misprints, screens, laying transparent colours one over the other, and usually prepared the printing plates himself. At Meijer Printers in Wormerveer, where he was free to make use of the firm's resources, he once said: 'Printing has to be a perfect miss'. As well as posters, including many for the Holland Festival, exhibition information and postage stamps, Elffers designed books in which the letters become illustrations. In the book *Op de bodem ligt lettergraniet* (On the Bottom Lies Letter Granite) of 1970, he evolved pure, new graphic symbols from letters, which interpret the contents of the text. It can be said that Elffers' work was determined by 'design and counterdesign', a theory concerning the organisational role of the designer and the 'poetic moment', about which he wrote a book in 1976.

Dick Elffers
Poster for the
*International Film Week
in Arnhem*, Holland
Festival, Arnhem
1959

Dick Elffers
Exhibition poster
Art Since 1950, Seattle
World's Fair, 1962

Dick Elffers
Booklet *Op de bodem
ligt lettergraniet* (On
the Bottom is Letter
Granite), De Bijenkorf
department store,
Amsterdam 1970.
The text was written
by Bert Schierbeek

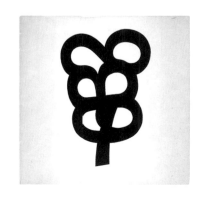

Printers Weekly (*Drukkersweeklad en auto-lijn*) was the official mouthpiece of the Federation of Employers' Organizations for the Printing Trade, or rather the journal of communication for the printing house bosses. It was not particularly remarkable, but once a year, at Christmas, there was a bumper issue. The tradition was established before the war and the varied, lavishly illustrated contents about topics from the printing world were followed by advertisements in the form of attached inserts. These inserts were technical masterworks from printers all over the country, and for the most part were extremely kitsch.

At the outbreak of the war, the publisher A.A.M. Stols succeeded in publishing for two years the finely produced magazine *Halcyon*. Every issue consisted of a portfolio with loose sections, each devoted to an aspect of the art of book design, printing and printmaking. These were separate contributions produced by various printers, such as Trio, Boosten & Stols, Enschedé and Thieme. In 1944 publication of the journal was forbidden by the German occupiers and after the war there was no money to continue with the magazine. However, the editorial staff of *Printers Weekly* paid homage to the high quality of *Halcyon*. The foreword of their Christmas 1949 issue states: 'It has gradually become a tradition that every year a number of Dutch printers, entirely voluntarily and without receiving compensation, contribute to elevating their profession. By so doing they intend first and foremost to fire their colleagues and the entire personnel of Dutch printers to greater effort and to increasing the quality of the work. At the same time they are mindful that printed matter reflects culture... Also some of them have now provided young graphic artists with the opportunity to show their talents, and who sometimes use the opportunity to experiment with drawing

Christmas issues of Printers Weekly

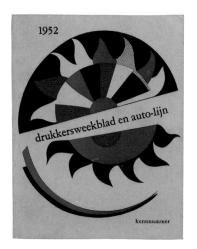

Dick Elffers
Front cover and
double-page spread of
the Christmas issue
of *Printers Weekly*,
Amsterdam 1952

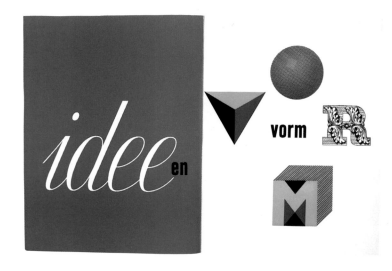

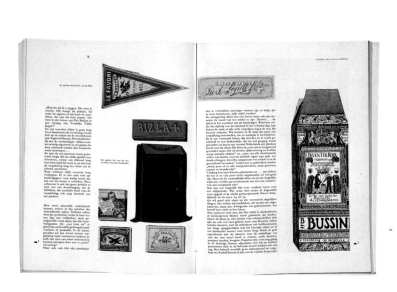

Jurriaan Schrofer
Title page spread and
back cover of the
Christmas issue of
Printers Weekly,
Amsterdam 1954.
The advertisement
is for the paper
merchant G.H.
Bührmann. Schrofer
described the type as
'attempting to
balance on the edge
of a grid, between the
two- and the three-
dimensional'

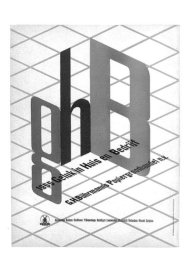

and colour.' Twelve printers had contributed the sections and the young
artists were Henk Krijger, Otto Treumann, Helmut Salden and Dick Elffers.

In subsequent years the editorial staff endeavoured to make each issue
more coherent in terms of content and design, so that the number of graphic
designers working on the Christmas issues gradually became smaller.
Eventually each number was devoted to a particular theme that was not
always directly related to the graphic industry, but gave printers and
platemakers the opportunity to show their talents. Designing the Christmas
issue, however, remained a splendid commission for a graphic artist and
brought a wide degree of recognition. Dick Elffers, Mart Kempers, Jurriaan
Schrofer, Hans Barvelink, Wim Crouwel and many more were all given the
opportunity. Every year devotees waited excitedly for the new Christmas
issue, wondering if it would again be designed by such a lunatic as last year,
or whether this time it would be a fine work of art.

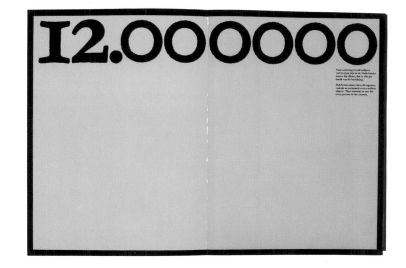

Jan van Toorn
Title page spread of
the Christmas issue
of *Printers Weekly*,
Amsterdam 1968. The
issue was devoted to
the fact that Dutch
museums had some
12 million objects in
their possession

Willem Sandberg
Front cover of the
Christmas issue of
Printers Weekly. The
theme of this number
was 'The Symbol'

Susanne Heynemann
Cover of *T.S. Eliot, The
Cocktail Party* (the play
was translated into
Dutch by M. Nijhof),
Querido, Amsterdam
1951

Henri Friedlaender
Page from *J. Slagter,
Leo Gestel*, L.J.C.
Boucher, The Hague
1948. The text for this
book, one of the St
Lucas series on
modern Dutch artists,
was set in sans-serif
Nobel

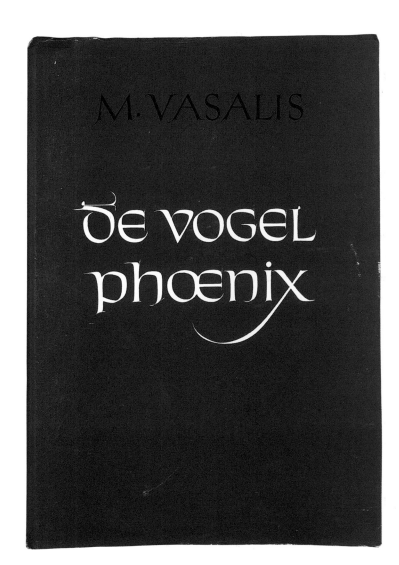

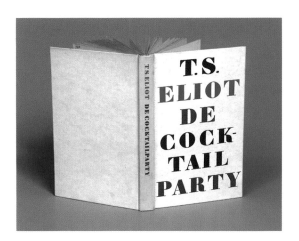

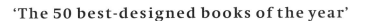

'The 50 best-designed books of the year'

Helmut Salden
Cover of the poetry
anthology *M. Vasalis,
De vogel Phoenix* (The
Phoenix Bird), A.A.M.
Stols, The Hague
1948. The publication
received one of the
'50 best-designed
books' awards for its
'remarkable cover'

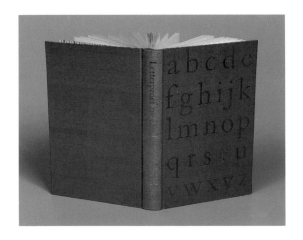

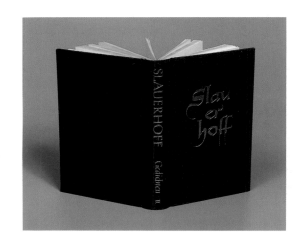

After the war the graphic industry slowly got into its stride, at first with a great shortage of raw materials; particularly restricting was the lack of paper. Thus it was not until 1948 that the pre-war institution of 'The 50 best-designed books of the year' was reinstated. An annually appointed jury of five book connoisseurs was put together by a commission responsible for promoting the Dutch book, supported by printers and booksellers. There was a great deal of reproach in the jury's general comments in the first few years that could not be explained away by the distressing economic circumstances. On each occasion they particularly lamented the fact that no schoolbooks or children's books deserved an award. Only during the 1950s did the jury begin to find the standard 'reasonable' or 'good'. Publishers were able to hire more graphic designers for book production and had increasing access to better materials. Monotype typesetting was more widely used, along with elegant book faces like Bembo, Baskerville, Garamond and Times. Meticulous calligraphic embossing was developed for more aesthetically pleasing covers and the standard of book illustration rose.

From 1953 onwards the jury produced a detailed critique for each selected book. A typical critique read: 'In this book the designer has been given the freedom to arrange text and illustrations in an accessible and pleasantly readable way. The whole shows a fresh and original approach. Much attention has been given to the quality of the illustrations; the only regrettable point is the noticeable difference in colour between the paper for the text and that for the illustrations. The table of contents is also accessible. Pleasing cover.'

In the first years there was special praise for the typography, embossing and covers done by Jan van Krimpen, Henri Friedlaender and Helmut Salden –

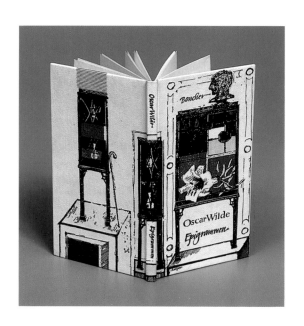

in particular the latter's designs for editions published by A.A.M. Stols of The Hague. For many years these designers had an important share of the '50 best designs'. Aldert Witte, Suzanne Heynemann and Theo Kurpershoek feature regularly in the history of the awards, and these design laureates have been joined by members of a younger generation, such as Karel Beunis, Jan Vermeulen, Jurriaan Schrofer, Frits Stoepman and Jan Kuiper. In the years prior to the award's temporary suspension in 1968 due to its perceived élitism, the designers Joost van de Woestijne, Harry Sierman, Wim Crouwel and Leendert Stofbergen were many times award winners. And for 20 years Helmut Salden was the most awarded designer for typography, covers and embossing. By this time the image of Dutch book production had drastically changed. The paperback, for instance, had found a firm niche – and was now included in the '50 best designs' – and new categories of books were added, such as illustrated art museum catalogues. Graphic designers continued to take over more of the design aspects that had once been the prerogative of typesetters and printers. No longer was the cover the sole domain conceded to designers; it became standard practice that they should determine every detail of the type matter. The fact that the designing of a book could be a creative challenge was many times demonstrated by the '50 best' awards.

Jan Bons
Double title page of
*Thomas Dekker, The Guls
Hornbooke*, De Roos
Foundation, Utrecht
1960. Jan Bons' design
and illustrations are
quite exceptional for
these largely
traditionally-designed
series of fine books

Thomas Dekker

the guls hornbooke

*first published at
London, 1609
reprinted in 1960
for the members of
de Roos, Utrecht*

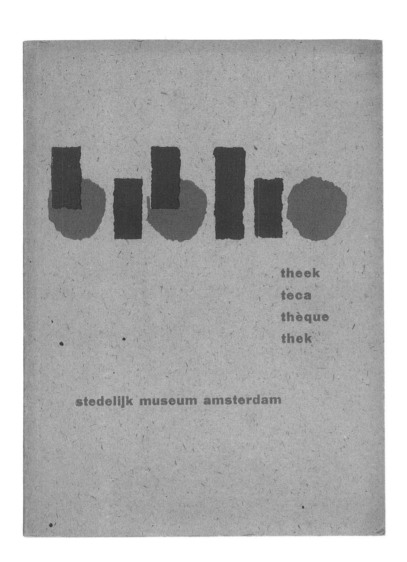

Willem Sandberg
Cover of the *Stedelijk
Museum's library
catalogue*, Amsterdam
1957

Hans Barvelink
Cover of a jury report
and catalogue for the
*50 Best-designed Books,
1962*, VBBB and CPNB,
Amsterdam 1963

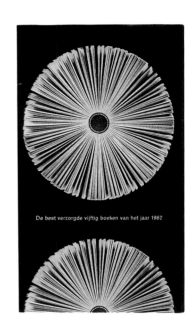

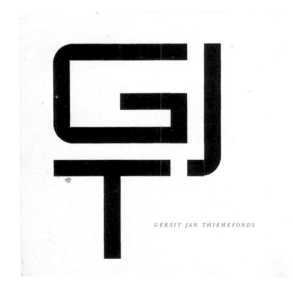

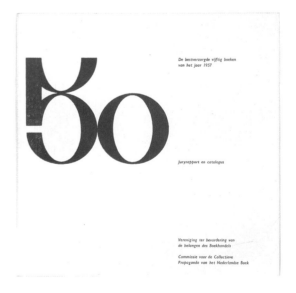

Hans Barvelink
Cover of a jury report
for a competition for
*Well-designed calendars
and office diaries*,
Gerrit Jan Thieme
Fund, Amsterdam
1962

Wim Crouwel
Cover of a jury report
and catalogue for the
*50 Best-designed Books,
1957*, VBBB and CPNB,
Amsterdam 1958

Jan van Krimpen
Spectrum, designed
1941-1943,
The Monotype
Corporation Ltd,
1955. This was
included in the type
reference book of the
well-known printing
house of Enschedé,
Haarlem c.1960

Classic typeface designers

SPECTRUM

48 p.
6-48D)

ABCDEFGHIJK
LMNOPQRST
UVWXYZ
1234567890
&
abcdefghijklmn
opqrstuvwxyzij
1234567890
.,:;!?""-(*[—

The long tradition of fine typography in the Netherlands was resumed after the war, but gradually, due partly to the disappearance of hot metal typesetting, it became absorbed in international production of electronic type. After 1945 the line followed by De Roos and Van Krimpen was taken up again by Sem Hartz who, like Van Krimpen, was closely associated with the Enschedé printers in Haarlem. His work was also influenced by Van Krimpen and this can be seen in Emergo, a type published right after the war, and in Juliana of 1958, both designed for the English firm Linotype. Other post-war typeface designers worked along similarly traditional lines, although often with greater contemporary awareness, such as Chris Brand.

Dick Dooijes joined the Amsterdam Type Foundry in 1926 as De Roos's assistant. He helped De Roos design the Nobel face among others, and in 1940 succeeded him as designer and librarian of the foundry's typographic library. Dooijes designed various faces, such as Mercator (1958), Contura (1964), and Lectura (1969), and completed a serif type that Stefan Schlesinger had begun. In 1968 Dooijes was appointed director of the Rietveld Academy, where Gerard Unger had completed his typographic training.

The calligrapher, typeface designer and typographer, Gerrit Noordzij, designed Dutch Roman (1980), Batavian (1980) and the more recent Remer, which have their roots in Van Krimpen's work. At The Hague Academy he had a strong influence on the young generation of typeface designers that are mentioned later in this book.

The typeface designer and calligrapher, Chris Brand, designed Albertina for the Monotype Corporation, and adapted it for a Greek and Cyrillic type. He also designed Delta Grotesque (1965-69) and a few Coptic (Dragnet) and Hebrew (Zippora) faces. He produced Denise in 1983 and designed the *Volkskrant* newspaper heading (1965), seen daily by thousands.

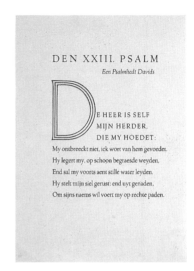

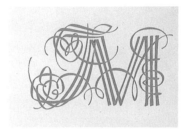

S.H. de Roos
De Roos Roman and Italic, Amsterdam Type Foundry, 1947. The letter was after a design by Dick Dooijes and used for a Christmas greeting for a prominent collector of fine books, Utrecht 1949

Henk Krijger
Raffia Initials, Amsterdam Type Foundry, 1952

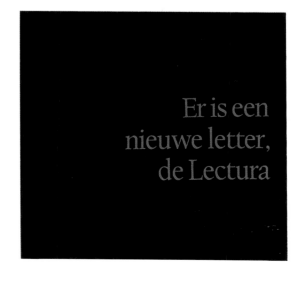

Chris Brand
Albertina, The Monotype Corporation Ltd., 1964

Dick Dooijes
Lectura, Amsterdam Type Foundry, 1969, from the first type reference sheets of the foundry

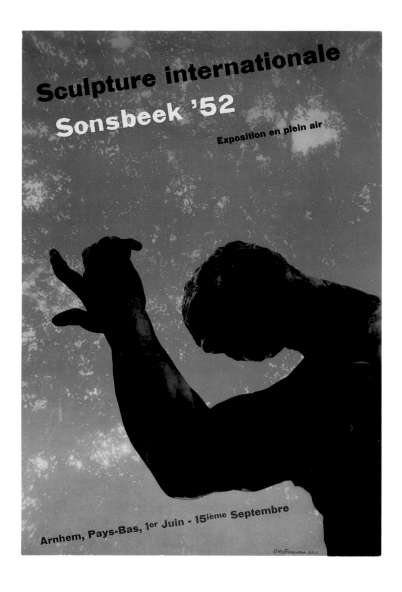

Otto Treumann

Otto Treumann arrived in the Netherlands from Bavaria after 1933 as a
refugee from the Nazis. His initial training was in design at the Amsterdam
School for Graphic Art, and in 1936 he became a student at Paul Citroen's
New Art School, which exerted the greatest influence on his work. Accepted
into the Amsterdam Resistance Movement during the war, he made
counterfeit documents such as fake passports, identity cards and ration
cards. At the same time, he learnt to master the printer's craft.

In 1945 Treumann began working as a freelance designer. His
commissions included posters (often for the annual Trade Fair and
museums), magazines, book covers, house styles and postage stamps.
His work displays a lucid combination of image and text and always carries
a characteristic and recognisable style, largely due to its composition and
unusual use of colour (for instance varied greens, particularly olive green,
burgundy and certain primary colours). The images were composed by
combining photography, asymmetrical typography and compositional
elements, shapes, geometric patterns and sometimes drawn figures. Most
of his posters have a strong spatial effect and the decorative aspect plays a
major role. In this sense, Treumann always retained a 'pre-war' poetic facet in
his work. One of his first post-war posters, for a PTT exhibition of stamps in
the Bijenkorf department store in Amsterdam, is reminiscent of Piet Zwart's
drawn paper man for *The PTT Book*. The commission to design the *Rayon Revue*
magazine for the rayon industry gave Treumann the opportunity to reveal
his talents and apply every possible graphic design technique.

Treumann often introduced changes and experimented with his work
while standing by the presses, aware of exactly what was and was not
possible – technically, aesthetically and economically. Content and form were

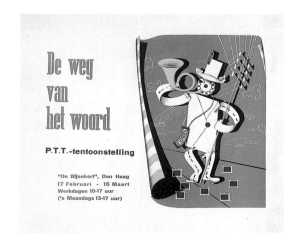

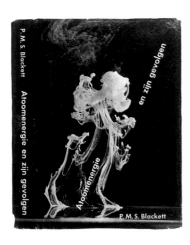

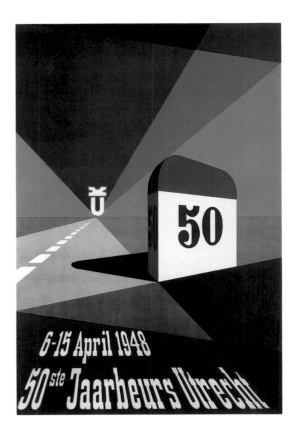

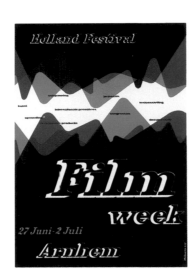

Otto Treumann
Cover of *P.M.S.
Blackett, Atoomenergie
en zijn gevolgen*
(Atomic Energy and
Its Effects), World
Library, Amsterdam,
1950

Otto Treumann
Poster for *Arnhem Film
Week*, Holland
Festival, Arnhem
1955

Otto Treumann
Poster for *Utrecht's
50th Trade fair*, Utrecht
1948

precisely attuned to one another and repeatedly considered from every angle.
While he was working, new possibilities would present themselves and this
reappraisal invariably led to a clear, definitive design. Typical examples of
Treumann's work are his three stamps with memorials honouring the
Resistance, which as a series of alternating images form a powerful unity.
His forceful logos for Wolters Noordhoff Publishers or for El Al airlines
offered many possible variations. His organisational talents were put to good
use at the GKf, the association of practitioners of the applied arts.

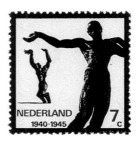

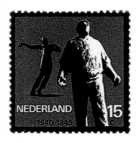

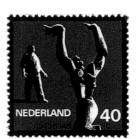

Otto Treumann
*Three commemorative
stamps*, PTT (Post
Office), The Hague
1965. The series
depicted three Dutch
war memorials

Jan Bons
Poster for a funfair
Lunapark, Amsterdam
c.1948

Jan Bons
Poster *Atomium –*
Visitez Bruxelles, World
Trade Fair, Brussels
1958

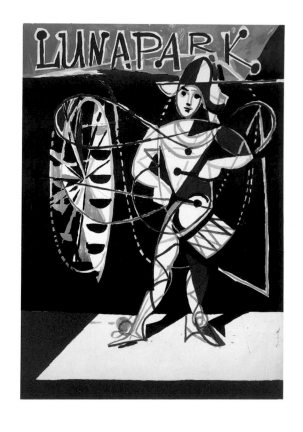

Jan Bons

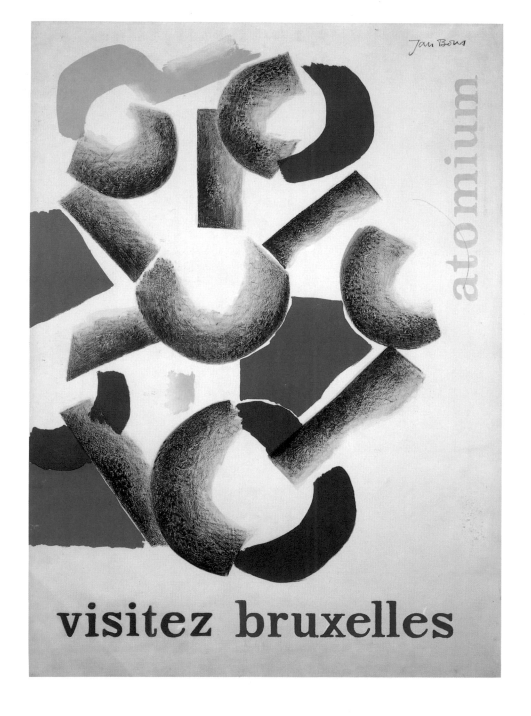

The Hague Academy, the New Art School in Amsterdam, and his contacts with Sandberg, Treumann and Duwaer printers have combined to mould Jan Bons into an idiosyncratic designer, who through the clarity of his use of typography, form and colour uses any graphic means in a spontaneous and piercing manner. Bons gained his experience during the war, making illegal documents and designing and publishing the first translation of Kafka in the Netherlands, as well as a book on Kandinsky – as part of the Duwaer series that he initiated – and publishing the *Waakzaam* (Watchful) publication against fascism (1939). These activities constituted the basis of his post-war work, which included murals, exhibition design, posters, calendars, postage stamps and other type matter. Bons is still the sort of craftsman who places his design for a poster over the screen frame at the printers himself. He made many posters for De Brakke Grond theatre in Amsterdam and since 1972 has produced all the posters and programmes for De Appel theatre group, as well as the annual calendars for the Van Ommeren shipping line in Rotterdam.

Similar to the other designers in his circle, such as Elffers and Treumann, Jan Bons managed to secure a great deal of artistic freedom from his clients. And not all clients could have Bons. This independent attitude found in some designers is characteristic of and unique to the Netherlands. Interference with their freedom could well result in their handing back a commission. Bons did this with the liberation stamps of 1985, which the PTT considered to be too provocative.

This liberality is also expressed in the way Bons uses typography. The letterform for him is not sacred, as it was for Van Krimpen, but provides many possibilities for emphasising the contents. For instance, Bons utilises the 'n' in his poster for the play *The Nuns* as a visual statement. He rarely used photography in his work, but there were many illustrations and an evocative use of areas of colour or colour accents; an example is *The Guls Hornbooke*, published by De Roos Foundation. The wall Bons painted in Mexico in 1952 for a Dutch exhibition is characteristic of his style: cheerful primary colours, stencilled letters and pictograms, treated with immediacy and without any frills. The mural was reproduced in one of the *Quadrate* magazines of Steendrukkerij De Jong (lithographers). He also worked with architect Gerrit Rietveld, for whom he designed a monumental poster in 1959. Bons, however, was also capable, depending on the commission, of revealing a totally different side to his talents. In one poster, for instance, he appears to be inspired by the work of the painter Jeroen Bosch. It is striking that the vision of Elffers, Treumann and Bons blossomed into such personal yet extremely varied styles. Their work is always recognisable.

Jan Bons
Foster *Roger Vitrac,*
Victor of de kinderen
aan de macht (Victor or
Children in Power),
De Appel Theatre
Group, The Hague
1982

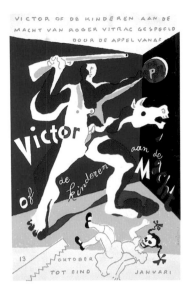

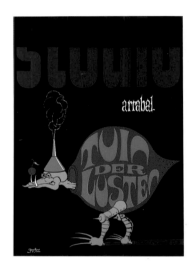

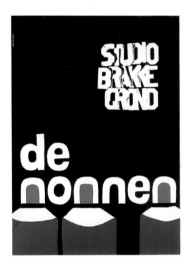

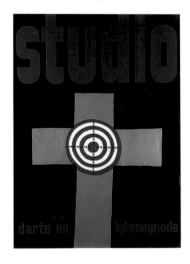

Jan Bons
Poster for *Fernando*
Arrabal, Tuin der Lusten
(Garden of Desire),
Studio Theatre Group,
Amsterdam 1969

Jan Bons
Poster for *Eduardo*
Manet, De nonnen (The
Nuns), Studio Theatre
Group, Amsterdam
1969

Jan Bons
Poster for *Lodewijk de*
Boer, Darts en
Lijkensynode (Arrows
and a Synod), Studio
Theatre Group,
Amsterdam 1968

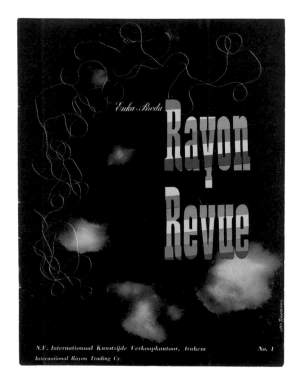

During the period of reconstruction the Dutch publishing industry sought to make itself known internationally for its dynamism and progressive ideas. The printing of informative magazines, quarterlies and yearbooks was one such customer-relations exercise, although in the world of paper and print, such magazines already existed. The Amsterdam Type Foundry published *Grafische Mededelingen* (Graphic Communications); paper wholesalers and binders Proost & Brandt issued its humorous *Proost Prikkels* (Proost Promptings); and the paper wholesaler Corvey produced *Het Model voor de Uitgever* (The Publisher's Model) designed by Johan H. van Eikeren.

Experimentation was not always eschewed, as is demonstrated by two publications from the royal paper manufacturers Van Gelder and Sons: *Aspects of Printing* and *The Language of Form*. In the first Dick Elffers, together with the young Jurriaan Schrofer, revealed an entire armoury of printing possibilities through the creative use of paper of various colours and textures combined with original illustration techniques, and by changing the colour-process printing order and choosing less obvious typefaces.

More industries became open to new ideas for their printed matter. Otto Treumann's design for the *Rayon Revue* journal caught the attention of the graphic design world. By employing photographic effects and an odd use of colour, certain covers and title pages appear like something from science fiction, while the contents are characterised by a stark, formal arrangement of type and illustration. Alexander Verberne and Ton Raateland gave Philips house magazine, *Range*, an open layout with classic type and a sparing use of illustrations and diagrams. Magazines that covered the realm of progressive architecture and interior design, such as the new architectural monthly *Forum* and *Good Living*, were designed by members of GKf, to which they were

New-style magazines and house journals

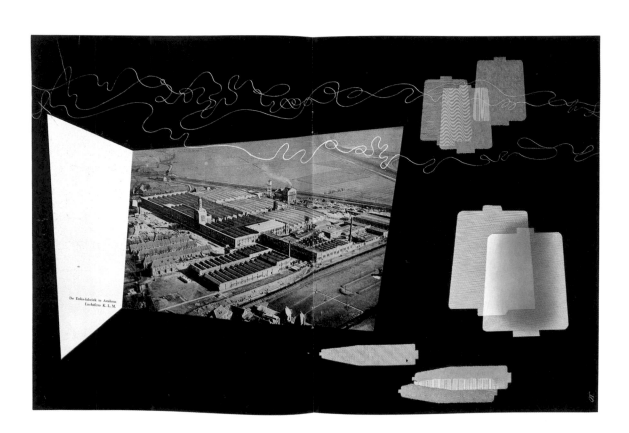

Otto Treumann
Cover and double-
page spread of *Rayon
Revue*, vol. 1, no. 1,
Breda/Arnhem 1947

affiliated – if not actually, then certainly regarding editorial content. In all these designs can be seen a continuing desire to experiment with shapes, colours and materials, which began with the Bauhaus, was handed on by the New Art School and by the end of the 1940s was valid once more. In one designer there was an overriding tendency towards clarity and geometry, in another the pleasure of painterly contrasts and an expressive use of colour, while a third might be concerned with the possibilities that experiments with the photographic image could provide.

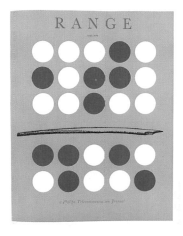
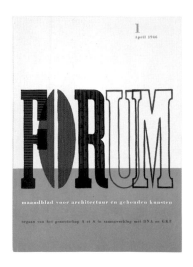

Alexander Verberne
and Ton Raateland
Cover of the quarterly
house journal *Range*,
Philips
Telecommunication
Division, Eindhoven
1950

Wim Brusse
Cover of *Forum*, vol. 1,
a monthly magazine
for architecture and
the applied arts,
Amsterdam 1951

Dick Elffers
Cover and double-
page spread from
*Cor Pels, Facetten van
boekdruk* (Aspects of
Letterpress), Van
Gelder Zonen,
Amsterdam 1952.
Jurriaan Schrofer
assisted in producing
the book;
Cas Oorthuys, Carel
Blazer and Emmy
Andriesse took the
pictures

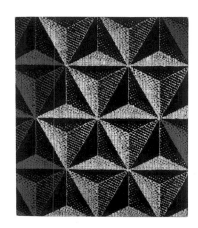

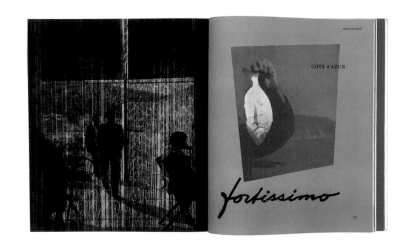

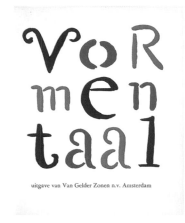

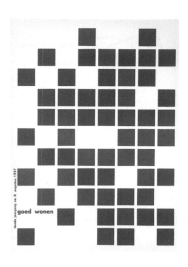

Jan van Keulen
Title page of
B. Majorick, Vormentaal
(The Language of
Design), Van Gelder
Zonen, Amsterdam
1955

Charles Jongejans
Cover of the monthly
magazine *Goed Wonen*
(Good Living), vol. 10;
Goed Wonen
Foundation,
Amsterdam 1957

Formal arrangement and variation

With the increasing prosperity of the 1960s the *ordenende* (formal arrangement of text and image) principle in design appeared to hold sway over the friendly and illustrative style of the 1950s. The straightforward approach, designing without frills as inspired by the Swiss school of design, tied in with a growing economy and the burgeoning of trade and industry. The prevailing mood of optimistic constructivism in the visual arts was a legacy from the 1920s. Practitioners hoped that the *ordenende* principle would 'make contemporaries familiar with the laws upon which our contemporary society rests' (H. Jaffé). A climate of reconstruction still prevailed, and there was a belief in a better world despite East-West tensions. This optimism was expressed in graphic design, which was nourished by the avant-garde of the inter-war period and by influences from Switzerland, Italy and the USA. The designs of Wim Crouwel, Total Design, Tel Design and BRS, and individuals like Jurriaan Schrofer and Pieter Brattinga for instance were objective, analytical, informative and in tune with the climate.

In 1955 Liga Nieuw Beelden, a society for artists and designers, was founded. It aimed at a synthesis of architecture, art and design, which, it felt, should be integrated in society and life. As Hartsuyker stated: 'A valuable human society is constructed on the basis of creativity. And the means of doing this is by transforming society through this creativity. Then "art" in its present meaning and form becomes irrelevant and the most important work of art is the constructing of interhuman relations.' In 1969 Liga was dismantled on the grounds that art would become institutionalised and lose its individuality. A relationship with society was sought in other ways: optimistic and constructive on the one hand and critical and challenging on the other.

A sector of trade and industry, as well as government bodies, began to see the relevance of design and commissioned logos, house styles and promotional advertising. Printing firms continued to give graphic designers the scope to experiment with type matter and make it interesting. The Nederlandse Bank introduced a series of new and – for those circles – exceptional banknotes, designed by R.D.E. Oxenaar. In 1969 the BRS design agency began working for the Ministry of Home Affairs, and the PTT continued its support of good design begun in the 1920s. The critical and provocative aspect that existed in graphic design paralleled the protest movements in politics and the fine arts. New printing and typesetting techniques changed the graphic industry and were responsible for the 'democratisation' of general printing, in which the graphic designer had an increasingly important role.

Jurriaan Schrofer
Exhibition poster
i 10: Internationale
Avantgarde 1927-1929,
Stedelijk Museum,
Amsterdam 1963. The
letters are composed
from two basic
elements: a square
and a quarter-circle

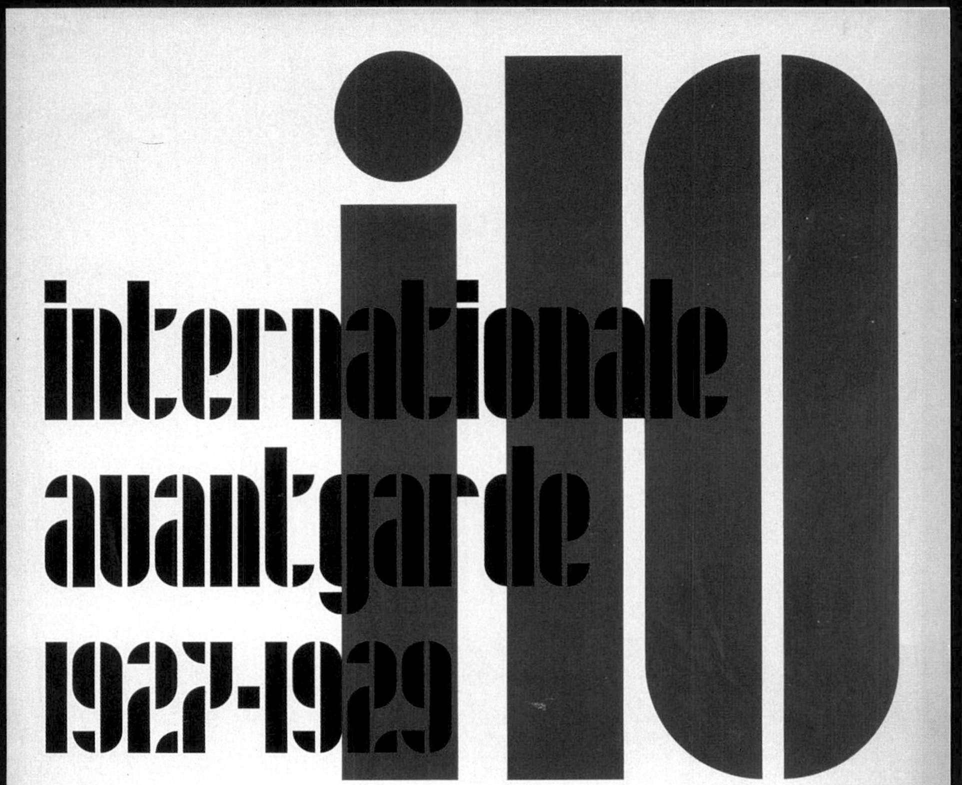
i10
internationale
avantgarde
1927-1929
stedelijk museum
amsterdam
18-10–18-11 '63

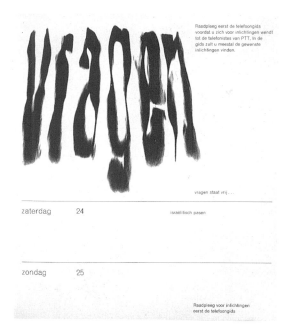

vragen staat vrij . . .

zaterdag   24   israelitisch pasen

zondag   25

Raadpleeg voor inlichtingen
eerst de telefoongids

Jurriaan Schrofer
Two pages from the
Staff agenda, 1965, PTT
(Post Office),
The Hague 1965. The
letters were distorted
in various ways

Jurriaan Schrofer: new forms of lettering

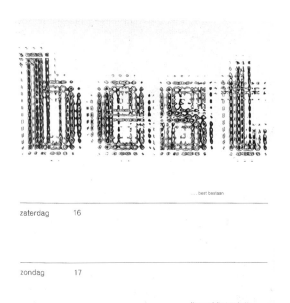

. . . best bestaan

zaterdag   16

zondag   17

Neem een beleggingsrekening
bij de Rijkspostspaarbank

Jurriaan Schrofer
Cover of the journal
*Cognition: International
Journal of Cognitive
Psychology*, Mouton,
The Hague and Paris,
1972. A typographic
design in which
three-dimensional,
geometric
letterforms are
arranged into an
improbable spatial
composition

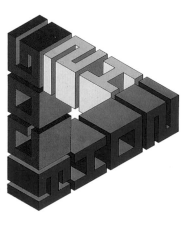

Jurriaan Schrofer was one of the more significant post-war designers. Reared in the anti-authoritarian climate of the teacher Kees Boeke, he became interested in philosophy, theatre, film and photography, and from his youth was fascinated by letters and type images. After a roving start to his career, he became assistant to Dick Elffers, from whom he learnt about the freedoms that can exist within design disciplines.

The progressive printing firm of Meijer was Schrofer's next employer. Here he immersed himself in the possibilities of Monotype setting and produced a type sample sheet. This experience formed the basis for his career as a freelance designer. He designed logos, book covers, diaries, brochures, advertisements, photographic books and so on for numerous companies, publishers and institutes, in which the layout and especially the type played an important role. Though Schrofer was a typographer he was more a conjurer with letters, which he designed himself. Under the influence of photography he began distorting the type image: his PTT staff diaries are fine examples of this. Increasingly, his experimentation with letters and his interest in the relation between type image and content, developed into one process. He combined size, structure, rhythm, spacial order and mathematical precision with his intense need for spontaneity and visual effects. Ultimately for Schrofer the word became the image and the image concealed the text.

The urge to break new ground was also demonstrated in his administrative talents. He did much for GVN, the association of graphic designers, and subsequently became co-director of the design agency Total Design. He was a lucid and inspiring instructor and taught at the Rietveld Academy in Amsterdam and at the Rotterdam Academy before becoming director of the Arnhem Academy. His work grew more simplified and muted, while in his word images he made greater use of light and space. The upper-case 'And And', two words raised and cut deeply into paper, can be seen to exemplify Schrofer's credo: no truth exists, only possibilities. His short verses – in which at first glance the hand-cut paper letters are often barely legible – form light, spatial structures that overstep the boundaries of functionalism to become poetical.

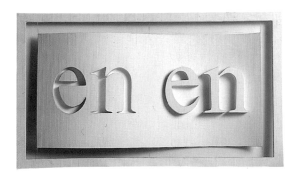

Jurriaan Schrofer
Three-dimensional
typographic
composition *en en*,
1988

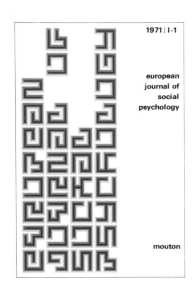

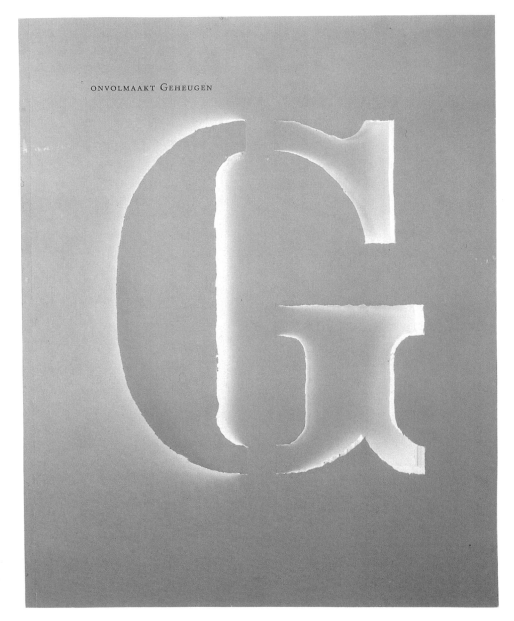

Jurriaan Schrofer
Covers of the *European
Journal of Social
Psychology*, Mouton,
The Hague and Paris
1971

Jurriaan Schrofer
Cover of *Jurriaan
Schrofer, Onvolmaakt
geheugen* (Imperfect
Memory), Bührmann-
Ubbens Papierprijs,
Amsterdam 1988

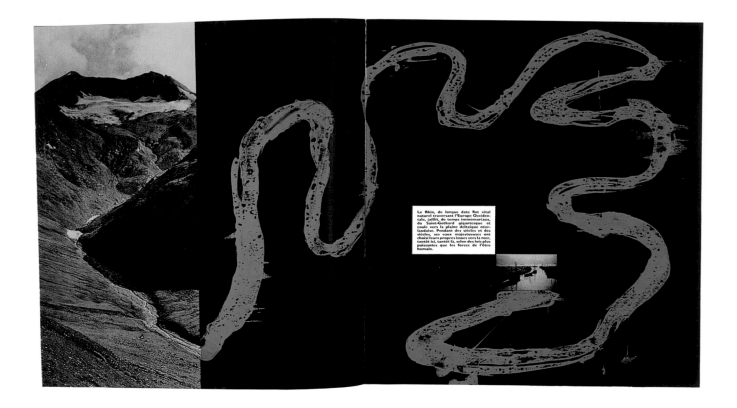

Dick Elffers
Double-page spread
for an advertising
book *Synthese*,
Kunstharsfabriek
Synthese, Katwijk
1950. Photography by
Cas Oorthuys

Books and photography:
a new association

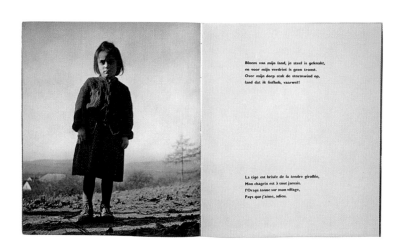

Jurriaan Schrofer,
Ata Kando and
Violette Cornelius
Photographic book
*Voor het kind uit
Hongarije* (For the
Hungarian Child),
Meijer Printers,
Wormerveer 1956

In 1939, when the rebellious young designers Dick Elffers and Wim Brusse pointed to the limitations of photography compared with freely-drawn illustration, the older generation pointed out to them the new perspectives that photography made possible. Their elders were right. Both Elffers and Brusse married photographers, Emmy Andriesse and Eva Besnyö respectively, and photography took on an importance in the work of these designers as never before.

Meanwhile, an entire generation of professional photographers had arisen in the Netherlands who moved beyond experimentation and photography for its own sake. This was made clear by GKf photographers at the 'Photo '48' exhibition in the Stedelijk Museum: 'The aim of photography is not a beautiful picture, but to say something about using a camera. This photography serves a purpose and in practice is dependent on a commission...Slowly one comes to realise that no new imagery has been created, and one returns to reality, the very straightforward reality.' Four years later at an important exhibition of photographs by Eva Besnyö, Emmy Andriesse, Carel Blazer and Cas Oorthuys, it was apparent that their work had developed towards a more functional use of the medium, embracing social realism and documentary record.

During the 1950s Meijer printers specialised in producing advertising booklets, yearbooks and commemorative books for commercial firms. Designers like Dick Elffers, Mart Kempers, Jan van Keulen and Benno Wissing produced the layouts and covers, and in addition to drawn illustrations more space was increasingly given to photography. Elffers' young assistant, Jurriaan Schrofer, later landed a job with Meijer and subsequently succeeded in making photography an integral part of the books published there.

Benno Wissing
Company brochure
4 Holes in the Ground,
Laura & Vereeniging,
Eygelshoven 1961.
Photography by Carel
Blazer

Jurriaan Schrofer
Company brochure
Fire by the Sea,
Hoogovens, IJmuiden
1958. The copy was by
Paul Rodenko and the
photographs were
taken by Violette
Cornelius, Ed van der
Elsken, Paul Huf, Ata
Kando and Cas
Oorthuys

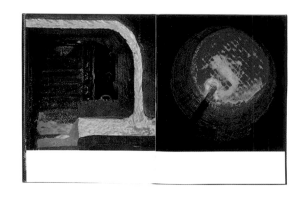

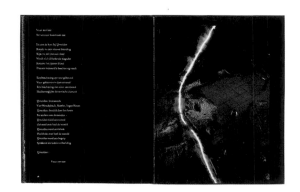

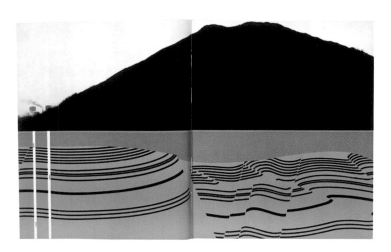

'What kept me totally occupied were the photographic books, and to control the entire editorial planning of these was a little like directing a film. At the same time I saw new distribution channels for the visual book. Not only for those meant for sale at bookshops, but the publications of local government, companies etcetera.' A good example of seamless interaction between typographer, copywriter and photographer was the book *Fire and Sea*, a eulogy in words and pictures to Hoogovens, a steel company in Ijmuiden. The photographs were by turn straightforwardly informative and social documentation, while lyrically portraying fire and steel in black and white and coloured photographic images.

By incorporating photography into his work, the graphic designer brought about a new type of book in which the purely visual elements were assigned an independent role alongside the text. The widespread development of offset printing at the expense of letterpress ultimately provided cheaper printing, such as the paperback, with the same illustrative possibilities.

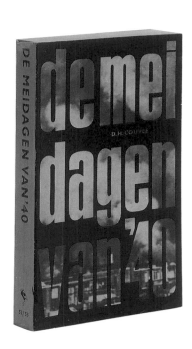

Jurriaan Schrofer
Cover of *D.H. Couveé,
De Meidagen van '40*
(The May Days of '40),
Bert Bakker, The
Hague 1960.
The design combines
photography with
cut-out letters

Wim Crouwel: function and form

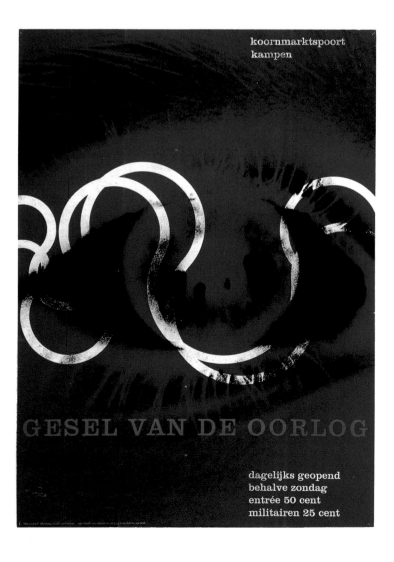

Wim Crouwel is a designer with an explicit vision, which he eloquently champions in his work and his words. He favours a methodical and systematic approach, but with a personal edge. In both his three-dimensional and two-dimensional designs he has excelled in the creation of functional and aesthetic forms.

Crouwel trained at the Minerva Academy in Groningen and at the Institute for Industrial Arts Education in Amsterdam. He began designing exhibitions (from 1957 to 1961) in close collaboration with the interior designer, Kho Liang Ie, with whom he also designed posters. In 1963 he was one of the founders of the design agency Total Design in Amsterdam. His interest in typography was inspired by his introduction to the strictly methodical Swiss typography, which influenced the developing principles of New Typography in the 1920s. Wim Crouwel made his first series of graphic designs in the latter half of the 1950s for the Van Abbemuseum in Eindhoven. These posters and catalogues became increasingly similar and their typographic design was in keeping with the contents of the exhibitions' themes. Sometimes Crouwel toyed with the letterforms on the posters or catalogue covers to create attention, but regarding the layout he worked systematically under the credo: 'Typography must be visually orderly for the purpose of good readability'.

When the Van Abbemuseum's director, De Wilde, took over from Sandberg at Amsterdam's Stedelijk Museum in 1962, he commissioned Crouwel to design new graphics for the museum. Crouwel, in his systematic way, introduced standard sizes, grids and types in order to guarantee continuity and visual unity, and a museum house style emerged. Crouwel denied this was his intention. He wanted to create 'a visual image of all the printed material which attempted to express what the basic premises of the museum as an institute had in common'. Despite the fact that Crouwel viewed design as a pragmatic means to an end, his fascination with letterforms remained, as his minimalist poster 'Forms of Colour' goes to prove. In the Christmas Issue of *Printers Weekly* that he designed in 1962 he was already saying 'We will have to divest ourselves of many things handed down. We are still stuck with those three type families to which after Bodini – which is a classic type – nothing more has been added in essence. We have to aim for a totally different letterform.' The annual calendars for the printing firm Van der Geer gave Crouwel the chance to experiment further – with the legibility of letter fragments (1975) and with creating new forms from a few basic rules (1976). In his poster for the 'Designers' exhibition and – to a greater degree – in his New Alphabet (a new type) he showed the unexpected results that methodology combined with inventiveness can produce.

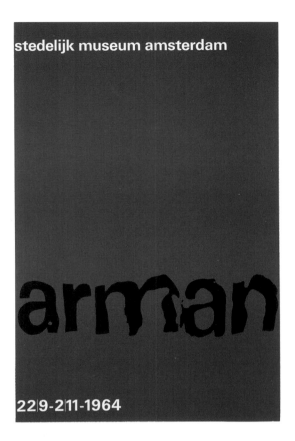

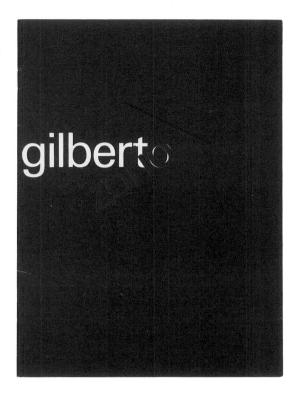

Wim Crouwel
Exhibition poster
Arman, Stedelijk
Museum, Amsterdam
1964

Wim Crouwel
Exhibition poster
Gilberto Zorio, Stedelijk
Museum, Amsterdam
1979

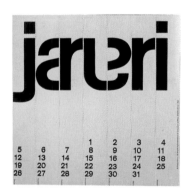

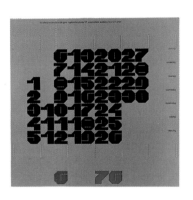

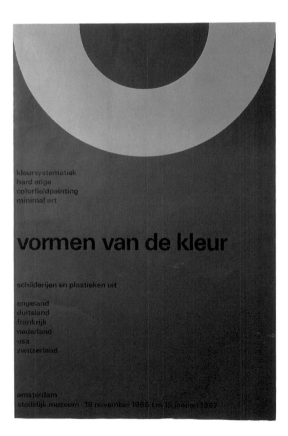

Wim Crouwel
Page from a *Calendar*
for 1975, Erven E. van
de Geer Printers,
Amsterdam 1974

Wim Crouwel
Page from a *Calendar*
for 1976, Erven E. van
de Geer Printers,
Amsterdam 1975

Wim Crouwel
Exhibition poster
Colour Forms, Stedelijk
Museum, Amsterdam
1966

Wim Crouwel
Number postage stamp,
PTT (Post Office),
The Hague 1976

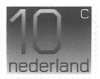

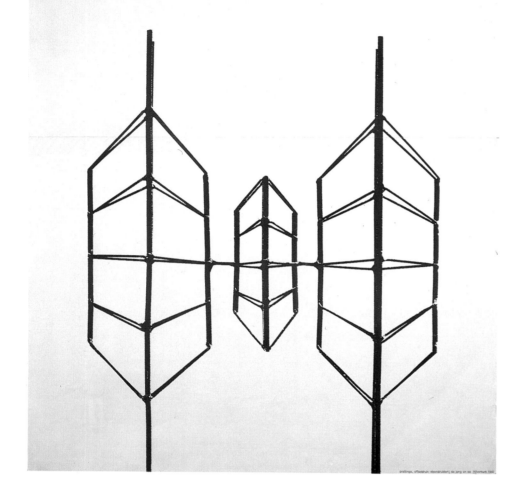

carel visser

van 20 mei tot 20 juni   stedelijk museum a'dam

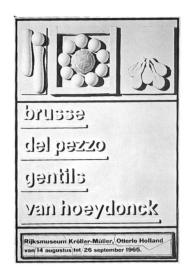

Pieter Brattinga
Poster for an
exhibition of work by
*Mark Brusse, Lucio del
Pezzo, Vic Gentils and
Paul van Hoeydonc,*
Rijksmuseum Kröller-
Müller, Otterlo 1965

Pieter Brattinga

Pieter Brattinga
Poster for an
exhibition on the
sculptor *Carel Visser,*
Stedelijk Museum,
Amsterdam 1960

Pieter Brattinga
Double-page
advertisement in the
Christmas issue of
Printers Weekly,
Amsterdam 1963.
This was based on the
logo, designed by Otto
Treumann, of
Steendrukkerij De
Jong, the printing
firm run by
Brattinga's father

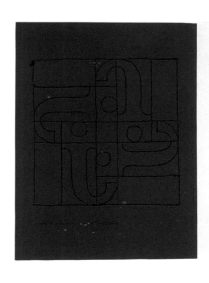
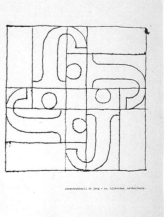

Pieter Brattinga spent his early years in his father's printing firm
Steendrukkerij De Jong in Hilversum, where he learnt the trade while coming
into contact with many designers and clients. He acted as a middleman for
printers and designers, whereby the wishes of the latter were respected as far
as possible. In this way he was able to bring many designers and clients into
association with the family firm. As the firm's representative he
commissioned a great deal of graphic design. This background enabled
Brattinga to harness his creative talent to a wide experience of organisational
and business management. Both aspects determined his design outlook, his
teaching at many institutes and his graphic design style.

From 1954 to 1973 Brattinga organised a series of exhibitions of avant-
garde art and design in the family firm's canteen. He designed the posters
himself, using a basic square grid. During this same period he edited a series
of experimental *Quadrate* journals. In his role as an intermediary, Brattinga
perceived gaps in the training of graphic designers and was invited by New
York's Pratt Institute to set up courses that covered every internal design
aspect – history of the profession, analysis, problem solving and new
technology – as well as every external aspect – public relations, clients and
marketing. Brattinga also mounted exhibitions, designed posters and laid out
typography for newspapers, books, magazines, catalogues, postage stamps
and house styles, including those for the Amsterdam Metro, the State Mines,
and Mercis, his own agency.

Since 1965 Brattinga has also worked as the house designer for the
Rijksmuseum Kröller-Müller in Otterlo, creating posters, catalogues and
layouts for several exhibitions. Having grown up with the work of such
functionalists as Piet Zwart (whom he knew well), Schuitema and Kiljan, and
inspired by his contact with Sandberg, Brattinga developed a personal, direct
manner of working in which the grid, the sans-serif letter and often the
square formed the basis. For him a graphic designer is an intermediary acting
between the client and the general public, and design plays an indispensable
background role. The canteen exhibitions begun at Steendrukkerij De Jong
were continued in 1972 in the print gallery of his design consultancy in
Amsterdam. Until the present day he has held a respectable number of
exhibitions there, all more or less aimed at providing information on
developments within the design profession.

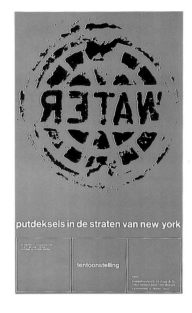

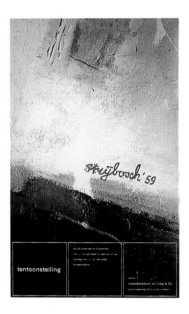

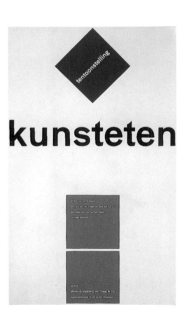

Pieter Brattinga
Exhibition poster
Manhole Covers,
Steendrukkerij de
Jong, Hilversum 1964

Pieter Brattinga
Exhibition poster on
the Dutch designer
Wim Strijbosch,
Steendrukkerij de
Jong Hilversum 1959

Pieter Brattinga
Exhibition poster *Eat
Art*, Steendrukkerij de
Jong, Hilversum 1965

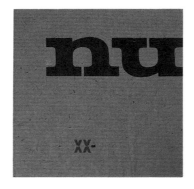 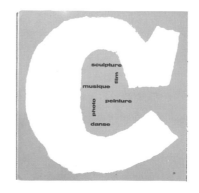 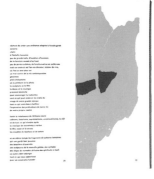

Willem Sandberg
Cover and spread of a
theme issue *NU: in het
midden van de
twintigste eeuw* (Now:
Half-way through the
20th Century) from
Kwadraatblad
(Quadrate journal),
Steendrukkerij de
Jong, Hilversum 1959.
Sandberg contributed
an article on
contemporary
museums

The De Jong Kwadraatblad Journals

The *Kwadraatblad* (Quadrate) journals of Steendrukkerij De Jong in Hilversum
were mailed to the printer's business contacts. The journals drew attention to
the firm and at the same time brought clients and designers into contact with
extremely diverse cultural topics, such as music, design, literature,
typography, architecture and the visual arts. Because of the journal's high
standards, the firm was able to show a cross-section of its work. Pieter
Brattinga was the editor and a new designer was invited to lay out every
issue. In total, 23 *Kwadraatblad* journals were produced, and for Brattinga the
main concern was the opportunity to demonstrate new trends and
discoveries. The idea for the *Kwadraatblad* publications stemmed from the
success of a brochure on the Sonsbeek Pavilion by Rietveld, published in 1956.
The square shape of the journal (25 x 25 cm) initially came in for much
criticism, but ultimately became its trademark. The first issue was devoted to
Marc Chagall's 'Clocks' (1957), and further publications covered Buckminster
Fuller, Sandberg (who designed his *NU* and *NU 2* magazines himself), music
and technology, the written language, Jan Bons' mural in Mexico, Katavolos'
organic architectural forms, Rietveld's Schröder House and Crouwel's newly
designed alphabet. The artist Les Levine used 'House'; designer Anthon Beeke
his controversial naked bodies alphabet; while Dieter Roth devoted his *Daily
Mirror* issue to the concept of 'quantity' by means of a number of square blow-
ups of the English newspaper of the same name.

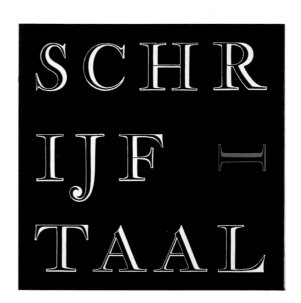

Ton Raateland
Cover of a
*Kwadraatblad with
the theme Schrijftaal 1*
(Written Language 1),
Steendrukkerij de
Jong, Hilversum 1961.
The issue featured
handwritten texts
from authors and
poets collected by the
poet Simon
Vinkenoog

Pieter Brattinga
Theme issue of
Kwadraatblad entitled
Number, comprising a
box of receipts;
Steendrukkerij de
Jong, Hilversum 1970

Anthon Beeke
Theme issue of
Kwadraatblad entitled
Antinon Beeke Alphabet,
Steendrukkerij de
Jong, Hilversum 1970.
Photographed by
Geert Kooiman and
produced by Anna
Beeke

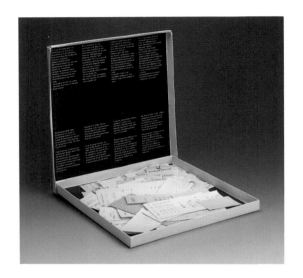

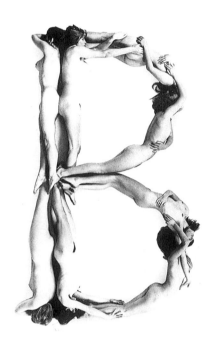

Jan Bons
Concertina-type
pages from
Kwadraatblad's issue
on the *Genesis of
Composition*,
Steendrukkerij de
Jong, Hilversum 1961.
B. Majorick
contributed an article
on a mural by Jan
Bons painted for a
Dutch exhibition in
Mexico in 1952

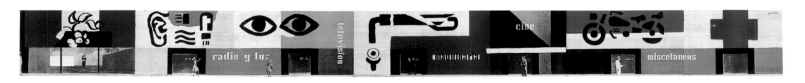

Freestyle approach vs. grid

The formally arranged and utilitarian graphic design style of the 1960s may have been determined by increased prosperity, yet in this geometric preserve there were dissidents, such as the provocative young designers Anthon Beeke and Swip Stolk. Their design style expressed the freedoms of neo-Dadaism, Fluxus and Provo, movements in art and politics that were at odds with the social order of the times, and they even attempted to discover new avenues for design. Their commissions came mainly from cultural bodies. In 1967 Gert Dumbar began working for the design agency Tel Design in The Hague, and alongside its formally ordered design style, as in Dutch Rail's house style, he introduced relatively freer graphic design approaches, employing among other things staged photography for the purpose. Jaap Drupsteen produced a new and challenging design style for television, a discussion of which is prevented by a lack of space. Jan van Toorn held a special position throughout this period with work that was clear and well ordered, but highly critical of society.

The 1970s saw a growing freedom and eclecticism, which again evoked reactions among such young typographic designers as Walter Nikkels and Karel Martens, who aspired to a restrained and classic design style. After 1980 these approaches were further expanded upon and refined by such design groups as Hard Werken and Wild Plakken. They have no uniform style, but take a free and eclectic design approach in which graphic achievements from the distant or recent past are quoted and reinterpreted.

The 'purposeful' aspect of design – still advocated by, among others, Kees Nieuwenhuijzen, Baer Cornet, René van Raalte, Hans Kruit and Paul Mijksenaar – had partly shifted towards 'design for design's sake' in which the artistry of the maker was becoming increasingly important. It was a trend to which clients had gradually become accustomed. The recent image of Dutch graphic design is one of a large quality of widely varying work, due in part to the many new graphic design techniques that now exist. But despite this plurality there is at the same time a certain mediocrity, due to the increasing number of designers, although individual approaches still remain that produce unexpected results and high-quality work. As a counterpart to the large design studios, there will always be designers who want to remain working independently and on a small scale.

Wim Crouwel
Exhibition poster
Designers, Stedelijk
Museum, Amsterdam
1968

stedelijk museum amsterdam
s april t/m 23 juni 1968

vorm
gevers

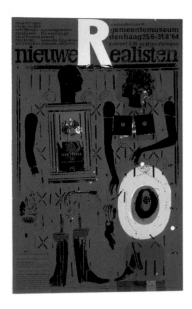

The Netherlands has several striking design products of public interest, such as its banknotes and postage stamps, which are highly acclaimed abroad. Over the last decades, R.D.E. Oxenaar has been responsible for designing several postage stamps and most of the Dutch banknotes. He trained at The Hague Academy, first as a fine artist (he was taught painting, drawing and illustration by W.J. Roozendaal, Bertram Weihs and Paul Citroen), before switching to the applied art department and specialising in graphic design. At the time this department had a reputation for promoting the New Functionalism, while a special feature of the academy was that the champions of very subjective art like Roosendaal and Citroen, taught alongside advocates of an extremely plain and objective visual style.

Both approaches led to Oxenaar's present interests and graphic design style and today he still looks to fine art as a visual source for graphic design. From the beginning he was particularly interested in German Expressionism, Marcel Duchamp and the Dada movement; yet he was also inspired by Constructivism, El Lissitzky, Tatlin and De Stijl. What struck him most in the work of these artists was their command and knowledge of content, their personal, yet at the same time broad and rational manner. In his work Oxenaar, too, has tried to combine by illustrative means the personal and general, and the constructively functional with the subjective. Similarly he was able to use these elements as a member of various committees and when teaching. He was a board member of the GKf and the international association of graphic designers, AGI; taught at The Hague Academy from 1958 to 1970; and was first an assistant then head of the Aesthetic Design service, now the Art and Design department, of Royal PTT Nederland. He is also visiting professor of visual presentation at Delft Technical University.

Oxenaar prefers the unexpected, the exceptional within the normal, and knows how to convey this to others. Often it is unexpectedly hidden, such as his nickname 'Ootje', which he incorporated in miniscule letters into the Dutch five guilder banknote, or the rabbit that can be detected in the watermark of the 250 guilder banknote. It is largely visible, too, in the primary iconography of his work. He also produced some monumental paintings, including those for The Hague's city police station, and together with Rietveld he organised the exhibition 'E55' on Dutch post-war reconstruction in Rotterdam.

As well as banknotes and postage stamps he has designed book covers, exhibitions and posters, such as the one for the 'New Realists' exhibition in The Hague's Gemeentemuseum. Despite his hankering after the unconventional, his work is recognisable and lucid. Content appears to be more important than design, though the attractiveness of the image, even if occasionally mildly impoverished, is always unmistakable.

R.D.E. Oxenaar

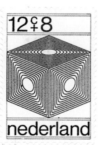

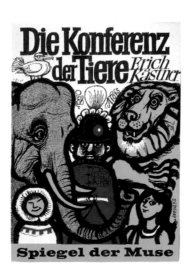

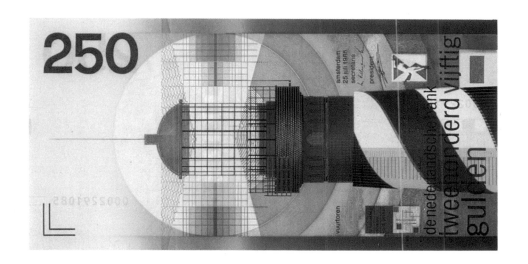

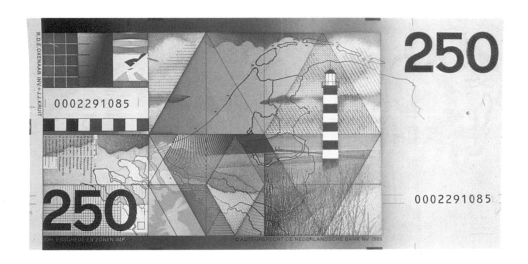

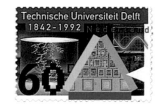

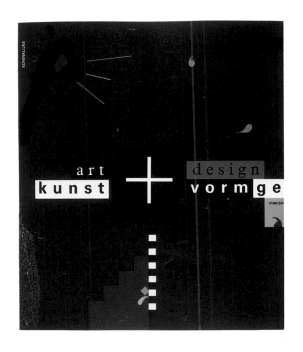

R.D.E. Oxenaar
and Hans Kruit
*A Bank note of 250
guilders*, Enschedé,
Haarlem 1986

R.D.E. Oxenaar
Cover of a book *10
years Art + Design*,
PTT (Post Office),
The Hague 1992

R.D.E. Oxenaar
Postage stamp
depicting *Delft
Technical University*,
PTT (Post Office),
The Hague 1992

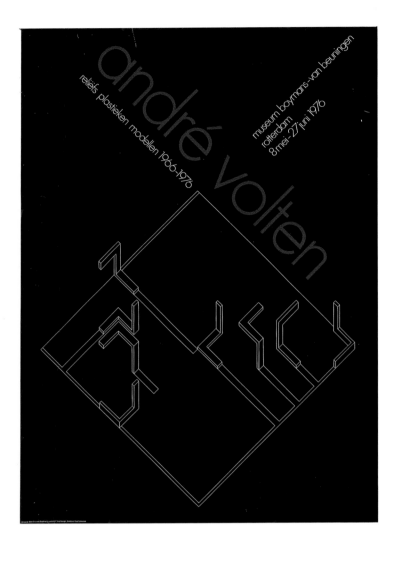

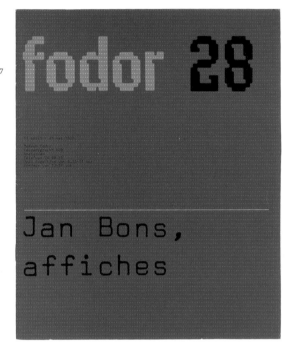

Total Design

In spring 1963 the Total Design studio in Amsterdam was founded by Wim Crouwel, Benno Wissing and industrial designer Friso Kramer, together with Dick and Paul Schwarz, who ran the organisational and business management side. The studio's somewhat immodest name, which quickly became known as TD, symbolised a collaboration from a collective viewpoint that would lead to two- and three-dimensional design for industry, government, trade and commerce.

Through teamwork the group designed large and complex commissions, such as corporate identities, that would reflect a 'total' design concept down to the finest details. This was achieved by combining the traditional innovations of the 1920s and New Architecture with the contemporary demand for visual recognition of their products required by companies. To begin with new design principles were introduced, described by Benno Wissing as: 'the module, simplification, standardisation, measurability, visual rhythms, functionality, visual expression of applied technology. Our earlier work was somewhat dogmatic looking.'

In the 1960s the studio expanded enormously and maintained a broad network of regular clients including Schiphol Airport, banks, companies, museums, festivals and far-reaching projects such as the Dutch pavilion at the Osaka World Trade Fair in 1970. Numerous young design students have done periods of practical training at the studio. Some of the original founders, such as Friso Kramer, left and the studio focused increasingly on the design of corporate identity programmes for institutes and firms, and other forms of visual communication.

In the 1970s the nature of the studio gradually changed. Alongside designers like Wim Crouwel, Ben Bos, Jolijn van de Wouw and Daphne

Paul Mijksenaar
(Total Design)
Graphics depicting
Payments,
Bankgirocentrale
Annual Report,
Amsterdam 1978

Ben Bos (Total Design)
Logo and poster for
Randstad office
employment agency,
Amsterdam c.1970

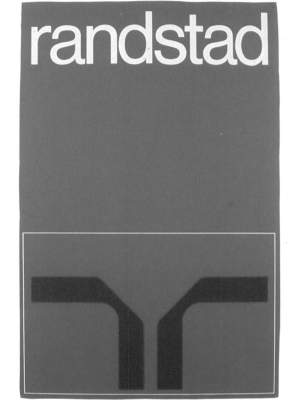

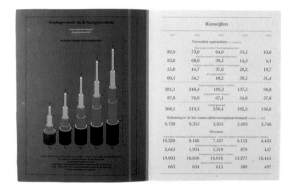

Duijvelshoff, who for many years had lent continuity to Total Design,
individual designers with their own personal - and often diverging –
contributions were associated with TD for short periods, such as Jurriaan
Schrofer, Anthon Beeke, Andrew Fallon and Paul Mijksenaar. Their
contribution ensured that TD's design did not lead to boring uniformity but
remained visually varied and lively and that the debate on the function of
graphic design was kept alive. In 1982 Jelle van der Toorn Vrijthoff joined TD,
representing a younger generation that was not averse to using
unconventional forms and introducing new techniques.

Jolijn van de Wouw,
Reynoud Homan,
Adth van Oyen and
Esther Verdonk (Total
Design)
Cover for *J.H.
Schuilenga et al, One
Hundred Years of the
Telephone*, Executive
Board, PTT
Telecommunications.
The Hague 1981

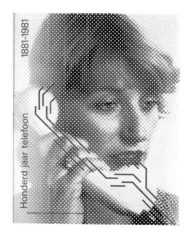

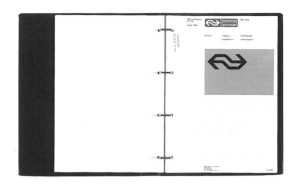

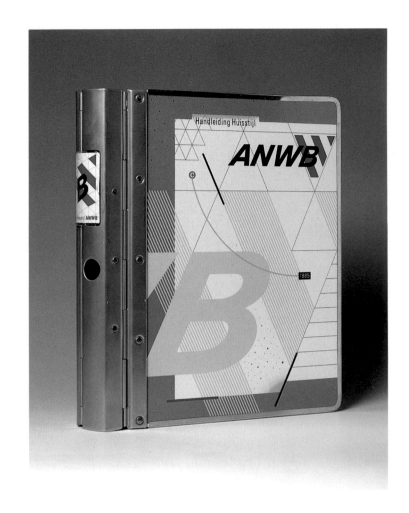

Logos and house styles

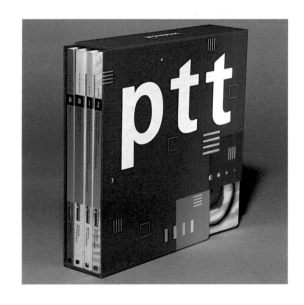

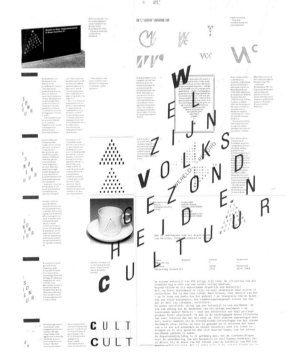

Tel Design
House style manual
for *Dutch Railways*,
Utrecht 1968

Studio Dumbar
House style manual
for PTT Post, The
Hague c.1989

Studio Dumbar
House style manual
for the motoring
association *ANWB*,
The Hague 1985

Walter Nikkels
Brochure to
introduce the new
logo of the *Ministry of
Welfare, Health and
Culture*, Rijswijk 1984

Since the 19th century industry has made use of an emblem in the form of a trademark or logo, which with separate or interwoven letters can further be used as a monogram. They rendered the product brand instantly recognisable everywhere. Well-known examples of logos are Coca-Cola and AEG, and in the Netherlands include KLM and PTT. The PTT has produced many variations on its three letters over the years, wherein sometimes the letters have formed an image of a dove, a man or a posthorn.

A trademark can represent an object or geometric figures, and can also be used together with a logo made up of letters. During the 1950s, the period of reconstruction, before the trend for full-blown house styles reached the Netherlands, trademarks and logos became increasingly in vogue. During this period Jurriaan Schrofer produced various logos and trademarks, including those for the 'E55' exhibition, for Hoogovens (steel foundry), and for the Dutch Opera Foundation. He combined an emblem with letters, mainly in a stylised way, based on basic geometric figures. Nowadays there is virtually no company that does not carry a trademark or logo. These emblems form the basis of a house style and are the first to draw attention to notepaper, buildings or rolling stock.

In the 1960s the interest in house styles shifted in industry to cover corporate identity programmes and corporate image. This was linked to growing competition and a realisation that a corporate image could be extremely important. Moreover, the number of companies in the world increased and existing companies, which due to mergers had become multinational enterprises, often required a new visual identity, or modification of their old one. In pre-Second World War Holland there were already a few companies that carried a form of identity, such as Van Nelle, Van Houten, De Gruyter, Bruynzeel and the PTT. After the war KLM and Dutch Rail were among the first to demand one. More companies followed suit and over the years government bodies, too, began to feel the need for an individual identity. The then state-owned PTT led the way, and now every ministry, university and practically every local council has a logo and house style to go with it.

The general trend towards privatisation led to many new identity images. Many design studios now specialise in this field. Originally, a house style largely consisted of a logo or trademark, but today a corporate image goes much further and is expected to be visible in every aspect of the company, both internally and externally, ranging from business cards, stationery, personnel files, signage and promotional gifts to advertisements, public relations, company clothing and the lettering on buildings and cars. Every visible manifestation must carry the company stamp, with guidelines on using the house style prescribed in a manual. Although in most cases a corporate identity programme is rigorously applied, there are companies that allow for a certain flexibility, thus leaving more scope for freedom in design and for modifications as and when changes occur in the company. Some graphic examples of logos and house styles are shown here.

Swip Stolk
Portfolio with folders
for travelling
exhibitions of the
government art body
*Rijksdienst Beeldende
Kunst*, The Hague 1985

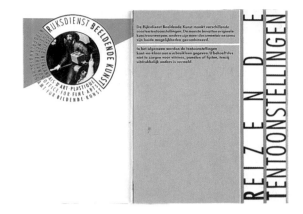

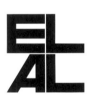

Jurriaan Schrofer
Logo for a national
exhibition *E55*,
Rotterdam 1955

Harry Disberg
Logo for PTT Post,
The Hague c.1950

G. Him and Otto
Treumann
Logo for the Israeli
airline *El Al*, c.1960

Wim Crouwel, Total
Design
Logo for the *City of
Groningen*, c.1970

Jurriaan Schrofer
Logo for *Hoogovens*,
IJmuiden c.1960

Total Design
Logo for the *Dutch
Pavilion of the World
Trade Fair*, Osaka 1970

Total Design
Logo for the *Office
Efficiency Fair*,
Amsterdam 1964

BRS (design collective)
Logo for the *Ministry
of Foreign Affairs*,
The Hague c.1980

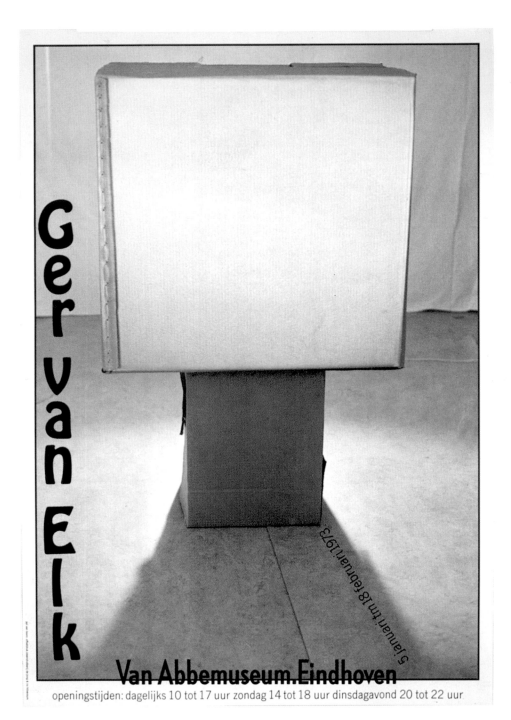

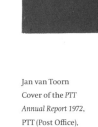

Jan van Toorn: art and society

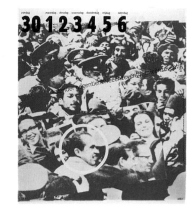

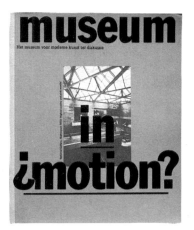

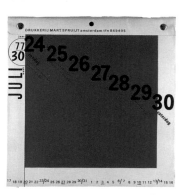

Jan van Toorn trained at the Institute for Industrial Arts in Amsterdam, later to become the Rietveld Academy. Under Mart Stam the curriculum was inspired by the Bauhaus and was thus not only subject-orientated, but above all had a strong social content. Van Toorn has always revealed this idealistic yet also realistic side in his work. Communication of the message, with all the positive and negative aspects, is for him a prerequisite: 'The apparent wide diversity of styles that you see now are only drawing attention to themselves in my opinion. They act as a veil over a situation in which hardly anything is raised. The designer can delightfully indulge in the most fantastic discoveries of form, yet this indulgence disguises a lack of real debate... Remember that printed matter is made to function within a situation. Thus its value should be determined here in the first place.' This attitude was echoed in his work, his essays and his teaching.

Van Toorn was hired chiefly by the cultural and educational sectors. His clients included museums, printers and the PTT. From 1960 to 1977 he produced and edited the annual calendars for Spruyt, the Amsterdam printing firm, which he illustrated with actual social and political world events. From 1965 to 1974 he was in-house designer for the Stedelijk Van Abbemuseum in Eindhoven, where architect Jean Leering was director. Both had strongly-held views on art and design and it relation to society at large. For them information on art went hand-in-hand with information on society's activities, and the concept of art for art's sake was something to be questioned. Exhibitions at the museum, for example on Piero Manzoni, El Lissitzky and themes like 'The Street', were placed in a broader context. Both Van Toorn and Leering were clear about the way a museum should present information to the public; they were diametrically opposed to the idea of artistic autonomy.

Van Toorn's work reveals rational and sequential compositions, with photography playing an important role. He sees the photograph as a pragmatic medium, indispensable for probing deeply into everyday reality. He used this theme for a series of posters, entitled 'People and Surroundings', for the De Beyerd Art Centre in Breda and he illustrated the PTT's Annual Reports of 1987 and 1988 with world events that had taken place during both years. The covers for the *Museumjournaal* symbolised more of the world in which the art was produced, than the art itself. He never displayed an artwork on its own, but always in the context of its surroundings and of society.

This principle has also defined Toorn's teaching at the Rietveld Academy and the Rijksacademie in Amsterdam. As director of the Jan van Eyck Academy in Maastrict he endeavoured to develop these ideas further within the climate of the present day. For him there should be no form just for form's sake, but rather it should be directed at the function of the image.

Jan van Toorn
Covers of the
magazine *DA +AT:
Dutch Art and
Architecture Today*,
Rijksdienst Beeldende
Kunst, The Hague

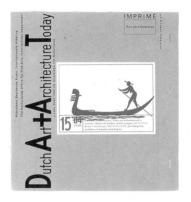

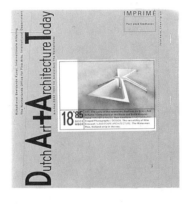

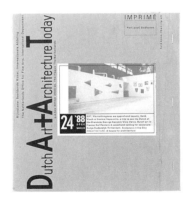

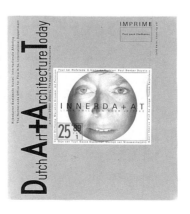

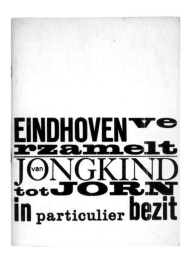

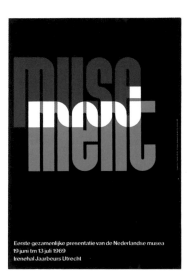

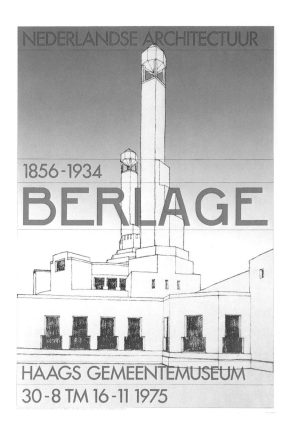

Graphics for museums

After the Second World War, the majority of Dutch museums had little interest in, or even the means to pay for, specially designed catalogues and posters. Their publicity was thus generally old fashioned and unappealing. However, due not only to an increasing awareness of the importance of good design in industry, and above all to the Stedelijk Museum's early example (under Sandberg), most museums have now followed suit.

The Stedelijk Van Abbemuseum hired Wim Crouwel as designer, who later continued this type of work for the Stedelijk Museum under its new director, E. de Wilde. In Eindhoven Jan van Toorn worked with Jean Leering, and later Walter Nikkels worked with Rudi Fuchs. Otto Treumann and Pieter Brattinga were virtually in-house designers at the Rijksmuseum Kröller-Müller, and the Gemeentemuseum in The Hague commissioned a variety of designers. Only one designer, however, ensured a consistent and recognisable image for the museum.

For a long time contemporary graphic design was associated with museums of modern art; now, no kind of museum can neglect its external image. The world-famous Rijksmuseum, for example, uses Studio Dumbar. Developments in graphic design for museums since 1960 give an interesting picture that not only runs parallel to general design advances, but also reveals the attitudes of the museum and curator. Clear examples are the different approaches towards imagery and typography in the work of Crouwel, Van Toorn, Brattinga and Nikkels. Crouwel's objectivity, diversity and informative approach is in sharp contrast to Van Toorn's almost subjective style and involvement with content. This controversy was to lead in the 1970s to two published polemics on the role of design in the museum. The nub was whether the museum wanted to be a medium for forming

independent opinion or, owing to its expertise, intended to position itself as an unassailable authority. Put another way, may a designer interpret and design what is being exhibited in his own way? Pieter Brattinga's clear, objective and almost static imagery stands alongside Walter Nikkels's carefully considered, art-inspired imagery or the more changing images in Lex Reitsma's posters for Museum Overholland. These contrast with Swip Stolk's work for the Groninger Museum. Nowadays there is a wealth of approaches, which sometimes impels a museum to choose a designer on the basis of what they happen to be exhibiting.

Anthon Beeke
Catalogue cover for a
Peter Struycken
exhibition, Centraal
Museum, Utrecht
1975

Jan van Toorn
Catalogue cover for
an exhibition *Three
Blind Mice*, Van
Abbemuseum,
Eindhoven 1968.
The exhibition drew
together works from
three private art
collections

Jan van Toorn
Posters for an
exhibition series
*Humankind and the
Environment*,
De Beyerd Centre for
the Visual Arts, Breda
1982

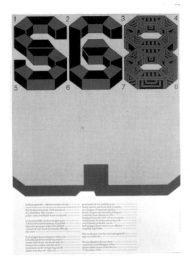

Swip Stolk

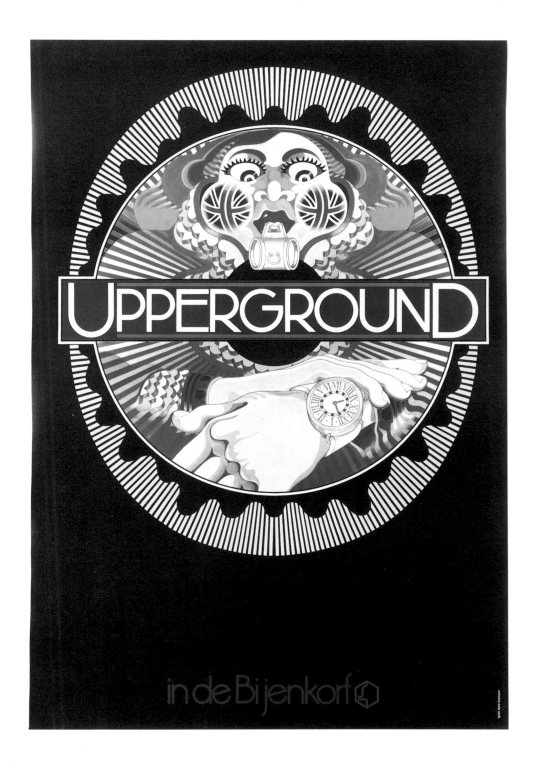

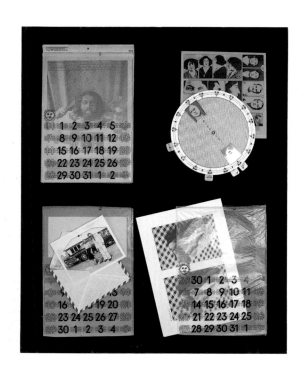

Swip Stolk
Poster advertising
forthcoming cultural
events at the
University of Utrecht,
1968

Swip Stolk
Four pages from a
*1974 Calendar 'Zakken
vol ongeloof'* (Bags Full
of Disbelief),
Grafische Industrie
De Boer en Vink,
Zaandijk 1974

Swip Stolk
Poster *Upperground*,
De Bijenkorf
department store,
Amsterdam c. 1966

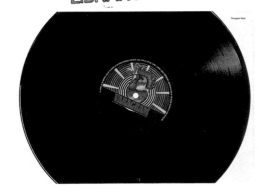

Swip Stolk's past and present work show similarities. Self-taught, he worked around 1960 for an advertising agency and is now 'publicity maker' of the Groninger Museum, which is run in a slightly offbeat and sometimes provocative manner by its director, Frans Haks. It is a fitting context for Stolk, who was involved with the 1960s alternative Provo movement and who, over the last 30 years, has worked with enormous energy and in a similarly quirky fashion as a graphic designer. He has been active in every area of graphic design. Although he was for some time a member of the Art Directors Club Nederland, mass communication is not his metier. His attitude, however, remains adventurous and he is always in search of a chance to create a provocative design. This is the reason he collaborated in the 1960s with the artist Wim T. Schippers and with Willem de Ridder as well as with his colleague, Anthon Beeke.

This provocative aspect is typically Dutch and has influenced the entire field of graphic design past and present. The political arena of the 1970s called for an anti-political approach: there was a movement against lethargy, and a need to show raw reality, mixed with a confusing and sometimes cynical humour. A pacesetter here was, and still is, the radio and television network, VPRO. On the other hand, in 1978 the left-wing but moribund VARA network rejected the house style designed for them by Stolk after having used it only for a short time. It was an exceptional and striking new image, dominated by the socialist symbol of the hen. Dutch Rail, too, had trouble with Stolk's poster campaign – it used slogans like 'Conductor, my hand is stuck between the doors' at a time when things were not going too well with this public transport company. However, in England Stolk received an award for this 'relativist' campaign.

For many years Stolk designed the annual calendars for the lithographic printers De Boer and Vink, which carried bizarre subject matter like 'visual irritation' encased in extraordinary wrappings. As a consultant he also produced layouts and designs for the many exhibitions organised by various ministries and by the state arts department Rijksdienst Beeldende Kunst. One such example was 'Sitting for a Lifetime', a documentary exhibition tracing the history of the chair in which no choices were made on purely aesthetic grounds. Every type of seating was shown, from a throne to a bidet and an electric chair. Thus was reality depicted in all its embarrassment without any conscious manipulation.

As a designer Swip Stolk is the visual mouthpiece of the Groninger Museum. His posters and catalogues reflect the museum's preference for controversial art and design. The examples shown here are from the exhibition of video clips held in pavilions especially designed by international architects; the exhibition of the Memphis design group; and the proposed new museum building from the architect Mendini.

Swip Stolk's graphic work is immediately recognisable from its use of shrill metallic colours or very soft pastels. The distorted typography is also striking, as is the form of some of his recent catalogues: folders with loose cards. As a teacher at the AKI in Enschedé and at the Rietveld Academy in Amsterdam, he taught more about attitude than about design, and this also characterises his own work.

Swip Stolk
Record label *Varagram* from a catalogue for an exhibition on the VARA broadcasting company, Groninger Museum, Groningen 1979

Swip Stolk
Posters for an exhibition *In Full Flow*, Groninger Museum, Groningen 1991

Swip Stolk
Poster *Summer Exhibition*, Groninger Museum, Groningen 1990

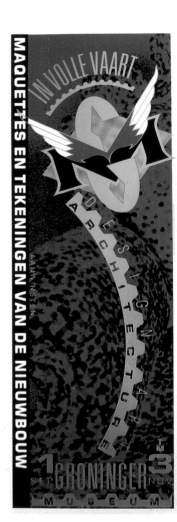

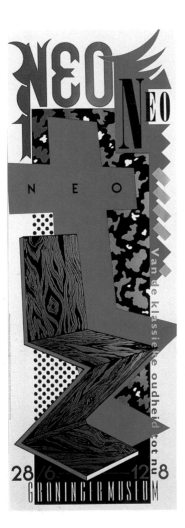

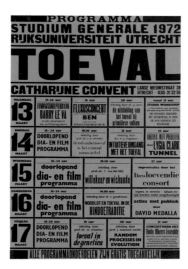

Anthon Beeke

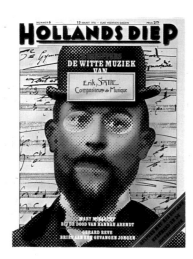

Anthon Beeke
Poster advertising
forthcoming cultural
events at the
University of Utrecht,
Utrecht 1972

Anthon Beeke
Cover of the
magazine Hollands
Diep, devoted to the
work of the composer
Erik Satie,
Amsterdam 1976

Anthon Beeke attended the School for Industrial Art in Amsterdam for only
one year, and having later gained experience abroad and assisted Jan van
Toorn, he regards himself as self-taught. Since 1963 he has worked
independently and now has a design studio in Amsterdam. In his early days
he was closely involved with the Fluxus movement, and took part in the
Fluxus festival at Scheveningen. This Fluxus background – unconventional,
unrestrained, provocative and imaginative – was very important to Beeke's
artistic development.

Beeke exploited this sense of freedom even further and his work shows
a compelling handling of imagery and an unexpected packaging of the
message. It runs through his entire oeuvre, including the catalogues and
regular newsletter for the Centraal Museum in Utrecht, where he also
worked together with artists. Concerning this, author K. Schippers wrote:
'The artists produced a design for a booklet and Beeke as designer carried it
out, taking wicked pleasure in being subordinate to them as if his ideas on
the design of a publication did not matter.' It was also the period when he
worked with Swip Stolk, among others, on a Christmas issue of *Grafisch
Nederland* (1970), which was never published. Beeke designed book covers, arts
magazines (*Hollands Diep* and *Kunstschrift*) and posters, particularly those for
the Globe theatre group, the Holland Festival and the Amsterdam Theatre
Group, in which the images were always immediate and sharply formulated.
Beeke's intuitive interpretation of the drama of the theatre was often
expressed through challenging images of the human form.

Beeke often uses a cliché where it is least expected. He breaks most
existing conventions, such as using a typeface more suitable for a tabloid
newspaper to grace the cover of a weighty treatise; or for a book cover on the
theory of form showing the book itself in perspective so that the front of the
cover becomes the back. For a series of publications entitled *Lives and
Literature* from De Bezige Bij publishers, he designed the covers to mimic the
front pages of newspapers. There is always something anarchistic in his
work: sometimes a mild and sometimes a consciously provocative way of
depicting imagery. Typography, for instance, appears to be an arsenal for
Beeke in which anything and everything is usable, according to the theme.
When he designed an alphabet himself, it consisted of 26 letters, each
composed of naked girls and published as a theme for one of Steendrukkerij
De Jong's *Quadrate* magazines.

Beeke worked for a short period for Total Design, where he was given every
opportunity to realise his own ideas – as can be seen in the posters for the
Globe theatre and the Holland Festival. In recent years Beeke has worked for
the French textiles fair Première Vision. He is an exponent of the autonomous
attitude of the Dutch graphic designer and his work, largely for cultural
bodies, reveals the scope and opportunities clients can allow their designers.

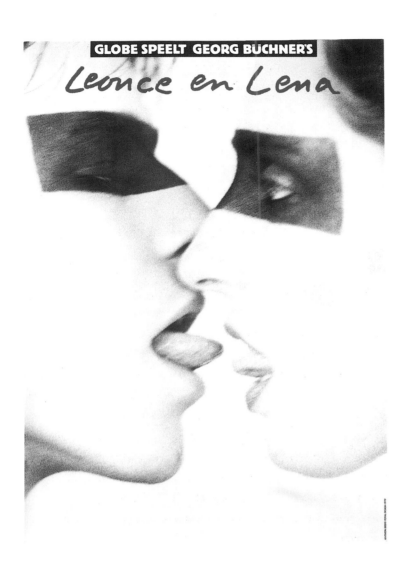

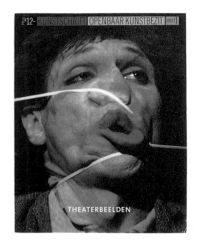

Anthon Beeke
Cover of the arts
magazine *Kunstschrift*,
Amsterdam 1987.
This particular issue
covered painting and
theatre

Anthon Beeke
Poster for *Georg
Büchner, Leonce and
Lena*, Globe Theatre
Group, 1979

Anthon Beeke
Poster for *Kazimir
Malevich Exhibition*,
Stedelijk Museum,
Amsterdam 1989

Anthon Beeke
Poster for *Gerardjan
Rijnders, Ballet*,
Amsterdam Theatre
Group, 1990

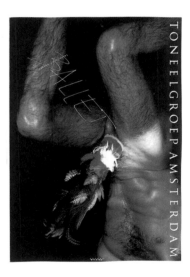

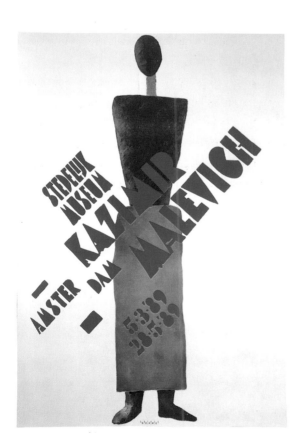

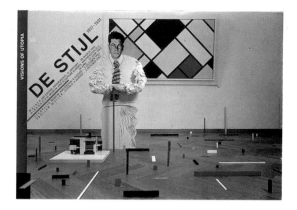

Gert Dumbar
Exhibition poster *De
Stijl 1917-1931 – Visions
of Utopia*, Walker Art
Center, Minneapolis
1982

Gert Dumbar and his studio

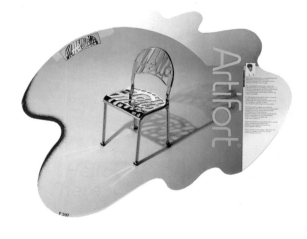

Studio Dumbar
Poster for *Artifort*
furniture, Maastricht
1985

Gert Dumbar
Cover of *Dutch
Railways timetable
booklet for 1985-1986*,
Utrecht 1985

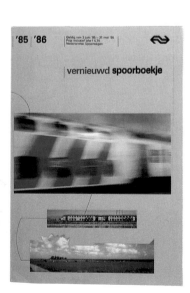

The fine arts have invariably provided a source of inspiration for Gert Dumbar's graphic work. The freedom he experienced while training as a painter at The Hague Academy, and later as a designer at the Royal College of Art in London, resulted in his developing a provocative and tantalising design style. Dumbar's fragmentary and freestyle design approach reflects recent trends in art and design. While functionalist graphic designers have rejected embellishment since the mid-1960s, meaningful decoration has in fact been a challenge for Dumbar. From 1967 he has put his ideas into practice at Tel Design in The Hague and later at his own Studio Dumbar. By consciously taking a polarised stand, he ultimately created a studio with a specific work climate that has occasionally evoked opposition from fellow designers. From early on the staged photograph dominated his work (most of these are taken by Lex van Pieterson), and initially they were of papier-mâché figures or objects. At the same time, he sometimes uses collages for the backgrounds. He breaks up the standard rectangular form of a poster by using cut-out shapes that follow the image. He then often uses typography to underline this chaotic and fragmented effect, making the message difficult to read. At the same time he reinterprets historic examples of Constructivism, Dada or Fluxus – depending on the subject matter – to create new, interesting forms. Dumbar has a fine feeling for contemporary movements and his studio uses these in all manner of variations; nothing is bound by regulations and much is left to chance.

Clients' briefings are interpreted in a practical way, but allow for variation and a relaxed design approach. The examples of his work reproduced here include the corporate identities for Dutch Rail (begun at Tel Design) and Royal Nederland PTT (in collaboration with Total Design).

At Studio Dumbar commissions are discussed and worked out as a team. Cooperation and dialogue largely determine the results. Dumbar himself runs as a 'red thread' through the whole design process, which helps make the work easily recognisable. As a person who 'challenges' others he has an inspiring effect on his staff. If initially the studio's work was reaction to the severe functionalism of the 1960s and 1970s, it now fits into the eclectic image of the day. Nevertheless, Dumbar endeavours to make his voice heard above this combined response and to arouse the curiosity of the viewer.

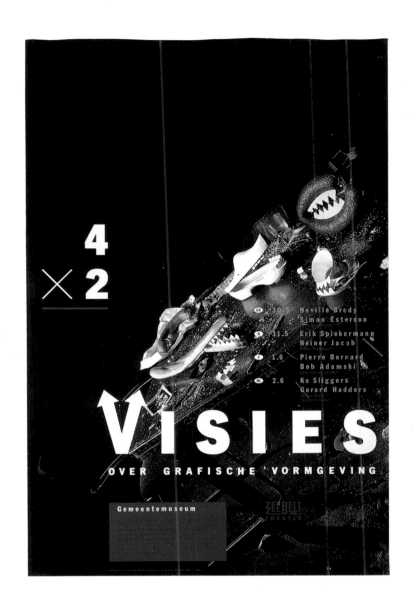

Studio Dumbar
Poster for a series of
seminars *4 × 2 Visions
on Graphic Design*,
Gemeentemuseum,
The Hague 1989

Studio Dumbar
Poster for *Zeebelt
Theatre*, The Hague
1986

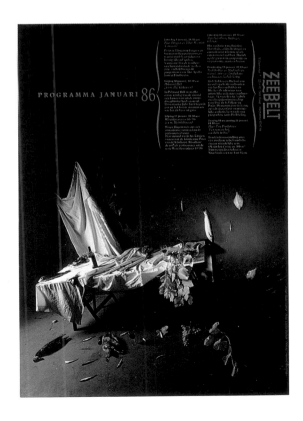

Walter Nikkels
Cover of an
exhibition catalogue
Lothar Baumgarten,
Tierra de los perros
mudos, Stedelijk
Museum, Amsterdam
1985

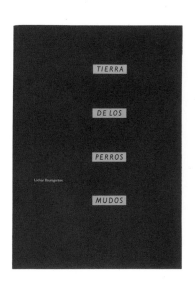

Walter Nikkels: balance and intuition

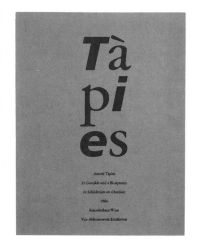

Walter Nikkels
Catalogue cover for
a *Lothar Baumgarten*
exhibition, West
German Pavillion,
Venice 1984

Walter Nikkels
Catalogue cover
of an *Antoni Tàpies*
Exhibition, Stedelijk
van Abbemuseum,
Eindhoven 1986

Walter Nikkels
Invitation to an
exhibition *Eye Level,*
Stedelijk Van
Abbemuseum,
Eindhoven 1986

Amid all the current battling design styles, there are a few restful corners where designers and typographers continue to work in the traditional mould of Dutch graphic design. One of these is provided by the typographer Walter Nikkels, who once wrote: 'When asked about my reasons for taking up typography, I thought – no matter how paradoxical this may seem about a profession that only contributes to a fleeting product like printed matter – that design as a rational activity always has another motive: namely to combat that fleetingness.' Nikkels trained at the academies of Rotterdam, Munich and Milan, almost as if to anticipate his present international fame. He currently lectures at the Düsseldorf Academy.

While Nikkels has been involved in various aspects of graphic design such as postage stamps and posters, he quickly arrived in the museum world. Catalogues, books, contemporary art posters, the redesigning of Dordrechts Museum and the mounting of exhibitions, including 'Bilderstreit' in Cologne and 'Documenta 7' in Kassel: all are his specialist fields. In this context typography is his speciality and Tschichold and Sandberg can be regarded as his mentors. No conventional, 'invisible' typography in the style of Van Krimpen for him, but lettering that is varied and visible in every respect. In fact, in his work he explores both modern and traditional typography. For Nikkels the type, size, weight, spacing, rhythm, appearance and composition of the type page, the tension, paper and colour of the paper, the size, the cover, the decision on margins, lines and the placing of a coloured dot – in fact the entire treatment of a book – evolve from balance and intuition.

Nikkels's typography is focused on content and its meaning in a broader sense. He perceives there to be a relationship between his work and conceptual art. Typography for him, however, is also a form of architecture on a small scale, in which the walls can be slanted or the windows tall and very narrow if the design demands. He almost always involves the client, exhibition director or the artist in the design process. By working in this way Nikkels is able to find a form that is compatible with his view of the function of typography, and at the same time reveals his adaptability.

Walter Nikkels
Exhibition poster
Rundgang,
Kunstakademie,
Düsseldorf 1986

Walter Nikkels
Catalogue for the
Remy Zaugg Exhibition,
Stedelijk Van
Abbemuseum,
Eindhoven 1987

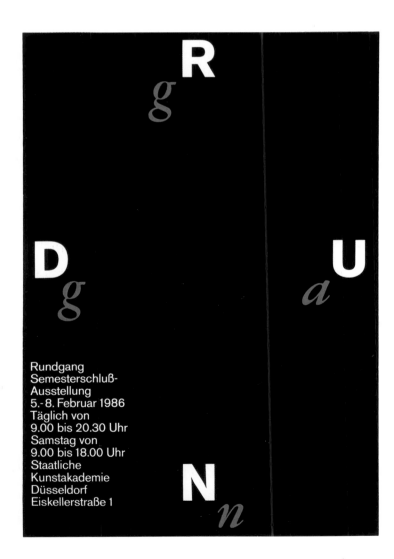

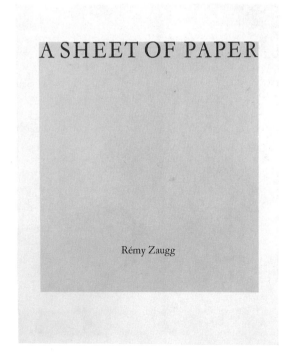

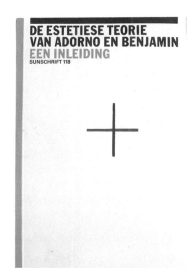

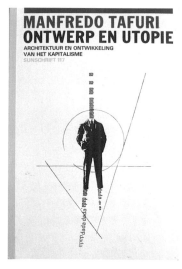

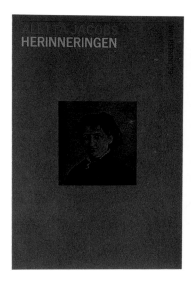

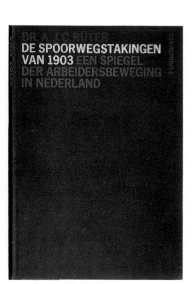

Karel Martens

The typographic task of positioning text and images on paper has another aspect for Karel Martens. He utilises type and paper as a medium for his freestyle art pieces, which he carries on in tandem with his graphic work. He has built up a wide experience over the years that can be traced in the books, magazines, catalogues and postage stamps he has designed. H.C. Boekraad, a former publisher, describes Martens' view of his profession as a 'commitment to content' and this is expressed in the choice of paper, type, colour and size. One might say that this is basic to the craft, but with Martens it has become his personal signature.

After studying, Martens went to work for the publishing company Van Loghum Slaterus, where the design of a book, its contents and cover, was not just geared to the marketplace. The company was eventually taken over by the Kluwer conglomerate, where commerce was the main concern and change and risk not tolerated. This encouraged Martens to stick increasingly to his own standards. The SUN publishing house, where he had worked from 1975 to 1981, hired him again to design their total book output. The content of SUN's publications, which leant towards social criticism and change, was in keeping with Martens' own researches into design. At SUN, he was able to reveal both sides of his work.

While certain periodicals like the *Sunschriften* boasted a clear, consistent design style, Martens was nevertheless able to create a new image within this framework. His work, however, became increasingly autonomous and in some instances clashed with the design brief and the text, which was no doubt his way of counterbalancing the sometimes doctrinaire contents of the books. Here the designer is acting as co-creator of the printed matter, putting forth his own ideas and viewpoints on form in relation to content.

This approach becomes increasingly difficult, however, as more editors and publishers want to be intensely involved with the content. Nonetheless, it is undoubtedly is a basis for original design and is also one of the precepts Martens teaches his students at the Arnhem Academy. In his lectures he upholds the philosophy of such typographic predecessors as Jan Vermeulen, and by so doing has created a 'school' at the academy, which has produced designers such as Stephan Saaltink and Wigger Bierma, who in their turn meticulously combine craftsmanship and content with individual views.

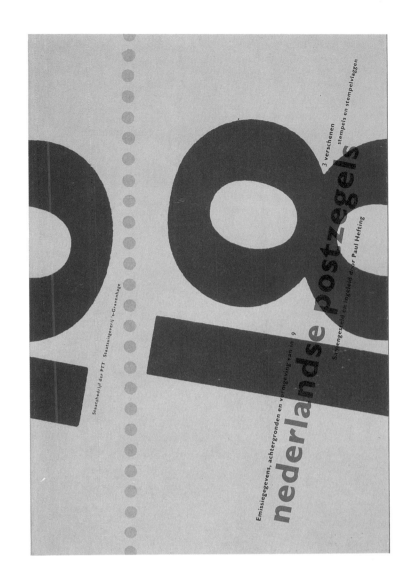

Karel Martens
Cover *Paul Hefting,*
Dutch Postage Stamps,
PTT (Post Office),
The Hague 1984

Redactioneel De moderne architectuur heeft het vraagstuk van de
vorm altijd trachten te omzeilen. Idealiter zou de vorm als
vanzelf moeten voortkomen uit een of ander proces, als het
zuiver logistieke resultaat van een aantal factoren, of als een
wat duistere intuïtie van een historische voortgang die zich
uitkristalliseert in een soort moment-opname. In de plattegrond levert dit niet direct problemen op; de scheidingen
en verbindingen binnen het horizontale vlak laten zich veelal
gemakkelijk lezen als een afspiegeling van een aantal
interne relaties. Anders ligt het in het verticale vlak, met
name aan de buitenzijde. Zoals Joost Meuwissen stelt in zijn
in deze OASE afgedrukte artikel: 'Van boven ziet het er
allemaal nog wel aardig uit als een plattegrond. Maar van
voren beginnen de problemen.' Een proces heeft geen
buitenkant. Aan een proces kun je niet vragen welke positie
het inneemt binnen een (historisch gegroeide) maatschap-
lijke constellatie; je kunt alleen maar het proces voor
'staat', je kunt alleen maar vragen of het 'werkt'. Het is
vermoedelijk vooral hierom dat de moderne architectuur
neigt naar een transparantie, die de historiek van het proces
min of meer volgens het modellen van aquarium poogt te
veraanschouwelijken of, wanneer we het begrip 'modern'
niet al te nauw definiëren, naar een gebruik van het gevelvlak als 'bill-board', als een soort reclamepaneel waarop los
van het eigenlijke gebouw tekens worden aangebracht. De
door het gebouw opgeroepen beelden zouden, in dit laatste
geval, als tekens mee moeten rouleren in de stedelijke
communicatie, maar krachtens het feit dat ze worden bevrijd
van elke consequentie, van elke binding aan een structuur,
nooit een werkelijke (maatschappelijk-algemene) betekenis.

In de moderne architectonische handboeken en
voorbeeldenboeken gaat de aandacht dan ook vrijwel volledig uit naar de plattegrond. Anders dan in de leerboeken uit
de renaissance en het classicisme ontbreekt een uiteenzetting
van de tektonische middelen waarmee de opstand van het
gevelvlak als architectonisch ontwerp zou kunnen worden
opgebouwd vrijwel volledig. Dan moet, natuurlijk, elk
architectonisch ontwerp uiteindelijk een precieze vorm
krijgen, ook aan de buitenzijde. Le Corbusier is een van de
weinige moderne architecten die zich welbewust en expliciet
hebben beziggehouden met het vraagstuk van de opstand; eerst

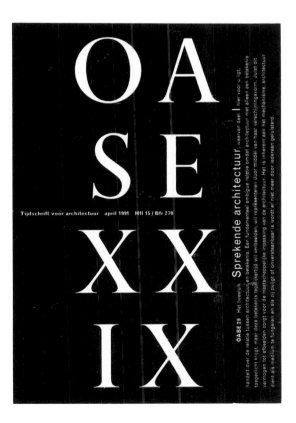

Karel Martens
Two covers for
Oase, an architectural
magazine, SUN
Publishers, Nijmegen
1991

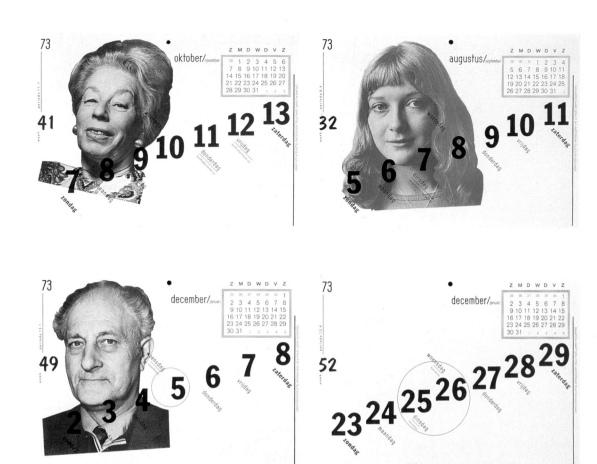

Printers and designers

The role publishers and printers have played this century within graphic design has already been discussed. Until now this interest was largely pursued through the initiatives of company directors, who felt very much involved in design, as well as being concerned with public relations. Calendars were always appropriate promotional gifts for printers to give to clients and they were created by the best designers. In the 20th century there have been many splendid examples of calendars, including those printed by Trio, Stadsdrukkerij Amsterdam and Van de Geer.

The calendars from Spruyt Printers, which have been published since the late 1950s and designed by well-known practitioners, have now become treasured collectors' items. Since 1959 Harry Sierman, Jan Van Toorn (who was involved for a long time as editor of the calendars), Paul Mijksenaar, Toon Michiels, Hard Werken, Anthon Beeke and the Samenwerkende Ontwerpers studio have all worked on them. The calendars also owe their fame in part to the subject matter covered: politics, sociology, eroticism and documentary.

In the area of type sample sheets, printers have also come up with exceptional works, such as Spruyt's loose-leafed book in which the back of each sheet contributes to a continuing story in changing typefaces. Chris Vermaas was responsible for the typography. Other printers, too, as well as the paper industry, now regularly publish booklets on graphic design. The printing firm of Rosbeek in Nuth has hired many designers for its series, which numbers 27 publications so far.

Lecturis Printers in Eindhoven produced similar editions to the *Quadrate* magazines of Steendrukkerij De Jong and a series of factual accounts on various aspects of graphic design. This series is still published and provides a good overview of developments and ideas within Dutch graphic design since 1970.

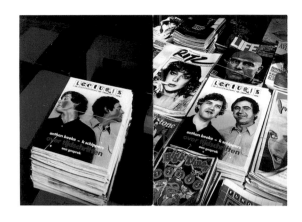

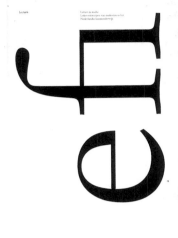

Anthon Beeke
Front and back cover
of *Anthon Beeke and
K. Schippers, Over
Tijdschriften* (About
Magazines), Lecturis,
Eindhoven 1979

Gerrit Noordzij
Cover of *Gerrit
Noordzij, A Study of
Lettering*, Lecturis,
Eindhoven 1983.
The letters 'e fi' were
designed by Frank
Blokland

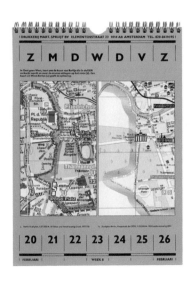

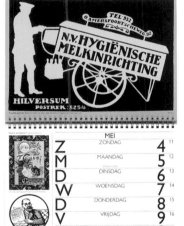

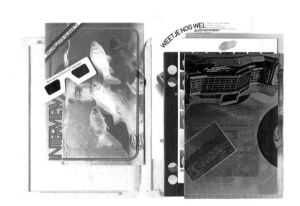

Paul Mijksenaar
Cover of a *1982-83
Calendar 'Street Plans
and Maps'*, Mart.
Spruyt, Amsterdam
1982

Paul Mijksenaar
Cover of a *1980
Calendar 'Trademarks'*,
Mart. Spruyt,
Amsterdam 1980

Will van Sambeek and
Martien Vissers
The Christmas issue
of *Grafisch Nederland
1971*, Amsterdam
1971. This was in the
form of a portfolio for
the year 2000

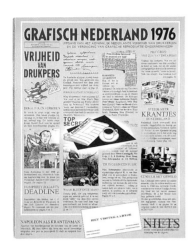

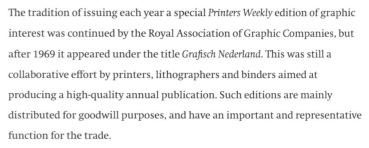

Paul Mijksenaar and
Piet Schreuders
Cover of the
Christmas issue of
Grafisch Nederland
1976, Amsterdam
1976. This particular
magazine focused on
'freedom of the
printing press'

Arlette Brouwers
Cover of the
Christmas issue of
Grafisch Nederland
1987, Amsterdam
1987. This particular
number covered the
history of recording
techniques

Grafisch Nederland

The tradition of issuing each year a special *Printers Weekly* edition of graphic interest was continued by the Royal Association of Graphic Companies, but after 1969 it appeared under the title *Grafisch Nederland*. This was still a collaborative effort by printers, lithographers and binders aimed at producing a high-quality annual publication. Such editions are mainly distributed for goodwill purposes, and have an important and representative function for the trade.

Designers and design studios were involved, who together with the editorial staff drew up a theme that was often related to the field of graphics, such as 'Printed Matter and Communication', 'Freedom of the Printed Press', 'Dutch Books', 'Photography in Design' and 'Four Centuries of Dutch Trading Catalogues'. Sometimes the editors chose a more general content or aimed at a particularly striking layout. It is interesting to see how the magazine's content reflected the ideals and beliefs of the day. The 1970 issue was never published as its design by Anthon Beeke and Swip Stolk was considered too controversial: a clear example of a generation gap and a clash of artistic ideals between designer and client. The 1971 issue, designed by Will van Sambeek, took the form of a bright yellow polystyrene box containing an imagined portfolio for the year 2000 with various types of 'magazines' printed on unusual paper. It came with special spectacles for the 3-D effect.

A concern for the environment and consumer society can be deduced from the magazine titles for 1974 and 1975: 'Recycling' and 'Back to Nature'. Designers apparently had also developed a critical eye for unbridled expansion. In the 1980s the trend was for historical themes and it was the turn of the younger generation of designers. Cees de Jong and Ernst Schilp experimented with pure typography and Hard Werken with highly contrasting photographic images. A second feminist wave also hit *Grafisch Nederland* in the form of Arlette Brouwers and Gracia Lebbink's ingenious and imaginative designs.

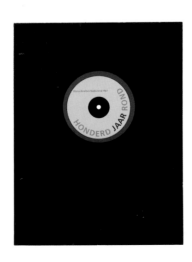

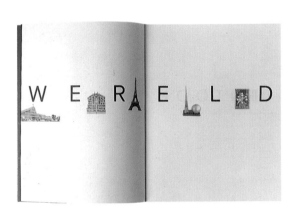

Gracia Lebbink
Title page spread of
the Christmas issue
of *Grafisch Nederland
1991*, Amsterdam
1991. The magazine
covered world trade
fairs held between
1851 and 1991

Cees de Jong and
Ernst Schilp
Double-page spread
of the Christmas
issue of *Grafisch
Nederland 1989*,
Amsterdam 1989

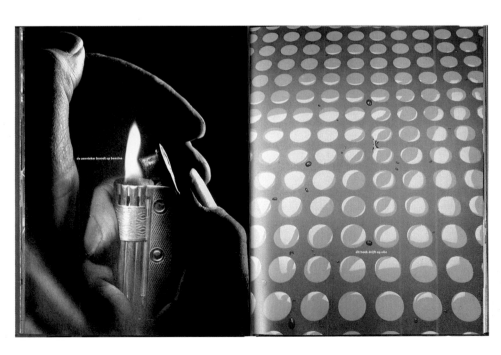

Hard Werken and
Gerard Hadders
Double-page spread
of the Christmas
issue of *Grafisch
Nederland 1990*,
Amsterdam 1990.
This number dealt
with the subject of oil

The recent past

From the 1960s, Total Design in Amsterdam and Tel Design in The Hague were the two leading graphic design studios in the Netherlands, executing important commissions for companies because of their size and specialisms. In the 1970s and 1980s the number of studios continued to increase, reflecting the growing demand for graphic design. In 1992 there were some 74 design studios, most of which were multidisciplinary as well as being members of the Union of Dutch Designers.

As the world has grown more complex, the plurality of styles in graphic design has correspondingly increased, and more value is placed on design as a visual phenomenon. Events in art and architecture during recent years – the rivalry between the conceptualists, minimalists, classicists, new expressionists and others – have been reflected in graphic design. The freedom and degree of autonomy allowed to designers is a typically Dutch phenomenon, and something of a luxury. Interest in the past among design professionals is enormous and, as in fine art, has led to much quotation from the past. An interest in Dutch developments in design comes also from abroad. In the United States, Dutch graphic designers are welcome visitors at the Rhode Island School of Design and the Cranbrook Academy of Art, and the Netherlands is rarely absent from international design exhibitions.

In the 1920s and 1930s functionalism and decoration were regarded as ideological opposites. Nowadays this dissimilarity has become a 'game' on a playing field without any rules. This has led some designers to yearn for a firmer theoretical basis for the profession. The differences which hitherto existed between decorators and rationalists have their parallel today in the difference between a small group of individual designers working conscientiously and in fine detail, and designers who are working either freelance or attached to design studios. Although the latter have more freedom, they are under pressure to maximise turnover and often work on commissions that in earlier times they would not perhaps have taken on. Economics clearly plays a major role in the profession and some form of selfpublicity must be undertaken in order to get the commissions coming in. Clients also make greater demands, and designers often have to make concessions; even so there is still a great degree of tolerance in the Netherlands among the customers of graphic design.

The reputation and status of design in the Netherlands has given the designer much scope. At the same time, a few designers are endeavouring to liberate themselves from the too-fashionable styles. Most designers have become dependent on the computer, not only because of its speed, but also because of the many opportunities that electronics presents. It has made many designers think long and hard about the nature of their profession.

Gielijn Escher
Poster for an annual
theatre event *Festival
of Fools*, Amsterdam
1982

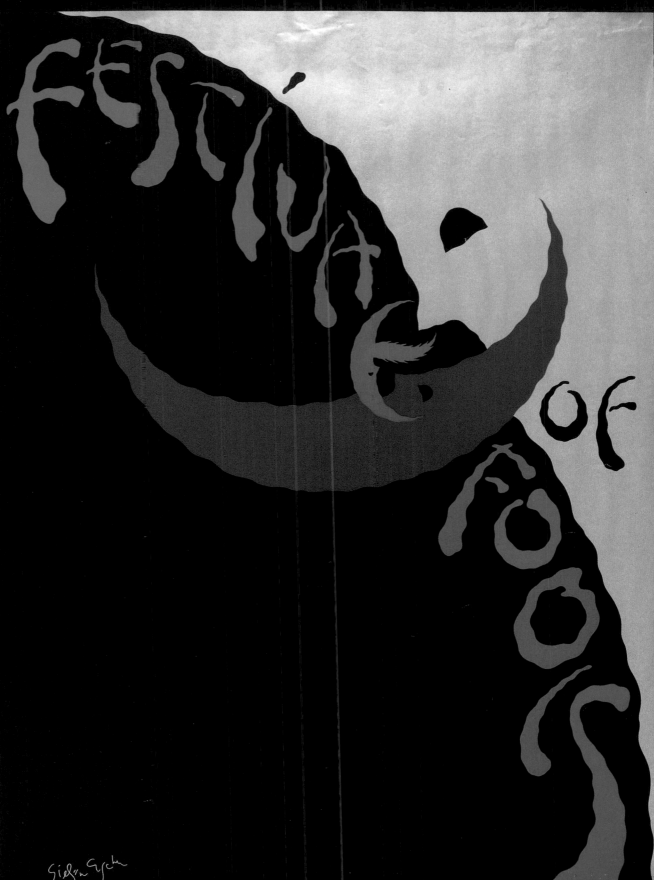

Gerard Unger
Bitstream Amerigo
designed in 1986

Bram de Does
Trinité 1,2,3 typeface,
designed in 1982 and
introduced by
Autologic SA and the
printing firm of
Enschedé in Haarlem.
Ascenders and
descenders are in
three different
lengths

Schrofer's computer-free typeface experiments and Wim Crouwel's controversial experimental alphabet of 1967 are the basis for most recent typeface experiments. If Crouwel's alphabet was, as he himself wrote, 'conceived as a body alphabet like that printed into the memory of the computer', since then computer technology has developed to the extent that lettering can be designed, distorted and manipulated. Since 1967 many special computer alphabets have been issued internationally, such as the OCR/A and B (1968), or exceptional alphabets like the special German DIN letter and the English BPR letter for road signs. Computer programmes are now available for designing letters, and there are programmes developed by designers themselves. There is also the Fontshop, which unites typeface designers from many countries, including Erik Spiekermann (Germany), Neville Brody (UK), Gerard Unger and Petr van Blokland from the Netherlands.

Gerard Unger is one of the most active Dutch typeface designers of recent years. He stands somewhere between the classic typeface designers and the contemporary ones. For Unger, aesthetics and functionality go hand in hand. He mainly designs lettering that suits modern typesetting and printing techniques, and special lettering for specific purposes, such as for the Amsterdam Metro MOL and the unique Swift newspaper type (1985). Unger works on commissions for Hell Digiset, and in 1986 designed for the US firm Bitstream the Bitstream Amerigo typeface for laser printers and desktop publishing. Together with designer Pieter Brattinga he also produced Primer for Philips Data Systems and was commissioned by the PTT, with Chris Vermaas, to update telephone directory numbers. Unger's typefaces are crisp and imaginative and frequently run counter to the conventional typographic climate. For Enschedé he designed Markeur (1972) as a type for signage, and

New typeface designers

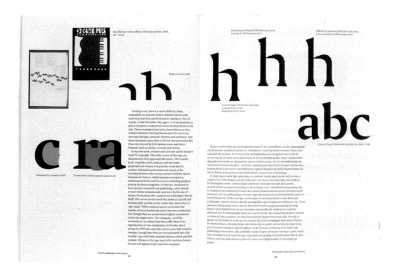

HadddpppeH

his other faces include Demos (1975), Praxis (1977), Hollander (1983), Flora (1984) and Ormanda (1986). For this book Unger's Swift typeface was used.

The classical line of Van Krimpen was continued in the Netherlands in a new, less 'hallowed' and sometimes controversial manner. A few years ago Bram de Does also designed a classic type, Trinité 1, 2, 3, for Enschedé, a face that befits the fine traditions of this printing house and which was to be the last type the firm produced. Young typeface designers were more inspired by Gerrit Noordzij and Petr van Blokland, lecturers in typography at the Royal Academy in The Hague, and by the Academy in Arnhem, where Jan Vermeulen, Alexander Verberne and Karel Martens enriched this specialist field. These academies spawned Just van Rossum, Erik van Blokland, Martin Majoor, Peter Verheul and the more traditionally minded Peter Matthias Noordzij as well as Stephan Saaltink, who under the aegis of his studio Typography & Other Serious Matters (Member of the League of Roman Alphabet Devotees) reacted against the moribund aspects of the profession. Max Kisman began designing type out of his interest in the computer, which has resulted in his experimental *TYP* magazine.

The letterforms designed by these type enthusiasts were generally unconventional. Justlefthand Regular from Van Rossum and Van Blokland was a type written shakily with the left hand and developed into an alphabet. From the same typeface designers is Beowolf, a type that appears to derive from the *Flintstones* TV programme and which can be manipulated in any direction. These are typographic jokes that have more serious companions, such as Evert Bloemsma's Balance. The field of type is filled with variety, and perhaps in the long run every designer will officially register his own 'self-portrait' typeface in order to be instantly recognisable.

ABCDEFGHIJK
LMNOPQRSTUV
WXYZ
abcdefghijklmn
opqrstuvwxyz
1234567890&
-.,:;!?„""''—

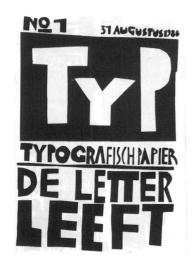

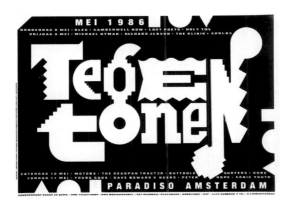

Erik van Blokland and Just van Rossum *Beowolf* typeface, designed in 1990

Max Kisman Magazine cover of *Typ: typografisch papier*, Stichting Typ, Amsterdam 1986

Max Kisman Poster for a music festival in Amsterdam's Paradiso, 1986

Within the world of contemporary Dutch graphic design Gielijn Escher holds a unique position. He mainly produces posters for cultural bodies and events and works on them from start to finish himself. Self-taught and the grandson of the graphic artist Jacob Jongert, Escher cherishes craftsmanship. He cuts the forms and letters for his posters himself, meticulously chooses the colours and makes changes and adjustments at the printing stage to achieve the desired result. In a sense Escher can be viewed as a direct descendent of William Morris and Walter Crane. He leaves nothing to chance, let alone to others. He says that by the age of ten, he had decided he wanted to make posters. The reason behind this youthful career decision was the combined beauty of type and image on orange wrappers and fruit crate labels, which Escher has collected by the thousand over the years.

The backgrounds of Escher's posters are often very dark in order to accentuate the colours of the type and image. He uses photography only occasionally. He prefers to draw everything himself, and while he is extremely precise in his spacing of letters, he can extract anything he wants from them. He uses image and typography to express his emotional involvement with the subject. An outstanding example of a typographic device is the poster for *Kaspar*, written by Peter Handke for the Baal theatre group. The Kaspar letters have been removed from the text and are fluttering down the poster; an inventive idea that unites text, image and content. As his work proves, Escher is more an artist than a graphic designer, and with his feeling for the broader perspective of the poster image on the street, his work belongs more to the French tradition of poster art.

The posters of Gielijn Escher

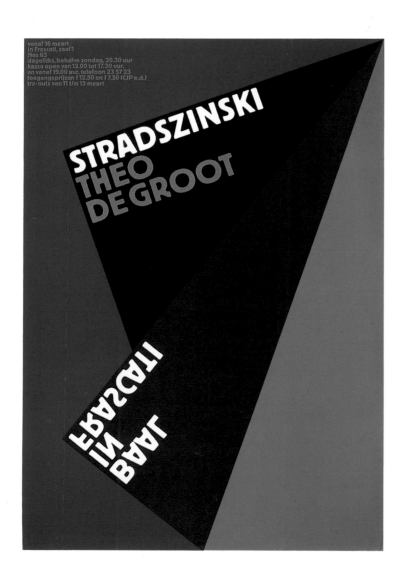

Gielijn Escher
Poster for *Theo de Groot, Stradszinski*, Baal Theatre Group, Amsterdam 1985

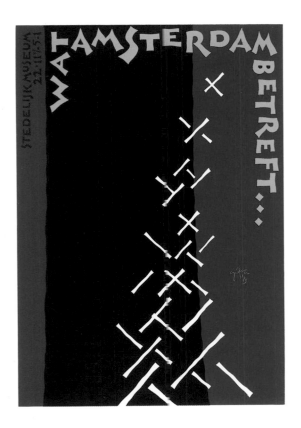

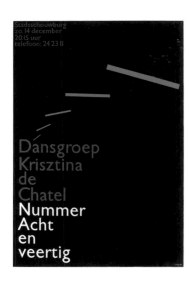

Gielijn Escher
Poster for a cultural
event 'Wat Amsterdam
betreft', Stedeljik
Museum, Amsterdam
1985

Gielijn Escher
Poster *Number Forty-
Eight*, Krisztina de
Chatel Dance Group,
Amsterdam 1986

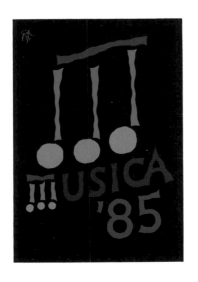

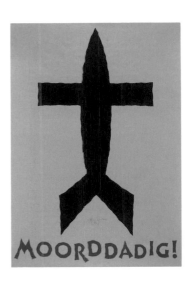

Gielijn Escher
Poster *Musica*,
Amsterdam 1985

Gielijn Escher
Poster depicting
opposition to
deploying cruise
missiles in the
Netherlands,
Amsterdam 1985

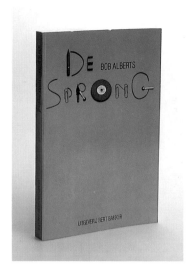

Hard Werken (Hard Working) is the name of a monthly publication founded by a group of Rotterdam designers in 1978. The group comprises Gerard Hadders, Rick Vermeulen, Willem Kars, Henk Elenga, Ton van den Haspel and Jan Willem de Kok, all of whom originated from the Graphic Workshop of the Rotterdam Art Foundation. The production of their own publication arose out of the wish – independent of clients and using every available graphic means – to shed more light on Rotterdam's social and artistic climate. The group had an expressive 'anything and everything is possible' approach to design that was in keeping with the mood of artists of the 1970s calling themselves the 'jong wilden'; (young wild ones), the Netherlands' answer to Germany's new expressionists. The group's eclectic approach to design perfectly reflected the complex image of the visual media at the time. They shared no specific design style or ideology and did not set out to be provocative. Following Provo-inspired design, however, there was a second wave of reaction against stark functionalism, which was seen as standing in the way of a more personal and subjective design approach. At Hard Werken every designer in the collective was responsible for their own commissions, or they were shared out. This relaxed approach led to much inventiveness and unexpected results. Design was not considered as holy ground, but the result of the moment, of an attitude.

Through their monthly publication the group became well-known and soon had its imitators. Hard Werken did not limit itself to graphic design, but created theatre décors, eye-catching furniture and lamps, as well as exhibition design and audiovisual presentation. Interior design has now developed into an essential and functional component of the group's work.

In Hard Werken's graphic designs photography (both 'found' images and staged photographs), unusual formats and every kind of typeface from the past and present is used. Anything that has ever been made is used or reinterpreted. They hold the conviction that content does in fact determine the design, the latter underlining the uniqueness of each message. Yet a certain form of gentle irony is indispensable in this type of design, and explains the reason for Hard Werken's vast away of styles from plain to chaotic. The majority of commissions have come from cultural bodies, galleries, museums, film festivals and universities. Publishers such as Bert Bakker have used Hard Werken to design book covers, such as the controversial one for Eco's *De Naam van de Roos* (The Name of the Rose) by Gerard Hadders. The design group soon received commissions from industry, which had discovered their unusual manner of communication. It produced annual reports for the National Investment Bank, brochures for car furniture and publications and stamps for the PTT. A branch was set up in Los Angeles, where Henk Elenga now works for Warner Brothers and Esprit among others.

Hard Werken in Rotterdam

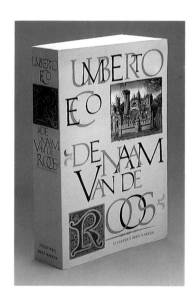

Hard Werken
(Rick Vermeulen)
Cover of Bob Alberts,
De sprong (The Jump),
Bert Bakker,
Amsterdam 1979

Hard Werken
(Rick Vermeulen)
Cover of Umberto Eco,
De naam van de roos
(The Name of the
Rose), Bert Bakker,
Amsterdam 1983

Hard Werken
(Gerard Hadders)
Poster for a dance
production *'Even'*,
Kunst Stichting,
Rotterdam 1981

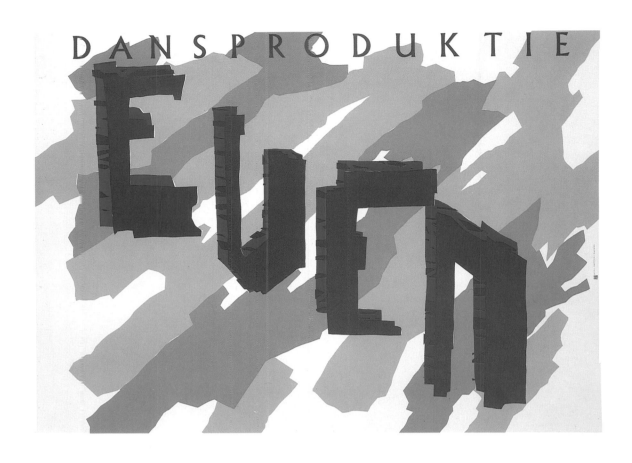

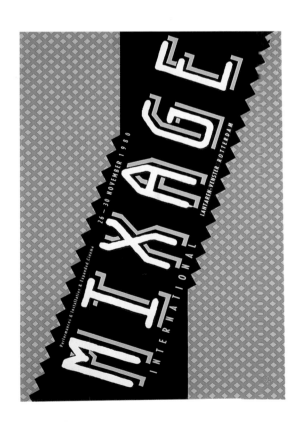

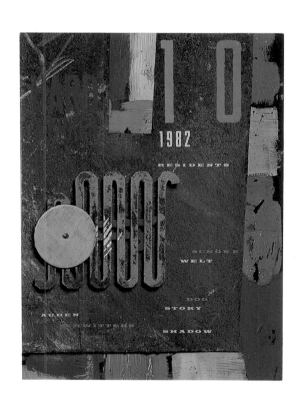

Hard Werken
(Gerard Hadders)
Poster *Mixage
International*, for a
multimedia show; De
Lanteren, Rotterdam
1980

Hard Werken
Cover of *Hard Werken*
no. 10, Rotterdam
1982

Wild Plakken
Poster for a national
Vietnam campaign,
Amsterdam 1975

Wild Plakken
Poster *Newborn Art*,
Wild Plakken,
Amsterdam 1984. The
text was by Willem
Sandberg: 'Newborn
art, uneducated and
demanding, does not
speak but shouts'

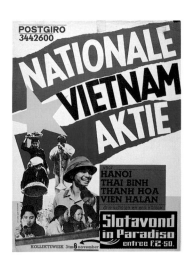

Wild Plakken
Poster for a national
Vietnam campaign,
Amsterdam 1975

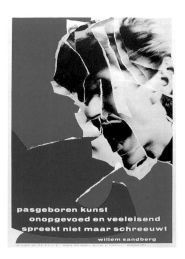

Wild Plakken
Poster *Newborn Art*,
Wild Plakken,
Amsterdam 1984. The
text was by Willem
Sandberg: 'Newborn
art, uneducated and
demanding, does not
speak but shouts'

Wild Plakken
in Amsterdam

After graduating from Amsterdam's Rietveld Academy – where they were taught, among others, by Jan van Toorn – Lies Ros, Rob Schröder and Frank Beekers began working together in 1977. They formed a collective with clear intentions: their work was at the disposal of groups who were actively involved in changing society in some way. Their design style was inspired by the idealists of the 20th century, such as El Lissitzky, John Heartfield and Paul Schuitema, and by the possibilities created by new technology, through which they discovered an experimental language of typographic form that conveys the message as clearly and plainly as possible.

At the Rietveld Academy they had already deployed their work for the democratisation movement in education, for pressure groups, community groups and political parties. As students they had long discussions on the relation of design to socially-motivated content. Called Wild Plakken (Flyposting) since 1981 – reflecting the illegal flyposting in the city – they have accepted or refused commissions depending on the ideological viewpoint.

As well as working within the collective, Schröder and Beekers were attached to the Rietveld Academy, with a view to providing students with practical experience. The 1970s, especially in Amsterdam, was a time of political unrest both nationally and internationally, with many demonstrations and protests. The Vietnam War, racism in South Africa, the housing shortage, the feminist movement, abortion and nuclear weapons were all subjects for action and Wild Plakken produced many posters, exhibitions, catalogues and banners. The group was also active on behalf of the Dutch communist party as well as working for such cultural bodies as Museum Fodor, the film magazine *Skrien*, the Sater theatre group, the Southern theatre group, De Balie theatre and the Dutch Opera company.

In contrast to Hard Werken, the group regarded each commission as a collective effort open to on-going discussion throughout the entire design process and, where necessary, to change. The group's design style makes clear its own attitudes on moral responsibility and values. Materials and resources are largely used in a direct way, with photocollage, typography, many diagonals and simple colour planes: a style initially harkening back to the 1920s and 1930s. Recently the work has become more varied and is no longer instantly recognisable as coming from Wild Plakken. As far as content is concerned, however, the group's firm stand has not diminished.

Wild Plakken
Poster for a West
German exhibition
*Begegnung mit den
Niederländer.*, Munich
1989

Wild Plakken
Poster for *Sergei
Prokofiev, l'Ange de feu*,
The Dutch Opera
Company,
Amsterdam 1990

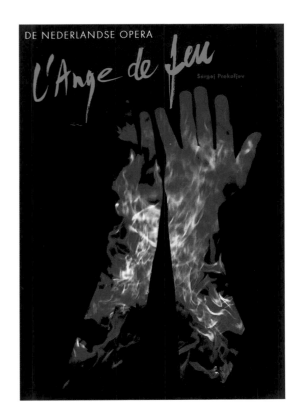

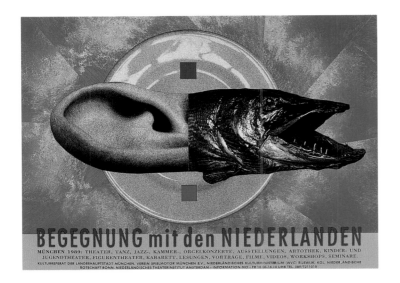

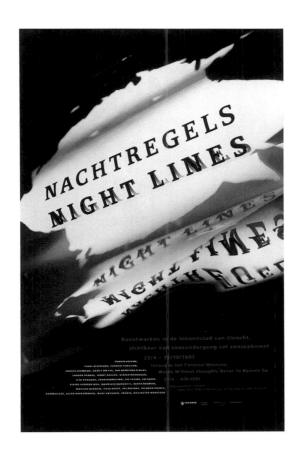

Wild Plakken
Poster for an
exhibition and
cultural programme
entitled *Nightlines*,
Central Museum,
Utrecht 1991

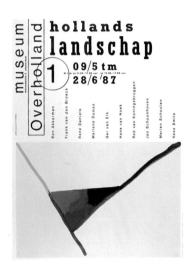

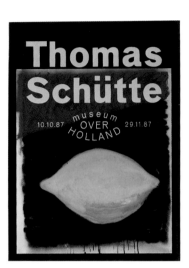

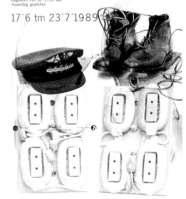

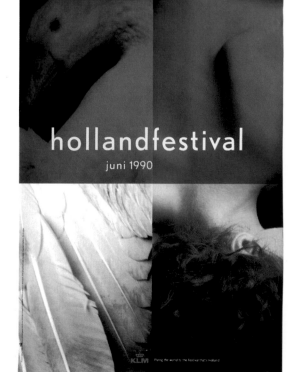

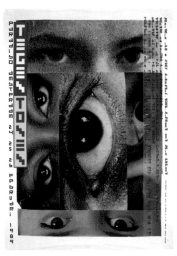

Max Kisman
Poster for a musical
festival in
Amsterdam's
Paradiso, 1989

Despite a greater interest in poster art nowadays, the commissions for graphic designers in this field are relatively small in number – although no fewer than before. Besides advertisements and flyposting everywhere on the streets, there are many posters created by graphic designers to promote cultural events such as exhibitions, theatre, opera, dance and concerts. By and large, designers working in this area are allowed more scope. Yet despite many exceptional designs it is difficult for them to stand out against the visual onslaught of the street. To do so requires aggressive images, but this does not always comply with the content. There currently exists no overview of what is taking place now in this field, even though trade publications regularly discuss the issues. In this book posters are reproduced from every period since 1890, and a few examples have been selected from the increasing number of contemporary posters.

Karel Kruijsen's poster is aimed at conveying pure information, while in his posters for the Overholland Museum Lex Reitsma adds pictorial fragments that evoke the atmosphere of the subject. Irma Boom goes further in her posters for the 1990 Holland Festival. She provides little information and the images are not specific, yet she still manages to illustrate the best aspects of the Holland Festival. In the words of the Russian designer V. Krichevski: 'It appears to be created from poetry and human feelings, while it absolutely does not contain any unusual form elements. The poster's clarity is mysterious.'

The computer has become a major tool for creating posters, as with it all manner of effects and visual manipulations can be achieved. Straight photography and staged photography are often used, and the layering of images on top of each other is a popular device. Much is done with typography, and the technical possibilities in this field are endless. However, notwithstanding the vast technical resources now available, posters are still produced which are comprised of collages, or are drawn or painted.

Posters: a continuing tradition

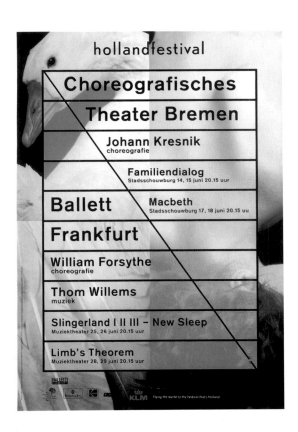

Irma Boom
Two posters for
Amsterdam's *Holland
Festival*, Amsterdam
1990. One of them
is a variation of the
standard festival
poster

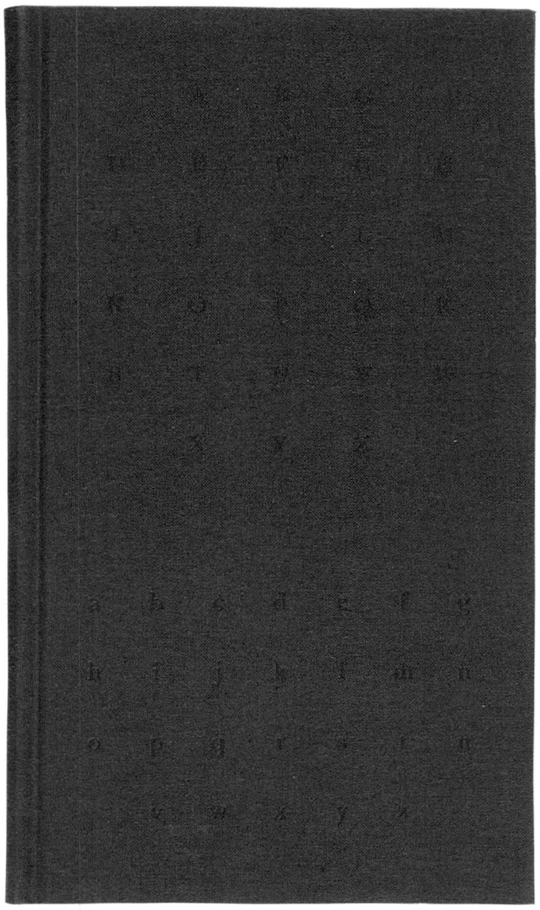

Gerrit Noordzij
Cover of a type
reference book, *Royal
Printers G.J. Thieme*,
Nijmegen 1986. The
work pays homage to
the type reference
book that Jan
Vermeulen designed
for the printing firm
in 1959

Return of the '50 best-designed books'

One of the recurrent issues when judging the graphic design of a book is
whether it should be assessed on its overall quality, or on exceptional
typographic presentation. Should books be judged on their own, often very
different, merits, or should their quality be compared, say, to a Jan van
Krimpen? Should the illustrations, and the originality and verve of the
design, be taken into account? The reason this annual award was disbanded
in 1970 was that the jury had been considered too 'one-sided' and too
concerned with the standards of classic typography as practised by De Roos
and Van Krimpen. New graphic design developments were ignored, and in
addition the concept of having awards had become discredited. When the
'50 best-designed books' awards were reinstated in 1986, the jury was much
more diverse, in background, age and personal taste. Among them were
typeface designers, graphic designers, printers, publishers and book retailers,
an eclecticism which is now reflected in the awards of recent years. Wide-
ranging design styles have been honoured from many different categories
such as literature, children's books, art books, museum catalogues,
photographic books, scholarly editions, scientific publications and general
non-fiction. Various illustrative styles are included here from Charles
Jongejans and Gerrit Noordzij, as well as those from a younger generation,
Wigger Bierma and Tessa van der Waals.

It is evident that these annual awards in recognition of good design are
an incentive to graphic designers as well as to printers and publishers, and
this can only be welcomed.

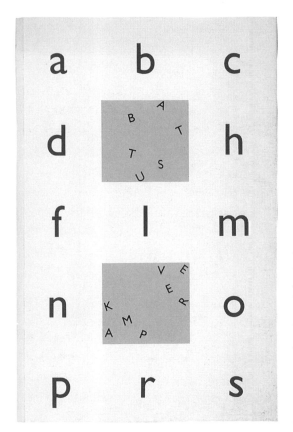

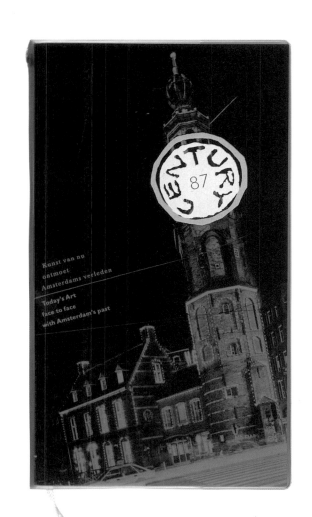

Wigger Bierma
Cover of *Battus and
Joost Veerkamp, Le
dichtstal, Lille fumière,*
Nova Zembla,
Arnhem 1988

Tessa van der Waals
Catalogue for an
exhibition and
cultural festival
Century '87,
Amsterdam 1987

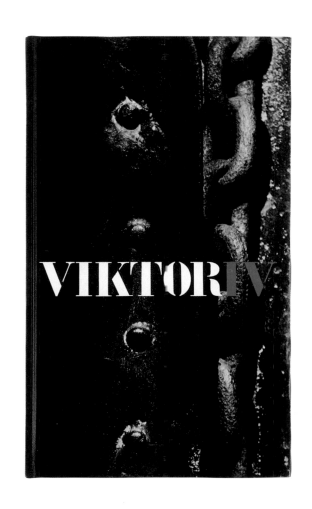

Charles Jongejans
Catalogue cover
Viktor IV, Stedelijk
Museum, Amsterdam
1990

E. Gruson and
E. Traast
Envelope DIN A4,
Centraal Museum,
Utrecht 1991

Gea Grevink
Envelope 'Doolhof' DIN
A5, Centraal Museum,
Utrecht 1991

It is virtually impossible to summarize recent developments in Dutch graphic design. The number of graphic designers graduating from the academies each year is roughly estimated at about two hundred, and interest in the profession is still growing. The field has various sectors, from typography to the design of packaging, exhibitions, corporate identities and signage.

It is not easy for freelance designers to find commissions. There are no manuals on how to do this, but experience shows that most good design graduates, working either on their own or with associates, have enough work within a few years of leaving college. Moreover, clients, especially cultural bodies, who want a different image from time to time, are aware of the great variety of possibilities, and no longer retain the services of one designer. A noteworthy example here is the Centraal Museum in Utrecht, which wanted to change its house style a few years ago. A few designers were invited to submit proposals, but it was concluded that choosing just one proposal would be arbitrary and would not reflect the museum's enormously diverse collection and exhibition agenda. Moreover, the museum needed a great variety of printed matter, such as posters, catalogues, stationery, business cards, folders, entrance tickets, information on works and so on. The museum decided to have all this various print material designed by different designers. Material was printed in small editions to give more designers the opportunity to work for the museum. A member of the museum staff was assigned the task of attracting young, good designers from art academies and elsewhere. The ministry of welfare, health and culture contributed to the design programme. This intriguing project, known as 'No Total' design, has given an impulse to the profession, and has resulted in the museum becoming widely known for its variety of house styles.

Today and tomorrow

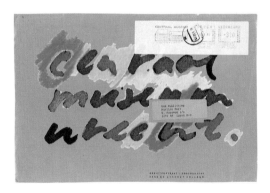

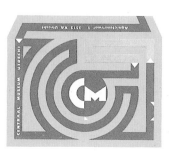

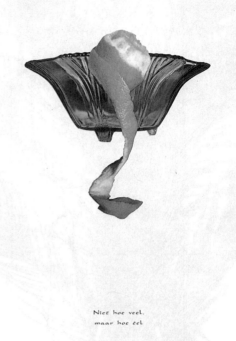

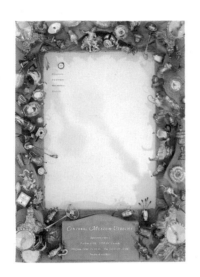

Martijn Swart
Letterhead, Centraal
Museum, Utrecht
1991

Mireille Geijsen
Letterhead, Centraal
Museum, Utrecht
1991

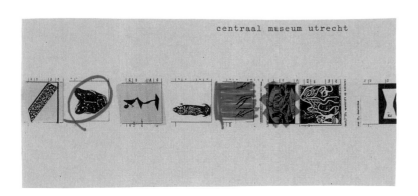

Mart Warmerdam
Information booklet,
Centraal Museum
and Rietveld
Schröderhuis,
Utrecht 1991

The Sandberg Institute, which has close ties with the Rietveld Academy, and the Jan van Eyck Academy in Maastricht are currently reappraising the place of the graphic designer in society. As the story of graphic design over the last hundred years draws to close, there is good reason to expect new developments in the future. No doubt the end of this century will reveal inspiring innovations in graphic design, as happened one hundred years ago.

Graphic design and training

In the Netherlands graphic design alternates between the functional and informative on the one hand and the freestyle and visual – often with an obscure message – on the other. There are designs based on content, designs allied to the past, and designs for their own sake. Nowadays, designers tend to prefer the photographic image, and drawn illustration is relatively rarely seen, yet it still belongs to the range of possibilities. The technical possibilities are virtually endless and the standard of lithography and printing is generally extremely high. The computer as a resource and a manipulator has become indispensable and provides ever increasing opportunities.

The various viewpoints found in the profession, here represented by a selection of postage stamp designs since 1946 (a much-loved exercise of the academies), arise in the first instance from design training. In fact they are the results of the work of the lecturers. Throughout the 20th century, teachers have played an essential role in the profession, particularly where courses were not simply practical, theoretical or traditional, but proceeded from the personal viewpoint of the teacher.

In the 1920s, the academies in Rotterdam and The Hague were crucial to the modernist movements. After the Second World War this role was taken over by the Rietveld Academy, where a large number of currently well-known designers were trained. The Hague Academy, together with designer Gerrit Noordzij, now mainly concentrates on letterforms. The Arnhem Academy pays attention to typography in a freer and yet more structural sense. The Academy St Joost in Breda, together with several influential teachers (Chris Brand, Henk Cornelissen, Karel Kruysen and René van Raalte) has contributed to new developments, while the AKI in Enschedé has attracted visiting lecturers such as Swip Stolk and Anthon Beeke, who have had a stimulating effect.

1 Jan van Krimpen
Postage stamp from a
Number series, PTT (Post
Office), The Hague 1946
2 Lex Horn
Postage stamp
depicting osier
workers from a set
issued on the
Deltaworks, PTT (Post
Office), The Hague 1959
3 Cas Oorthuys
Postage stamp
depicting a *1964 Electric
Train*, to celebrate the
anniversary of Dutch
Railways, PTT (Post
Office), The Hague 1964
4 Jurriaan Schrofer
Postage stamp to mark
the 50th anniversary
of the *International
Labour Organisation in
Geneva*, PTT (Post
Office), The Hague 1969
5 Wim Crouwel
Postage stamp issued
for the *World Trade Fair
in Osaka*, PTT (Post
Office), The Hague 1970
6 Jan Slothouber and
William Graatsma
Child Welfare stamp, PTT
(Post Office),
The Hague 1970
7 Karel Kruijsen
Postage stamp to
promote *Dutch bulb
exports*, PTT (Post
Office), The Hague 1974
8 Cas Oorthuys
Postage stamp to
commemorate *30 years
of Liberation*, PTT (Post
Office), The Hague 1975
9 Marte Röling
Postage stamp *Tennis*,
PTT (Post Office),
The Hague 1974
10 René van Raalte
Child Welfare stamp
1977, from a set
depicting risks
children face,
including traffic
11 Willem Diepraam
and Jan van Toorn
Child Welfare stamp PTT
(Post Office),
The Hague 1979, from
a series entitled
Children's Rights.

12 Jo Coenen
Postage stamp
depicting the *Royal
Palace, Amsterdam*, PTT
(Post Office),
The Hague 1982.
The designer is also an
architect
13 Kees
Nieuwenhuijzen
Commemorative
stamp for the 500th
birthday of *Martin
Luther*, PTT (Post
Office), The Hague 1983
14 Joost Swarte
Child Welfare stamp,
from a set depicting
children changing
places with adults, PTT
(Post Office),
The Hague 1984
15 Anthon Beeke
Postage stamp from a
series on *Endangered
animals*, PTT (Post
Office), The Hague 1985
16 Swip Stolk
Postage stamp for the
75th anniversary of
the Royal Dutch
Draughts Association
17 Irene Klinkenberg
and Nicole van
Schouwenburg
Postage stamp to
celebrate the
completion of the
Deltaworks, PTT (Post
Office), The Hague 1986
18 Cees de Jong
Europe CEPT stamp
depicting part of a
design by Rem
Koolhaas for the
Scheveningen
Danstheater
PTT (Post Office),
The Hague 1987
19 Charlotte Mutsaers
Child Welfare stamp, in
this serie women are
working on the land,
on the sea and in the
air, PTT (Post Office),
The Hague 1987
20 Wild Plakken
Postage stamp for the
*Dutch Trade Union
movement*, PTT (Post
Office), The Hague 1989

21 Robert Nakata
Postage stamp to
commemorate the
*150th anniversary of
Dutch Railways*, PTT
(Post Office),
The Hague 1989
22 Joke Ziegelar
Postage stamp
depicting *Hortus
Botanicus in Leiden* to
commemorate the
400th anniversary of
one of the oldest
university botanical
gardens in the world,
PTT (Post Office),
The Hague 1990
23 Menno Landstra
Postage stamp of
Rotterdam, PTT (Post
Office), The Hague 1990
24 Jaap Drupsteen
Postage stamp on *Air
pollution*, one of three
stamps dealing with
environmental
protection, PTT (Post
Office), The Hague 1991
25 Paul Mijksenaar
Summer postage stamp,
depicting an old
Frisian farmhouse;
PTT (Post Office),
The Hague 1991
26 Marten Jongema
Europe CEPT stamp on
space research, PTT
(Post Office),
The Hague 1991
27 Alex Scholing
Postage stamp
depicting the annual
*Dutch Four-Day Walking
Event*, with over 30,000
ramblers taking part
28 Gerard Hadders
Child Welfare Stamp,
depicting one of the
Dutch national sports;
PTT (Post Office),
The Hague 1991
29 Karel Martens
Postage stamp to mark
the *New Civil Code*, PTT
(Post Office),
The Hague 1992
30 Victor Levie
Commemorative
stamp for the Second
World War, depicting
Westerbork transit
camp; PTT (Post
Office), The Hague 1992

1

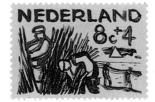

2

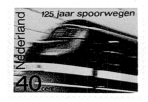

3

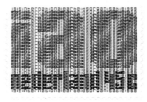

4

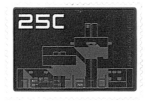

5

6

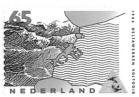

7

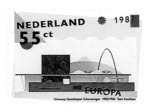

8

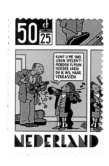

9

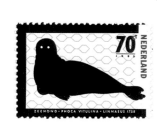

10

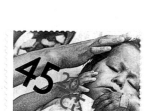

11

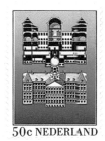

12

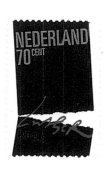

13

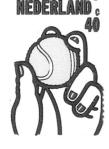

14

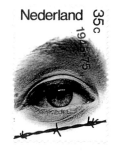

15

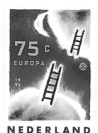

16

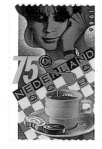

17

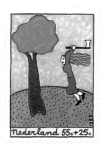

18

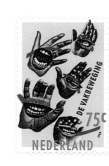

19

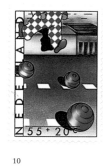

20

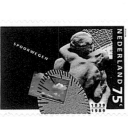

21

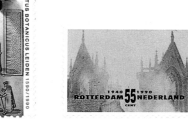

22

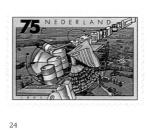

23

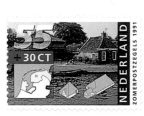

24

25

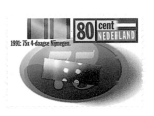

26

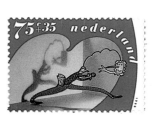

27

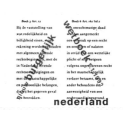

28

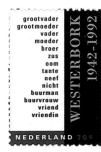

29

30

Biographies and selected bibliography

Alma, Peter
1886 Medan – 1969 Amsterdam
Artist, graphic artist
lit: cat. *Peter Alma*, Stedelijk Museum, Amsterdam
1960.

Arntz, Gerd
1900 Remscheid (Germany) – 1988 The Hague
Graphic artist, designer of pictograms
lit: Flip Bool, Kees Broos, *Gerd Arntz – kritische
grafiek en beeldstatistiek*, Haags Gemeentemuseum /
SUN, The Hague / Nijmegen 1976 (with
bibliography); Gerd Arntz, Kees Broos, *Symbolen
voor onderwijs en statistiek*, Mart. Spruijt,
Amsterdam 1981; Kees Broos, 'Bildstatistik
Vienna-Moskau-The Hague', in: *Arbeiterbildung in
den zwanziger Jahren*, Gesellschafts- und
Wirtschaftsmuseum, Vienna / Munich 1982,
p.214.

Arondeus, Willem
1894 Naarden – 1943 Haarlem
Artist, graphic artist, author

Baanders, Tine
1890 Amsterdam – 1971 Maarssen
Illustrator, calligrapher

Bazel, K.P.C. de
1869 Den Helder – 1923 Amsterdam
Architect
lit: J.L.M. Lauweriks, *De houtsneden van K.P.C. de
Bazel*, Amsterdam 1925; A.W. Reinink, *K.P.C. de
Bazel*, Amsterdam 1965; Fanelli 1978.

Beeke, Anthon
b. 1940 Amsterdam
Graphic designer
lit: Anthon Beeke, K.Schippers, *Over tijdschriften*,
Lecturis, Eindhoven 1979; *Pro-fil* 19, 1985; 60,
1989.

Beekers, Frank
b. 1952 Zaandam
Graphic designer
lit: Hefting 1982; *Pro-fil*, 20, 1985; 57, 1989.

Berlage, Hendrik Petrus
1856 Amsterdam – 1934 The Hague
Architect, industrial designer
lit: *Berlage 1856-1934. Een bouwmeester en zijn tijd*,
Nederlands Kunthistorisch Jaarboek 15 [1975],
Bussum 1975; Fanelli 1978; Umberto Barbieri,
Evert Rodrigo, Mariet Willinge, *Hendrik Petrus
Berlage – disegni, tekeningen*, Biennial Venice 1986;
Tanja Ledoux, *H.P. Berlage als boekbanddesigner,
illustrator en typograaf*, Fine & Rare Books,
Wageningen 1988; P. Singelenberg, *H.P. Berlage,
Idea and Style*, Utrecht 1972; Sergio Polano,
Henrik Petrus Berlage: Het complete werk, Alphen
a/d Rijn, 1988.

Besnyö, Eva
b. 1910 Budapest (Hungary)
Photographer
lit: Carrie de Swaan, *Eva Besnyö – 'n halve eeuw
werk*, Sara, Amsterdam 1982; Tineke de Ruiter,
'Eva Besnyö', *Geschiedenis van de Nederlandse
fotografie*, Samsom, Alphen aan den Rijn, vol. 5,
1986; Broos / Bool 1989.

Bierma, Wigger
b. 1958 Hengelo
Graphic designer, typographer
lit: *Pro-fil* 58, 1989.

Bijvoet, Bernard
1889 Amsterdam – 1979 Amsterdam
Architect
lit: Fanelli 1978.

Bleekrode, Meyer
1896 Amsterdam – 1943 Sobibor
Painter, graphic artist
lit: Carry van Lakerveld (ed.), *Meyer Bleekrode –
schilder, ontwerper, socialist 1896-1943*, Van Gennep /
Amsterdams Historisch Museum, Amsterdam
1983.

Blokland, Erik van
b. 1967 Gouda
Typeface designer

Blokland, Petr van
b. 1956 Gouda
Typeface designer
lit: 'Petr van Blokland', *Items* 2 (1982) p.48.

Bons, Jan
b. 1918 Rotterdam
Graphic designer, mural artist
lit: Jan Bons, 'De Nieuwe Kunstschool van Paul
Citroen', in: Löb 1974, p.62; cat. *Jan Bons, Posters*,
Museum Fodor, Amsterdam 1975.

Boom, Irma
1960 Lochem
Graphic designer

Bos, Ben
b. 1930 Amsterdam
Graphic designer
lit: Ben Bos, *Indruk in druk*, Lecturis, Eindhoven
1977; Ben Bos, *Huisstijl*, Van Loghum Slaterus,
Deventer 1986.

Brand, Chris
b. 1921 Utrecht
Typeface designer, calligrapher
lit: Carter 1987, p.140; Lommen 1987, p.43 (with
list of publications).

Brattinga, Pieter
b. 1931 Hilversum
Graphic designer
lit: B. Majorick, 'De Jong, Hilversum', *Typographica*
2, 1960; Pieter Brattinga, *Planning for Industry, Art
& Education*, Bruna / Van Nostrand, Utrecht / New
York; Pieter Brattinga, *Influences on Dutch Graphic
Design*, Amsterdam 1987; Geneviève Waldmann,
De activiteiten van Pieter Brattinga, een tijdsbeeld,
SDU / Kodansha, The Hague / Tokyo 1988.

Briedé, Johan
1885 Rotterdam – Amsterdam
Painter, graphic artist

Brouwers, Arlette
b. 1956 The Hague
Graphic designer
lit: *Pro-fil* 76, 1991.

Brusse, Wim
1910 Rotterdam – 1978 Amsterdam
Graphic designer, photographer

Cahn, Henny
1908 Hengelo
Graphic designer
lit: Broos / Bool 1989.

Caspel, Johann Georg van
1870 Amsterdam – 1928 Laren
Poster designer, architect
lit: Peter van Dam, *Johann Georg van Caspel*,
Stadsuitgeverij, Amsterdam 1990.

References in
abbreviated form (eg.
Hefting 1982) refer to
general bibliography

Coenen, Jo
b. 1949 Hoensbroek
Architect
lit: Hans van Dijk, 'Jo Coenen', *Archis*, July 1989;
Aart Oxenaar, *Jo Coenen*, Rotterdam 1993.

Cohen, Fré
1903 Amsterdam – 1943 Hengelo
Graphic designer, illustrator
lit: Dick Dooijes et al, *Rond Paasheuvel en Prinsenhof – Fré Cohen*, Stadsdrukkerij, Amsterdam 1977;
Nees Westerhout et al, *Fré Cohen*, Broekhuis,
Hengelo 1985.

Crouwel, Wim
b. 1928 Groningen
Graphic and industrial designer
lit: Wim Crouwel, *New Alphabet*, De Jong,
Hilversum 1967; Wim Crouwel, 'Type design for
the computer age', *The Journal of Typographic
Research*, January 1970; Wim Crouwel, *Vormgeving - door wie?*, Waltman, Delft 1973; Wim Crouwel,
Ontwerpen en drukken, G.J. Thiemefonds,
Amsterdam 1974; Wim Crouwel, *Vormgeven voor
een groot publiek*, Total Design, Amsterdam 1876;
Wim Crouwel, *Om de kunst*, Lecturis, Eindhoven
1978; Bibeb, *Wim Crouwel*, Thieme, Nijmegen
1978; Wim Crouwel, 'Experimental Typography
and the need for the experiment', in: *Idea*, sec.
issue, Tokyo 1980; Wim Crouwel, 'Total Design',
in: *Graphis*, 38 (1982) 220, p.8; Wim Crouwel,
Vormgeving: zin en onzin, Lecturis, Eindhoven
1985; Wim Crouwel, *Over functionalisme en stijl*,
Rosbeek, Nuth 1988.

Derkinderen, Antoon
1859 's Hertogenbosch – 1935 Amsterdam
Mural artist
lit: A.J. Der Kinderen, *De jeugd van Antoon Der
Kinderen door hemzelf beschreven anno 1892*, Van
Dishoeck, Bussum 1892; Maureen Trappeniers
(ed.), *Antoon Derkinderen*, Noordbrabants Museum,
's-Hertogenbosch 1980.

Diedenhoven, Walter van
1886 Amersfoort – 1915 Apeldoorn
Graphic artist

Diepraam, Willem
b. 1944 Amsterdam
Photographer
lit: Merlo 1980.

Dijsselhof, Gerrit Willem
1866 Zwollerkerspel – 1924 Overveen
Painter, applied artist

Does, Bram de
b. 1934 Amsterdam
Typeface designer
lit: Carter 1987, pp. 142, 165; Lommen 1987, p. 55
(with list of publications).

Doesburg, Theo van [pseud. C.E.M. Küpper]
1883 Utrecht – 1931 Davos
Artist, architect, author
lit: Spencer 1969; cat. *Theo van Doesburg 1883-1931*,
Van Abbemuseum, Eindhoven 1969; Joost Baljeu,
Theo van Doesburg, Studio Vista, London 1974;
Fanelli 1978; H.L.C. Jaffé, *Theo van Doesburg*,
Meulenhoff-Landshoff, Amsterdam 1983;
Evert van Straaten, *Theo van Doesburg 1883-1931*,
Staatsuitgeverij, The Hague 1983; Evert van
Straaten, *Theo van Doesburg – schilder en architect*,
SDU, The Hague 1988.

Domela [Nieuwenhuis], Cesar
1900 Amsterdam – 1992 Paris (France)
Artist, graphic designer
lit: Kees Broos, Flip Bool, *Domela*, Gemeente-
museum, The Hague 1980; G.B. Martini, A.
Ronchetti, *Cesar Domela – Fotografie, Fotomontaggi,
Disegni*, Bonini, Genova 1981; Marie-Odile Briot,
Domela, 65 ans d'abstraction, MAM Paris / Musée de
Grenoble, Paris / Grenoble 1987; Frits Bless, Evert
van Straaten, *Domela – schilderijen, reliëfs, grafisch
oeuvre*, Van Reekum Museum / Institut
Néerlandais, Apeldoorn / Paris 1990.

Dooijes, Dick
b. 1909 Amsterdam
Typaface designer, typographer, author
lit: Dick Dooijes, *Traditie en vernieuwing*,
Nederlandse vereniging voor druk- en boekkunst, Amsterdam 1959; Dick Dooijes,
Boektypografische verkenningen, De Buitenkant,
Amsterdam 1986; Lommen 1987, p. 19 (with list
of publications); Dick Dooijes, *Wegbereiders van de
moderne boektypografie*, De Buitenkant,
Amsterdam 1988; Dick Dooijes, *Mijn leven met
letters*, De Buitenkant, Amsterdam 1991.

Drupsteen, Jaap
b. 1942 Hasselt Ov.
Graphic designer, animator
lit: cat. *Jaap Drupsteen – televisiewerk en grafische
ontwerpen*, Groninger Museum, Groningen 1982;
Pro-fil, 72, 1991.

Duiker, Johannes
1890 The Hague – 1935 Amsterdam
Architect
lit: Fanelli 1978.

Dumbar, Gert
b. 1940 Jakarta (Indonesia)
Graphic designer
lit: 'Paul Hefting over Gert Dumbar', *Kunstschrift*,
2 1986.

Duyvelshoff-van Peski, Daphne
b. 1942 Geneva (Switzerland)
Graphic designer

Ehrlich, Christa
Industrial designer
lit: Kees Broos, 'Zilver voor mensen', *Museumjournaal 21* (1976) 1, p.12; cat. *Christa Ehrlich –
Weens ontwerpster in Nederland*, Dutch Gold, Silver
and Clock Museum, Schoonhoven 1988.

Elffers, Dick
1910 Rotterdam – 1990 Amsterdam
Graphic designer
lit: Lies Ros, Rob Schröder, 'Grafisch ontwerpen
vroeger en nu – een gesprek met Dick Elffers',
in: Ros, Schröder, *Ontwerpproces*, 1986, p. 93; Max
Bruinsma, *Een leest heeft drie voeten: Dick Elffers en
de kunst*, De Balie / G.J. Thiemefonds, Amsterdam
1989.

Escher, Gielijn
b. 1945 Oegstgeest
Poster artist
lit: *Pro-fil*, 11, 1984; 17, 1985.

Friedlaender, Henri
1904 Lyon (Fr.)
Typeface designer, typographer
lit: Henri Friedlaender, *Typografisch ABC*, Boucher,
The Hague 1937; Kurt Löb, 'Drei deutschsprachige
graphische Gestalter als Emigranten in Holland',
Philobiblon 33 (1989) 3, p. 177; Kurt Löb, 'Die
Buchgestaltungen Henri Friedlaenders für die
Amsterdamer Exil-Verlage Querido und Allert de
Lange 1933-1940', *Philobiblon 34* (1990) 3, p. 207.

Gerbrands, Roelf
1891 Groningen – 1954 Haarlem
Painter, applied artist

Gestel, Leo
1881 Woerden – 1941 Hilversum
Painter
lit: cat. *Leo Gestel als modernist*, Frans Halsmuseum /
Noordbrabants Museum, Haarlem / Den Bosch
1983.

Gidding, Jaap
1887 Rotterdam – 1955 Hillegersberg, Rotterdam
Painter

Gispen W. H.
1890 Amsterdam – 1981 The Hague
Industrial designer, painter
lit: André Koch, *Industrieel ontwerper W.H. Gispen
(1890-1981) – een modern eclecticus*, De Hef,
Rotterdam 1988.

Graatsma, William
b. 1925 Burchty
Artist, architect
lit: 'Cubische vormgeving 1955-1970', *Revue
Integration 11-12 1976*.

Hadders, Gerard
b. 1954 Rotterdam
Graphic designer
lit: Hefting 1982; *Pro-fil*, 14, 1985.

Hart-Nibbrig, Ferdinand
1866 Amsterdam – 1915 Laren
Painter, graphic artist

Hartland, Paul
1910 Apeldoorn – 1991 Amsterdam
Photographer, graphic designer

Hartz, S.L.
b. 1912 Leiden
Typeface designer, typographer
lit: cat. *S.L. Hartz in de grafische wereld*, Museum
Meermanno-Westreenianum, The Hague 1969;
Carter 1987, p. 109; Lommen 1987, p. 31 (with list
of publications).

Hofman, Pieter A.H.
1885 Teteringen – 1965 The Hague
Painter, graphic artist

Homan, Reynoud
1956 Eindhoven
Graphic designer
lit: *Pro-fil*, 23, 1987; 46, 1988.

Horn, Lex
1916 Nijmegen – 1968 Vannes (France)
Mural artist

Hoytema, Theo van
1863 The Hague – 1917 The Hague
Graphic/applied artist
lit: cat. *De grafiek van Theo van Hoytema*,
Rijksmuseum, Amsterdam 1977.

Huszár, Vilmos
1884 Budapest, Hungary – 1960 Harderwijk
Painter, designer
lit: Sjarel Ex, Els Hoek, *Vilmos Huszár – schilder en
designer 1884-1960*, Reflex, Utrecht 1985.

Hynckes, Raoul
1893 Brussel, (Belgium) – 1973 Blaricum
Painter
lit: Mona Brouwer-Verzaal, *Raoul Hynckes 1893-
1973 – Het grafische werk*, Gemeentemuseum
Arnhem 1991.

Jong, Cees de
b. 1945 Amsterdam
Graphic designer
lit: *Pro-fil*, 34, 1987.

Jongejans, Charles
b. 1918 Borneo (Indonesia)
Graphic designer
lit: Charles Jongejans, *Letterbeelden*, Wolters-
Noordhoff / De Jong, Groningen / Hilversum
1970; Charles Jongejans, *De letter buiten z'n boekje*,
Lecturis, Eindhoven 1984; Charles Jongejans,
'45'85 typografisch Nederland, G.J. Thiemefonds,
Amsterdam 1984; Charles Jongejans, *Allebehalve
plat*, De Buitenkant, Amsterdam 1989; Koosje
Sierman, 'Charles Jongejans – Portret van een
eigenzinnig estheet', *Items 31* (1989) p. 12.

Jongema, Marten
b. 1952 Schalkhaar
Graphic designer
lit: *Pro-fil*, 77, 1991.

Jongert, Jac.
1883 Wormer – 1942 Reeuwijk
Painter, graphic artist, designer
lit: Emy Hoogenboezem, *Jac. Jongert 1883-1942 –
graficus tussen kunst en reclame*,
Gemeentemuseum, The Hague 1982.

Kalff, Louis Christiaan
1897 Amsterdam – 1976
Industrial designer

Kamman, Jan
1898 Schiedam – 1983 Woudrichem
Photographer
lit: Broos / Bool 1989.

Kempers, Mart
b. 1924 Enschede
Graphic artist, illustrator

Kiljan, Gerard
1891 Hoorn – 1968 Leidschendam
Graphic and industrial designer, photographer
lit: Ankie de Jongh-Vermeulen en Hripsimé
Visser, 'Gerrit Kiljan', *Geschiedenis van de
Nederlandse fotografie*, Samsom, Alpen aan den
Rijn, vol. 6, 1987.

Kisman, Max
b. 1953 Doetinchem
Graphic designer
lit: *Pro-fil*, 36 1987; Marjan Unger, 'Max Kisman',
Items 38 (1991), p. 48.

Klaarhamer, P.J.C.
1874 Swiep – 1954 Ede
Architect
lit: Fanelli 1978.

Klerk, Michel de
1884 Amsterdam – 1923 Amsterdam
Architect
lit: Fanelli 1978.

Klinkenberg, Irene
b. 1957
Graphic designer
lit: *Pro-fil*, 28, 1986.

Konijnenburg, Willem van
1868 The Hague – 1943 The Hague
lit: Mieke Reinders, *Willem van Konijnenburg
1868-1943*, Rijksdienst Beeldende Kunst / Centraal
Museum / Drents Museum, The Hague / Utrecht /
Assen 1990.

Koo, N.P. de
1881 – 1961
Graphic designer, interior designer
lit: Egbert van Faassen, *N.P. de Koo designer*,
Gemeentemuseum/PTT Art and Design
department, The Hague 1988.

Krijger, Henk
b. 1914 Karoengi (Indonesia)
Graphic artist, typeface designer

Krimpen, Jan van
1893 Gouda – 1958 Haarlem
Typeface designer, typographer
lit: John Dreyfus, *The work of Jan van Krimpen*, Joh.
Enschedé en Zonen / De Haan, Haarlem / Utrecht
1952; John Dreyfus, 'Jan van Krimpen, 1892-
1958', *Typographische Monatsblätter* 80 (1961), 8/9,
p.471; Carter 1987, p.101; Jan van Krimpen, *Over
het ontwerpen en bedenken van drukletters*, De
Buitenkant, Amsterdam 1990.

Kruit, Hans
b. 1951 The Hague
Graphic designer
lit: *Pro-fil* 61, 1989.

Kruijsen, Karel
b. 1951 Oisterwijk
Graphic designer
lit: Max Bruinsma, 'De ontwerper', *Items* 28 (1988)
p.18; *Pro-fil* 64, 1990.

Kuiper, Jan
b. 1928 Heemstede
Painter, graphic designer, typographer

Landstra, Menno
b. 1961 Emmeloord
Graphic designer

Lauweriks, J. L. Mathieu
1864 Roermond – 1932 Amsterdam
Architect, applied artist
lit: Nic. H.M. Tummers, *J.L. Mathieu Lauweriks, zijn
werk en zijn invloed op architectuur en vormgeving
rond 1910 – De Hagener impuls*, Utrecht 1968;
Fanelli 1978.

Lebeau, Chris
1878 Amsterdam – 1945 Dachau
Painter, graphic artist, industrial designer
lit: Mechteld de Bois, *Chris Lebeau 1878-1945*,
Drents Museum / Frans Halsmuseum, Assen /
Haarlem 1987.

Lebbink, Gracia
b. 1963 Geldrop
Graphic designer
lit: *Pro-fil*, 76, 1991.

Leck, Bart van der
1876 Utrecht – 1958 Blaricum
Painter, interior designer
lit: R.W.D. Oxenaar, *Bart van der Leck, 1876-1958*,
Kröller-Müller / Stedelijk Museum, Otterlo /
Amsterdam 1976.

Levie, Victor
b. 1955 Amsterdam
Graphic designer
lit: *Pro-fil* 35, 1987; 89, 1992.

Lion Cachet, C.A.
1864 Amsterdam – 1945 Vreeland
Graphic artist, applied artist

Martens, Karel
b. 1939 Mook en Middelaar
Graphic designer, typographer
lit: *Pro-fil* 4, 1984; 49, 1988; cat. *Papier,
Commanderie van St. Jan*, Nijmegen 1985;
Hugues C. Boekraad, 'Het gezicht van een
uitgeverij – over het werk van Karel Martens voor
de SUN', in: Ros Schröder, *Het Ontwerpproces*, 1986,
p.69; Goder van Colmjon, 'Karel Martens', *Items*
23 (1987) p.70.

Michiels, Toon
b. 1950 Boxtel
Graphic designer
lit: cat. *Ontwerpen, Toon Michiels*, Kruithuis, Den
Bosch 1987.

Mijksenaar, Paul
b. 1944 Amsterdam
Graphic and industrial designer
lit: Paul Mijksenaar, *Heeft grafische vormgeving nut?*,
Lecturis, Eindhoven 1974; *Pro-fil* 6, 1984; 56, 1989.

Molkenboer, Anton
1872 Leeuwarden – 1960 Haarlem
Painter, mural artist
lit: Ellen Muller en Magda Kyrova, *Antoon
Molkenboer: ontwerpen voor muziek en toneel 1895-
1917*, Gemeentemuseum, The Hague 1982.

Molkenboer, Theo
1871 Leeuwarden – 1920 Lugano (Switzerland)
Graphic artist

Mus Jnr, Cor
1886 Edam – The Hague
Painter

Mutsaers, Charlotte
b. 1942 Utrecht
Painter, author
lit: *Pro-fil* 39, 1989.

Nakata, Robert
b. 1960
Graphic designer
lit: *Pro-fil* 56, 1989.

Neuhuys, Theo
1878 Edam – 1921 The Hague
Graphic artist

Nieuwenhuis, Theo
1866 Noordscharwoude – 1951 Hilversum
Applied artist
lit: Hanneke Oldyslager, *Theo Nieuwenhuis 1860-1951*,
010 Publishers, Rotterdam 1991.

Nieuwenhuijzen, Kees
b. 1933 Utrecht
Graphic designer
lit: Paul Hefting, 'Over Kees Nieuwenhuijzen',
Industrieel Ontwerpen, November 1992; *Pro-fil* 2,
1983; 23, 1985; 38, 1987.

Nieuwenkamp, Wijnand O.J.
1874 Amsterdam – 1950 San Domenico di Fiesole
(Italy)
Painter, graphic artist
lit: W.O.J. Nieuwenkamp, *Leven & werken, bouwen &
zwerven van de kunstenaar W.O.J. Nieuwenkamp
opgetekend door zijn kleinzoon*, Bruna, Utrecht /
Antwerpen 1979.

Nikkels, Walter
b. 1940 Lobith
Graphic designer, typographer
Roelof van Gelder et al, *Rijn – Rhein over het werk
van Walter Nikkels*, Rosbeek, Nuth 1989.

Noordzij, Gerrit
b. 1931 Rotterdam
Calligrapher, typeface designer, typographer
lit: Gerrit Noordzij, *The Stroke of the Pen:
Fundamental Aspects of Writing*, Royal Academy of
Art, The Hague 1982; Gerrit Noordzij, *Letters in
studie- Letterontwerpen van studenten in het
Nederlandse kunstonderwijs*, Lecturis, Eindhoven
1983; Gerrit Noordzij, *De streek, theorie van het
schrift*, Van de Garde, Zaltbommel 1985.

Nypels, Charles
1895 Maastricht – 1952 Groesbeek
Typographer
lit: M. en K. van Laar, *Charles Nypels, Meester-
drukker*, Charles Nypels Stichting / Rosbeek,
Maastricht / Nuth 1986.

Oorthuys, Cas
1908 Leiden – 1975 Amsterdam
Photographer
lit: Sybrand Hekking, *Cas Oorthuys fotograaf
1908-1975*, Fragment, Amsterdam 1982.

Oxenaar, R.D.E.
b. 1929 The Hague
Graphic designer
lit: Ada Lopez Cardozo, 'Ootje Oxenaar', *Items* 20
(1985) p.22.

Raalte, René van
b. 1946 Amsterdam-Nieuwendam
Graphic designer
lit: Ada Lopez Cardozo, 'René van Raalte', *Items* 20
(1986) p.38; *Pro-fil* 29, 1986.

Raateland, Ton
b. 1922 Laren
Graphic designer

Reitsma, Lex
b. 1958 Delden
Graphic designer
lit: *Pro-fil* 51, 1989.

Roland Holst, Richard N.
1868 Rotterdam – 1938 Bloemendaal
Monumental artist, graphic artist
lit: R.N. Roland Holst, *Brieven over de tentoonstelling
van den Duitschen Werkbund te Keulen*, Brusse,
Rotterdam 1914; H. Roland Holst – van der
Schalk, *Kinderjaren en jeugd van R.N. Roland Holst*,
Ploegsma, Zeist 1940; W.L.M.E. van Leeuwen,
B. Spaanstra-Polak, *Roland Holst*,
Kunstenaarscentrum, Bergen 1972; A. Roland
Holst, *Briefwisseling met R.N. Roland Holst en
H Roland Holst- van der Schalk*, Arbeiderspers,
Amsterdam 1990.

Röling, Marte
b. 1939 Laren
Artist
lit: *Pro-fil* 53, 1989.

Roos, Sjoerd H. de
1877 Smallingerland, Drachten – 1962 Haarlem
Typeface designer, typographer
lit: A.A.M. Stols, 'S.H. de Roos en zijn Heuvelpers',
Halcyon, 9-10, 1942; G.W. Ovink, 'De letters van
S.H. de Roos' *Halcyon* 9-10, 1942; Dick Dooijes,
Sjoerd H. de Roos, zoals ik mij hem herinner, Museum
Meermanno-Westreenianum, The Hague 1976;
Dick Dooijes, *Over de drukletterontwerpen van Sjoerd
H. de Roos*, Bührmann-Ubbens, Zutphen 1987;
Carter 1987, p.87, 102; Sjaak Hubregtse (ed.), Jan
Boterman, *S.H. de Roos Typografische geschriften*,
SDU, The Hague 1989.

Ros, Guus
b. 1940 Amsterdam
Graphic designer
lit: *Pro-fil* 9, 1984.

Ros, Lies
b. 1952 Hengelo
Graphic designer
lit: Hefting 1982; *Pro-fil* 20, 1985; 52, 1989.

Rose, Hajo
1920 Mannheim – 1989 Leipzig
Graphic designer
lit: cat. *Nieuwe Kunstschool*, Stedelijk Museum,
Amsterdam 1992.

Rossum, Just van
b. 1966 Haarlem
Typeface designer

Royen, J.F. van
1878 Arnhem – 1942 Amersfoort
lit: G.H. 's-Gravesande, *Mr J.F. van Roven en zijn
betekenis voor de boekkunst*, The Hague 1946;
Hammacher, A.M., *Jean François van Royen 1878-
1942*, Daamen / Stols / Dutch Post Museum, The
Hague 1947; cat. *Jean François van Royen*, Museum
Meermanno-Westreenianum, The Hague 1964;
Visser, J.G., 'Mr Jean François van Royen 1878-
1942', *Het PTT-Bedrijf*, XXIII (1983) 1, p.5.

Saaltink, Stephan
b. 1953 Wageningen
Graphic designer, typographer
lit: *Pro-fil* 71, 1990.

Salden, Helmut
b. 1910 Essen (Germany)
Typographer, typeface designer

Sambeek, Will van
b. 1935 Rosmalen
Graphic designer

Sandberg, Willem J.H.B.
1897 Amersfoort – 1984 Amsterdam
Typographer, museum director, graphic designer
lit: Bibeb, *Sandberg*, Thieme, Nijmegen 1969;
Ad Petersen, Pieter Brattinga, *Sandberg – een
documentaire*, Kosmos, Amsterdam 1975;
Ad Petersen et al., *Sandberg – typographer als
museumman*, De Zonnehof, Amersfoort 1982;
Adri Colpaart, *Sandberg*, De Librije, Zwolle 1986;
Ank Leeuw-Marcar, *W.J.H.B. Sandberg 1897-1984*,
Meulenhoff, Amsterdam 1987.

Schlesinger, Stefan
1896 Vienna (Austria) – 1942 Auschwitz (Poland)
Graphic designer, typeface designer
lit: Stefan Schlesinger, *Lettervormen*, Ahrend,
Amsterdam 1937; Stefan Schlesinger, *Voorbeelden
van moderne opschriften voor decoratieschilders*,
Veluvine, Nunspeet 1939; Stefan Schlesinger,
'Lettercomposities', *Halcyon* 5, 1941; F. Kerdijk,
'Stefan Schlesinger, grafisch kunstenaar', *Tété* 1
(1946) 12, p.247; Kurt Löb, 'Drei deutschsprachige
graphische Gestalter als Emigranten in Holland',
Philobiblon 33 (1989) 3, p.177.

Scholing, Alex
b. 1961 Arnhem
Graphic designer
lit: *Pro-fil* 70, 1991.

Schouwenburg, Nicole van
b. 1958 The Hague
Graphic designer
lit: *Pro-fil* 28, 1986.

Schreuders, Piet
b. 1951 Rotterdam
Graphic designer, author

Schröder, Rob
b. 1950 Oegstgeest
Graphic designer
lit: Hefting 1982; *Pro-fil* 20, 1985; 52, 1989.

Schrofer, Jurriaan
1926 The Hague – 1990 Amsterdam
Graphic designer
lit: Bibeb, *Jurriaan Schrofer*, Thieme, Nijmegen
1972; Hein van Haaren, 'Jurriaan Schrofer', cat.
Jurriaan Schrofer, Museum Fodor, Amsterdam;
Pro-fil 10, 1984; Paul Hefting, 'Jurriaan Schrofer',
Graphis 41 (1985) 235, p.74; Jurriaan Schrofer,
Letters op maat, Lecturis, Eindhoven 1987; Jurriaan
Schrofer, *Onvolmaakt geheugen – met een
denkbeeldige rondgang door K. Schippers*, Bührmann-
Ubbens, Zutphen 1988.

Schuitema, Paul
1897 Groningen – 1973 Wassenaar
Graphic designer, photographer
lit: Benno Wissing, 'Paul Schuitema',
Typographica, 8, 1963; Spencer 1969; Flip Bool,
'Paul Schuitema', *Geschiedenis van de Nederlandse
fotografie*, Samsom, Alphen aan den Rijn, 1, 1984;
D.F. Maan, *Paul Schuitema*, Museum Boymans –
van Beuningen, Rotterdam 1986.

Slothouber, Jan
b. 1918 Boskoop
Industrial designer

Sluijters, Jan
1881 's-Hertogenbosch – 1937 Amsterdam
Painter, graphic artist
lit: Kurt Löb, *De onbekende Jan Sluijters*, Bruna,
Utrecht 1968; cat. *Jan Sluijters*, Noordbrabants
Museum / Frans Halsmuseum, 's-Hertogenbosch /
Haarlem 1981.

Sluiter, Willy
1873 Amersfoort – 1945 The Hague
Painter, graphic artist

Stolk, Swip
b. 1944 Zaandam
Graphic designer
lit: cat. *De Varahaan 2 jaar vormgeving en presentatie*,
Groninger Museum, Groningen 1979; *Pro-fil*, 27
1986.

Stols, A.A.M.
1900 Maastricht – 1973 Tarragona (Spain)
Publisher, typographer
lit: A.A.M Stols, *Het schoone boek*, Brusse,
Rotterdam 1935; C. van Dijk, *Alexander A.M. Stols
1900-1973*, Zutphen 1992.

Strijbosch, Wim
1928 Amsterdam – 1968 Amsterdam
Painter, graphic designer

Swarte, Joost
b. 1946 Heemstede
Graphic artist and illustrator
lit: *Pro-fil* 12, 1984; Joost Swarte, *Joost Swarte,
Moderne kunst*, De Harmonie, Amsterdam 1986;
Joost Swarte, *Cultuur & techniek*, De Harmonie,
Amsterdam 1990; Jack Meijers, 'Joost Swarte –
een interview', *Items* 11, 2 (1992) p.34.

Thorn Prikker, Johan
1868 The Hague – 1932 Cologne
Painter, applied artist

Toorn Vrijthoff, Jelle van der
1946 The Hague
Graphic designer

Toorn, Jan van
1932 Tiel
Graphic designer
lit: cat. *Jan van Toorn*, Museum Fodor, Amsterdam
1972; Jan van Toorn, Jean Leering, *Vormgeving in
functie van museale overdracht*, Lecturis, Eindhoven
1978; *Pro-fil* 1, 1983; Evert Rodrigo, William
Rothuizen, in: *Ontwerpen – Jan van Toorn*,
De Beyerd, Breda 1987.

Toorop, Jan
1858 Poerworedjo (Indonesia) – 1928 The Hague
Painter, graphic artist
lit: Victorine Hefting, *J.Th. Toorop – de jaren 1885 tot
1910*, Rijksmuseum Kröller-Müller, Otterlo 1979.

Treumann, Otto
b. 1919 Fürth (Germany)
Graphic designer
lit: Bibeb, *Otto Treumann*, Thieme, Nijmegen 1970.

Unger, Gerard
b. 1942 Arnhem
Typeface designer
lit: Gerard Unger, *Een tegenvoorstel*, De Gong,
Hilversum 1967; Gerard Unger, *Tekst over tekst –
een documentaire over typografie*, Lecturis,
Eindhoven 1975; Gerard Unger, *Kijk...je kunt er mee
lezen en schrijven*, G.J. Thiemefonds, Amsterdam
1979; Ada Lopes Cardozo, 'Gerard Unger', *Items* 16
(1985) p.20; Gerard Unger, *Typografie –
grondbeginselen en toepassingen*, Ocè,
's-Hertogenbosch 1986; Carter 1987, p.143;
Lommen 1987, p.67 (with list of publications).

Urban, Paul L.
1901 Munich – USSR after 1937 (date unknown)
Graphic artist, illustrator
lit: Kurt Löb, 'Drei deutschsprachige graphische
Gestalter als Emigranten in Holland', in:
Philobiblon 33 (1989) 3, p.177; Kurt Löb, 'Die
Buchgestaltungen Paul L. Urbans für die
Amsterdamer Exil-Verlage Querido und Allert de
Lange' (1933-1936/7), *Philobiblon* 53 (1991) 4,
p.302.

Vecht, Nicolaas J. van der
1886 Abcoude – 1941 Velsen
Graphic/applied artist

Veldheer, J.G.
1860 Haarlem – 1954 Blaricum
Painter, graphic artist

Verberne, Alexander
b. 1924 Den Helder
Graphic designer

Vermeulen, Jan
1923 Leiden – 1985 Slijk-Ewijk
Graphic designer, typographer
lit: Hans van Straten et al, *Leven in letters. Over Jan
Vermeulen*, Gelderse Culturele Raad, Arnhem
1992.

Vermeulen, Rick
b. 1950 Schiedam
Graphic designer
lit: Hefting 1982; *Pro-fil* 40, 1988; 48, 1988.

Vordemberge-Gildewart, Friedrich
1899 Osnabrück – 1962 Ulm
Painter, graphic designer
lit: Volker Rattemeyer, Dietrich Helms, *Friedrich
Vordemberge-Gildewart – Typographie und
Werbegestaltung*, Landesmuseum / Sprengel
Museum / Museum für Gestaltung, Wiesbaden /
Hannover / Zürich 1990-1991.

Vossen, André van der
1893 Haarlem – 1963 Bloemendaal
Graphic artist

Waals, Tessa van der
b. 1960 Groningen
Graphic designer
lit: *Pro-fil* 41, 1988.

Warmerdam, Mart
b. 1955 Tilburg
Graphic designer

Werkman, H.N.
1882 Leens – 1945 Bakkeveen
Typographer, painter
lit: Hans van Straaten, *Hendrik Nicolaas Werkman –
de drukker van het paradijs*, Meulenhoff,
Amsterdam 1963; H.W. van Os, *H.N. Werkman*,
Niemeijer, Groningen 1965; J. Martinet, *Bij de
heruitgave van de Chassidische Legenden van H.N.
Werkman*, Corbey, Amsterdam 1967; Spencer
1969; J. Martinet, *Werkman 'druksels' en
gebruiksgrafiek*, Amsterdam 1977; Fie Werkman,
Herinneringen aan mijn vader H.N. Werkman,
Wolters Noordhoff, Groningen 1987.

Wijdeveld, H. Th.
1885 The Hague – 1987 Amsterdam
Architect, author
lit: Hans Oldewarris, 'Wijdeveld Typografie'
Forum 25 (1975) 1; Fanelli 1978; H. Th. Wijdeveld,
Mijn eerste eeuw, Ravenberg Pers, Oosterbeek 1985.

Wilmink, Machiel
1894 Zwolle – 1963 Voorburg
Commercial designer

Wils, Jan
1891 Alkmaar – 1972 Voorburg
Architect
lit: Fanelli 1978.

Wissing, Benno
b. 1923 Oosterbeek
Graphic designer

Wouw, Jolijn van de
b. 1942 's-Hertogenbosch
Graphic designer
lit: *Pro-fil* 68, 1990.

Ziegelaar, Joke
b. 1943 Sassenheim
Graphic designer

Zon, Jacques
1872 The Hague – 1932 The Hague
Painter, poster artist

Zwart, Piet
1885 Zaandijk – 1977 Leidschendam
Interior designer, graphic and industrial
designer, photographer
lit: H.L.C. Jaffé, 'Piet Zwart: a Pioneer of
Functional Typography, *New Graphic Design*, June
1961; Fridolin Mülle and Peter F. Althaus, *Piet
Zwart*, Arthur Niggli, Teufen 1966; Spencer 1969;
Kees Broos, *Piet Zwart en PTT*, Gemeentemuseum,
The Hague 1968; Kees Broos, *Piet Zwart*,
Gemeentemuseum, The Hague 1973; *Piet Zwart
1885-1977*, Van Gennep, Amsterdam 1982; Kees
Broos, 'Piet Zwart', *Studio International* 185 (1973)
954, p.176; Kees Broos, *Piet Zwart – Fotograf*,
Marzona, Düsseldorf 1981; Paul Hefting,
'Inleiding bij Piet Zwart', *Herdruk Het Boek van PTT*,
PTT, The Hague 1985; Bruno Monguzzi, 'Piet
Zwart – The Typographical Work 1923-1933',
Trimestrale, IX (1987) 30/2; Kees Broos, Piet Zwart',
Geschiedenis van de Nederlandse Fotografie, Samsom,
Alphen aan den Rijn, 12, 1989.

General bibliography

Beekers, Frank, Lies Ros and Rob Schröder. *Het ontwerpproces - grafisch designers en hun opdrachtgevers*, G.J. Thiemefonds / De Populier, Amsterdam 1986.

Bosters, Cassandra. *Ontwerpen voor de Jaarbeurs*, Walbur Pers / Centraal Museum, Zutphen / Utrecht 1991.

Boterman, Jan (ed.). *Rietveld Idiotenband*, Gerrit Jan Thiemefonds, Amsterdam 1983.

Braches, Ernst. *Het boek als Nieuwe Kunst - een studie in Art Nouveau 1892-1903*, Oosthoek, Utrecht 1973.

Brattinga, Pieter. 'Einflüsse auf die niederländische Plakatkunst in der ersten Hälfte des 20. Jahrhunderts', in: cat. *60 Plakate / Neun Holländische Graphiker / 1956-1970*, De Jong, Hilversum 1970.

Broos, Kees. 'Affiches', in: *Museumjournaal 20* (1975) 3, p.112

Broos, Kees. *Dutch Design II*, Gemeentemuseum / Cultural Ministry, The Hague 1978.

Broos, Kees. 'From the Fine Book to Visual Communication', in: *Dutch Art + Architecture Today* 10 (1978) 3, p.14

Broos, Kees. 'Dutch design for the public sector', in: *Graphis* 35 (1979/1980) 206, p.478.

Broos, Kees. 'Typografie', in: *Berlijn Amsterdam 1920-1940 wisselwerkingen*, Querido, Amsterdam 1982, p.246.

Broos, Kees. 'From De Stijl to a New Typography', in: *De Stijl 1917-1931 Visions of Utopia*, Abbeville/Phaidon, Minneapolis and New York/Oxford 1982.

Broos, Kees. *Ontwerp: Total Design*, Relfex, Utrecht 1983.

Broos, Kees. 'Hard Werken', in: *Dutch Art + Architecture Today*, 17 (1985) 26, p.26.

Broos, Kees. *Vorm in de maak*, Rosbeek, Nuth 1988.

Broos, Kees. *Architekst*, Lecturis, Eindhoven 1989.

Broos, Kees. 'Das kurze, aber heftige Leben des Rings "neue werbegestalter"', in: *"Typographie kann unter Umständen Kunst sein" – Ring 'neue werbegestalter' – Die Amsterdamer Ausstellung 1931*, Landesmuseum / Sprengel Museum / Museum für Gestaltung, Wiesbaden / Hannover / Zürich 1990-1991.

Broos, Kees and Flip Bool. *De Nieuwe Fotografie in Nederland*, Fragment / SDU, Amsterdam / The Hague 1989, Sebastian Carter, *Twentieth Century Type Designers*, Trefoil, London 1987.

Craig, James and Bruce Barton. *Thirty Centuries of Graphic Design*, Watson-Guptill, New York 1987.

van Dijk, C. *Halcyon*, Bührmann-Ubbens Papier, Zutphen 1989.

Dooijes, Dick and Pieter Brattinga. *A history of the Dutch poster 1890-1960*, Scheltema & Holkema, Amsterdam 1968.

Dooijes, Dick. *Boeken maken 1890-1940 – De Collectie Nijkerk*, Stedelijk Museum, Amsterdam 1975.

Drukkersjaarboek, Ipenbuur en Van Seldam, Amsterdam 1906-1910.

'The Dutch Issue', *Print*, November/December 1991.

van Fassen, Egbert. *Drukwerk voor PTT*, SDU, The Hague 1988.

Fanelli, Giovanni. *Moderne architectuur in Nederland 1900-1940*, Staatsuitgeverij, The Hague 1978.

Fioravanti, Giorgio. *Grafica & Stampa*, Zanichelli, Bologna 1984.

Gans, L. *Nieuwe kunst*, Oosthoek, Utrecht 1966.

Gouwe, W.F. *De grafische kunst in het praktische leven*, W.L. & J. Brusse, Rotterdam 1926.

Graphic Design and Typography in The Netherlands – A View of Recent Work, The Herb Lubalin Study Centre of Design and Typography / The Cooper Union and Princeton Architectural Press, New York 1992.

van Haaren, H. 'De vormgeving van de Nederlandse postzegel', in: *Nederlandsch Maandblad voor Philatelie*, October 1973.

Hefting, Paul. *Hard Werken / Wild Plakken*, Lecturis, Eindhoven 1982.

Hefting, Paul. *Nederlandse Koning- en koninginnezegels van 1852 tot en met 1981*, Staatsuitgeverij / PTT, The Hague 1982

Hefting, Paul. 'De dienst voor Esthetische Vormgeving', *Kunst en Beleid in Nederland*, Amsterdam 1986.

Hefting, Paul. *Operatie Bedrijfsstijl*, The Hague 1988.

Hefting, Paul. 'The Royal PTT Netherlands – Tradition in a new form', *The Image of a Company*, Architecture, Design and Technology Press, London 1990.

Hefting, Paul. 'A Certain Commitment – Art and Design at the Royal PTT', *Print*, November-December 1991.

Hefting, Paul and R.D.E. Oxenaar. 'Achtergronden, Wordingsgeschiedenis en inhoud van de PTT-bedrijfsstijl', in: *Het PTT-bedrijf*, XXIII (1983) 1, p.21.

Hofland, H.J.A., Marius van Leeuwen, Nel Punt, *Een teken aan de wand – Album van de Nederlandse samenleving 1963-1983*, Bert Bakker, Amsterdam 1983.

Hofstätter, Hans H. *Jugendstil Druckkunst*, Holle Verlag, Baden-Baden 1968.

de Jong, Dirk. *Het vrije boek in onvrije tijd*, Sijthoff, Leiden 1958.

Kinross, Robin. *Modern Typography*, Hyphen Press, London 1992.

Knuttel Wzn, G. *De letter als kunstwerk*, Amsterdam Type Foundry, 1951.

Kras, Reyer, et al. *Industrie & Vormgeving in Nederland 1850-1950*, Stedelijk Museum, Amsterdam 1986.

Lewin, Lisette. *Het clandestiene boek 1940-1945*, Van Gennep, Amsterdam 1983.

Lewis, John. *The Twentieth Century Book*, Studio Vista, London 1967.

Lewis, John. *Anatomy of printing*, Faber and Faber, London 1970.

Löb, Kurt (ed.). *Paul Citroen en het Bauhaus*, Bruna, Utrecht/Antwerp 1974.

Lommen, Mathieu. *Typeface designers*, Joh. Enschedé en Zonen, Haarlem 1987.

Lommen, Mathieu. *De grote vijf*, Zutphen 1991.

Lopes Cardozo, Ada. 'Ontwerpen op klein formaat', *Items* 17 (1985) p.16.

Maan, D.F. *De Maniakken*, Lecturis / Meermanno, Eindhoven / The Hague 1982.

Maan, D. and John van der Ree, *Typofoto*, Veen-Reflex, Utrecht 1990.

Malke, Lutz (ed.). *Europäische Moderne – Buch und Graphik*, Kunstbibliothek Berlin / Dietrich Reimer Verlag, Berlin 1989.

Meggs, Philip B. *A History of Graphic Design*, Van Nostrand Reinhold / Allen Lane, New York / London 1983.

de Moor, Chris. *Postzegelkunst – de vormgeving van de Nederlandse postzegel*, Staatsuitgeverij, The Hague 1960.

Ovink, G.W., et al. *Anderhalve eeuw boektypografie*, Thieme, Nijmegen 1965.

Pannekoek, G.H. *De verluchting van het boek*, W.L. & J. Brusse, Rotterdam 1927.

Petersen, Ad. *De Ploeg*, Bzztôh, The Hague 1982.

Prokopoff, Stephen S. (ed.). *The Modern Dutch Poster, The First Fifty Years 1890-1940*, Krannert Art Museum / MIT Press, Illinois / Cambridge Ma. / London 1987.

Purvis, Alston W. *Dutch Graphic Design 1918-1945*, Van Nostrand Reinhold, New York 1992 (bibliography).

Radermacher Schorer, M.R. *Bijdrage tot de geschiedenis van de renaissance van de Nederlandse boekdrukkunst*, School voor Grafische Vakken / Stichting De Roos, Utrecht 1951.

Reinders, Pim, Rudy Kousbroek, Jeroen Stumpel et al. *Schip & Affiche – Honderd jaar rederijreclame in Nederland*, Veen-Reflex, Utrecht / Antwerpen 1987.

Reinders Pim and Wilmy Oosterwijk. *Neem de Trein! Spoorwegaffiches in Nederland*, Veen-Reflex, Utrecht / Antwerpen 1989.

Schnid, Helmud. 'Typography seen and read', *Idea*, special issue, Tokyo 1980.

Spencer, Herbert. *Pioneers of Modern Typography*, Lund Humphries, London 1969.

Staal, Gert and Hester Wolters (eds.). *Holland in Vorm - Vormgeving in Nederland 1945-1987*, Stichting Holland in Vorm, The Hague 1987.

Staal, Gert. 'Design for communication', *Holland Herald*, October 1988.

Stols, A.A.M. *Het schoone boek*, W.L. & J. Brusse, Rotterdam 1935.

van Vliet, H.T.M. *Louis Couperus en L.J. Veen – Bloemlezing uit hun correspondentie*, Veen, Utrecht / Antwerp 1987.

Yocarini, Titus. *Vak in beweging*, Lecturis, Eindhoven 1976.

cat. *Affiches honderd jaar kunstleven in The Hague 1866-1966*, The Hague [Gemeentemuseum] 1966.

cat. *Art & pub – Art & publicité 1890-1990*, Centre Georges Pompidou, Paris 1990.

cat. *The Dutch PTT – Design in the Public Service*, Design Museum, London 1990.

cat. *Gedrukt in Nederland*, Rijksmuseum, Amsterdam 1960

cat. *Het Nederlandse boek 1892-1906*, Universiteitsmuseum, Utrecht 1965.

cat. *Ontwerpen voor een drukkerij*, Stedelijk Museum, Amsterdam 1963.

cat. *Typomundus 20*, Reinhold / Studio Vista / Otto Maier, New York / London / Ravensburg 1966

cat. *Vrij en gebonden*, Gemeentemuseum Arnhem 1965.

Index of names

Numbers in *italic*
refer to captions and
illustrations

Albers, Josef *131*
Alkema, Wobbe *71*
Allner, Heinz *131*
Alma, Peter *74, 75, 124, 125, 133*
Altink, Jan *71*
ANDO, Drukkerij *135*
Andriesse, Emmy *162*
Apollinaire, Guillaume *58*
Arntz, Gerd *114, 122, 123, 125*
Arondeus, Willem *118, 119*
Arp, Hans *92, 114, 135*
Arrighi, Ludovico degli *128*
Baanders, Tine *107, 108*
Bakker, Bert *135*
Balkema, A.A. *135*
Bantzinger, Cees *135*
Barr, Alfred *138*
Barvelink, Hans *145, 149*
Bauer, Marius *35*
Bayer, Herbert *131*
Bazaine, Jean *142*
Bazel, K.P.C. de *16, 22, 23, 45, 53, 56, 74, 94*
Becht, Uitgeverij H.W.J. *27*
Beckmann, Max *142*
Beeke, Anthon *168, 169, 170, 175, 181, 182, 183, 184, 185, 192, 193, 194, 195, 212, 213*
Beekers, Frank *204*
Berkovich, Elmar *111*
Berlage, H.P. *13, 15, 16, 21, 22, 23, 25, 27, 32, 45, 65, 67, 78, 96*
Bernhard, Lucien *104*
Besnyö, Eva *121, 162*
Beunis, Karel *146*
Bierma, Wigger *190, 208, 209*
Bijvoet, B. *12*
Bissière, Roger *142*
Blazer, Carel *120, 121, 162*
Bleekrode, Meyer *112, 113*
Bloem, J.C. *46, 48*
Bloemsma, Evert *199*
Blokland, Erik van *199*
Blokland, Petr van *198, 199*
Blommestein, Ch. van *135*
Bodon, A. *131*
Boekraad, H. *190*
Bons, Jan *8, 120, 131, 134, 136, 140, 148, 154, 155, 168, 169*
Boom, Irma *206, 207*
Boosten & Stols, Drukkerij *135, 144*
Bos, Ben *174, 175*
Bosch, Jac. van den *45*
Boucher, L.J.C. *126*
Braak, Menno ter *126*
Braakensiek, Johan *35*
Bradley, Will *35*
Brand, Chris *151, 212*
Braque, Georges *99*
Brattinga, Pieter *136, 158, 166, 167, 168, 169, 180, 198*
Breitner, G.H. *39*
Bremmer, H.P. *65*
Briedé, Joh. *51*
Brinkman, J.A. *84*
Brody, Neville *198*
Bromberg, Paul *111, 133*
Brouwers, Arlette *194*
BRS *158, 177*
Brusse, Wim *92, 97, 116, 118, 119, 120, 121, 136, 138, 157, 162*
Brusse, Uitgeverij W.L. & J. *13, 46, 82, 86, 96*
Buckland Wright, John *9*
Buckminster Fuller, R. *168*
Cahn, Henny *92, 116, 117-119*
Caldecott, Randolph *29*
Campendonk, Heinrich *114*
Cantré, Jozef *103*
Caspel, J.G. van *35, 39*
Cassandre, A.M. *101*
Chazal, Marc *168*
Chéret, Jules *35*

Chevalier, Drukkerij C. *81*
Citroen, Paul *114, 131, 152, 172*
Cobden-Sanderson, T.J. *40, 47*
Cochius, P.M. *13*
Coenen, Jo *213*
Cohen, Fré *112, 113, 133*
Cornelissen, Henk *212*
Cornelius, Violette *131*
Cornet, Baer *170*
Couperus, Louis *27*
Crane, Walter *16, 19, 25, 29, 32, 40, 45, 56, 200*
Crop, Duco *23*
Crouwel, Wim *9, 136, 145, 146, 149, 158, 164, 165, 168, 171, 174, 177, 180, 192, 198, 213*
Cuijpers, P.J.H. *32*
Day, Lewis F. *19*
Denijs, Job *108*
Derkinderen, Anton *24, 25*
Diedenhoven, Walter van *41, 50, 51*
Diepraam, Willem *213*
Dijck, Christoffel van *128*
Dijkstra, Johan *71*
Dijsselhof, G.W. *19, 24, 23, 25, 32, 33, 35*
Disberg, Harry *177*
Dishoeck, Uitgeverij C.A.J. van *27*
Does, Bram de *198, 199*
Doesburg, Theo van *23, 58, 60-63, 69, 73, 91*
Domela, Cesar *76, 90, 91*
Dooijes, Dick *105, 128, 151*
Dordrecht, Fred van *120*
Dreyfus, John *48*
Drupsteen, Jaap *170, 213*
Duchamp, Marcel *58, 172*
Duijvelshoff, Daphne *174, 175*
Duiker, J. *12, 74*
Dumbar, Gert *170, 176, 180, 186, 187*
Duwaer, Frans *135*
Duwaer en Zonen, Drukkerij J.F. *47, 103, 131, 135, 155*
Ehrlich, Christa *98*
Eikeren, Joh. van *156*
Eisenstein, Sergej *82*
Elenga, Henk *202*
Elffers, Dick *92, 94, 111, 116, 117, 120, 136, 140, 141, 142-144, 145, 155, 156, 157, 160, 162, 207*
Elsken, Ed van der *9*
Enschedé en Zonen, Lettergieterij Joh. *47, 48, 128, 135, 144, 151*
Ernst, Helen *131*
Escher, Gielijn *6, 10, 197, 200, 201*
Eyck, P.N. van *45, 46, 48*
Fallon, Andrew *175*
Fauconnier, H. le *51*
Feininger, Andreas *131*
Finsterlinn, Herman *74*
Flakkeesche, Drukkerij De *96*
Friedlaender, Henri *126, 127, 146, 147*
Fuchs, Rudi *180*
Gabo, Naum *133*
Geer, Drukkerij Erven van de *164, 192*
Gelder Zonen, Kon. Papierfabrieken Van *156*
Gerbrands, Roelf *96*
Gestel, Leo *50, 51*
Geijsen, Mireille *211*
Gidding, Jaap *41, 51*
Gill, Eric *128*
Gispen, W.H. *74, 92, 101*
Gogh, Vincent van *40, 55*
Graadt van Roggen, C.J. *82*
Graatsma, William *213*
Grasset, Eugène *35*
Gray, Eileen *74*
Greenaway, Kate *29*
Greshoff, Jan *46, 48*
Grevink, Gea *210*
Gropius, Walter *76*
Gruson, E. *210*
Guermonprez, Paul *114, 131*
Hadders, Gerard *195, 202, 203, 213*
Hahn, Albert *113*

Hammacher, A.M. 84
Hard Werken 192, 194, 202
Hart Nibbrig, F. 35
Hartland, Paul 130
Hartz, Sem 151
Haspel, Tom van den 202
Hausmann, Raoul 63, 91
Heartfield, John 113, 120, 126, 204
Heine, Th. Th. 35
Hem, Piet van der 55, 113
Hendriks, Jan 135
Henkels, F.R.A. 135
Heynemann, Suzanne 135, 146
Him, G. 177
Hoffman, Josef 74
Hofman, P.A.H. 51, 99
Hohlwein, Ludwig 101
Holkema & Warendorf, Van 27
Homan, Reynoud 175
Horn, Lex 213
Howard, Helen 192
Hoytema, Theo van 28-31, 32
Huszár, Vilmos 58, 59, 60, 61, 63, 65, 67, 69, 74, 75,
    85, 96, 101, 107, 119, 133
Hynckes, Raoul 55, 98, 114
Israëls, Joseph 35
Itten, Johannes 131, 133
Jaffé, H.L.C 138, 158
Jenson, Nicolas 45
Johnston, Edward 51
Jong, Cees de 194, 195, 213
Jong, Steendrukkerij de 138, 167, 168, 183, 192, 198
Jongejans, Charles 136, 140, 141, 157, 208, 209
Jongema, Marten 213
Jongert, Jac. 41, 74, 81, 92, 93-95, 101, 116, 200
Jordaan, L.J. 113
Kalf, Jan 25
Kalff, L.C.J. 100, 101
Kamman, Jan 81, 89
Kampen, Uitgeverij P.N. van 27
Kandinsky, Wassily 155
Kars, Willem 202
Kempers, Mart 141, 145, 162
Kerdijk, F. 13, 104, 107
Kesten, Hermann 126
Keulen, Jan van 157, 162
Kho Liang Ie 164
Kiljan, G. 77, 82, 84, 92, 94, 116, 120, 131, 133, 136,
    167, 172
Kirchner, Emil Ludwig 71
Kisman, Max 199, 207
Klaarhamer, P.J.C. 64, 65
Klee, Paul 114
Kleinmann, Uitgeverij 16, 30
Klerk, Michel de 56, 74
Klimt, Gustav 74
Klinger, Julius 104
Klinkenberg, Irene 213
Kloos, J.P. 138
Kluzis, G. 76
Kok, Anthony 63
Kok, Jan Willem de 202
Kolthoff, Mark 120
Konijnenburg, Willem van 34, 35, 74
Koo, N.P. de 94, 95, 101, 118, 119, 124, 133
Kramer, Friso 174
Krijger, Henk 145, 151
Krimpen, Jan van 9, 10, 13, 46, 47-49, 96, 103, 128,
    129, 135, 146, 150, 151, 189, 199, 208, 213
Kröller-Müller, H. 65
Kroonder, Uitgeverij F.G. 135
Krop, Hildo 74
Kruit, Hans 170, 173
Kruijsen, Karel 206, 207, 212, 213
Kuiper, Jan 146, 147
Kurpershoek, Theo 146
Kurvers, Anton 74
Landshoff, Fritz 126
Landstra, Menno 213
Lange, Uitgeverij Allert de 126

Larisch, Rudolf von 51
Laurens, Henri 91
Lauweriks, J.L.M. 22, 23, 53, 73, 74, 96
Le Corbusier 84
Lebbink, Gracia 194, 195
Lebeau, Chris 9, 23, 27, 52, 53, 57
Leck, Bart van der 58, 61, 64, 65, 69, 110, 111
Lecturis, Drukkerij 192
Ledoux, C.-N. 73
Leering, Jean 180
Leeuw, J. de 13, 111
Léger, Fernand 99
Lettergieterij 'Amsterdam' 45, 128, 151, 156
Levie, Victor 213
Levine, Les 168
Linotype 151
Lion Cachet, C.A. 14, 18, 19, 30, 32, 33, 35, 39, 50,
    51, 73, 74
Lissitzky, El 58, 61, 63, 74, 76, 114, 120, 125, 172, 179,
    204
Looy, Uitgeverij S.L. van 27
Majoor, Martin 199
Mallarmé, Stéphane 58, 63
Manutius, Aldus 45
Manzoni, Piero 179
Marc, Franz 142
Marinetti, F.T. 58, 63
Marken, J.C. van 13, 39
Marsman, Hendrik 126
Martens, Karel 170, 190, 191, 199, 213
Matisse, Henri 142
Mayakovski, Vladimir 63
Meijer, Drukkerij 135, 143, 162
Mendelsohn, Erich 74
Mendes da Costa, J. 74
Metz & Co., 65, 104, 111
Michiels, Toon 192
Mijksenaar, Paul 170, 175, 192, 193, 194, 213
Modley, Rudolf 125
Moholy-Nagy 58, 76, 82, 91, 114, 130
Molkenboer, Anton 57
Molkenboer, Theo 17, 34, 35, 39
Mondriaan, Piet 58, 61, 65, 91, 114
Monotype Corporation 128, 151
Morison, Stanley 48, 128
Morris, William 16, 19, 25, 40, 45, 56, 73, 200
Moser, Koloman 23, 51
Mouton, Drukkerij 126
Müller-Lehning, Arthur 91, 131
Mus jr, C. 99
Mutsaers, Charlotte 213
Nakata, Robert 213
Neuhuys, Theo 26, 27
Neurath, Otto 122, 123, 125, 133
Niegemann, Johan 131
Nieuwenhuijzen, Kees 170, 213
Nieuwenhuis, Th. 25, 32, 33, 35, 37, 39
Nieuwenkamp, W.O.J. 24, 25
Nijlen, Jan van 48
Nikkels, Walter 170, 176, 180, 188, 189
Noordzij, Gerrit 151, 193, 199, 208, 212
Noordzij, Peter Mathias 199
Nypels, Charles 45, 46, 102, 103
Oorthuys, Cas 111, 113, 120, 121, 157, 162, 213
Oud, J.J.P 111
Ovink, G.W. 74
Oxenaar, R.D.E. 158, 172, 173
Oyen, Adth van 175
Paul, Bruno 35
Penaat, W. 111
Picabia, Francis 58
Picasso, Pablo 58, 142
Pieck, Anton 39
Pieck, Henri 51
Pieterson, Lex van 186
Pissarro, Lucien 47
Poliakoff, Serge 142
Proost & Brandt, Papiergroothandel 156
Pudovkin, V. 82
Querido, Uitgeverij Emm. 55, 126

Raalte, René van 170, 212, 213
Raateland, Ton 156, 157, 168
Raemaekers, Louis 51, 113
Reidemeister, Marie 123
Reiner, Imre 104
Reitsma, Lex 180, 206, 207
Renner, Paul 128
Richter, Hans 91
Ricketts, Charles 40
Ridder, Willem de 183
Rietveld, Gerrit 61, 111, 138, 155, 168, 172
Rodchenko, Alexander 76, 120
Röling, Marte 213
Roland Holst, Richard N. 25, 26, 27, 39-41, 51, 55,
    74, 94, 99
Roller, Alfred 51
Roos, S.H. de 13, 44, 45, 46, 47, 56, 74, 94, 96, 103,
    128, 129, 151, 208
Ros, Lies 204
Rosbeek, Drukkerij 192
Rose, Hajo 114, 121, 130, 131
Rossum, Just van 199
Roth, Dieter 168
Rouault, Georges 142
Royen, J.-F. van 13, 43, 45, 46, 47, 56, 74, 84, 103,
    114, 119
Rozendaal, W.J. 172
Rueter, Georg 32, 35
Rueter, Pam G. 107
Saaltink, Stephan 7, 190, 199
Salden, Helmut 114, 126, 127, 145, 146, 147
Sambeek, Will van 193, 194
Samenwerkende Ontwerpers 192
Sandberg, Willem 3, 7, 71, 114, 119, 125, 132, 133,
    135, 136, 138, 139, 141, 142, 145, 149, 155, 164,
    167, 168, 180, 189
Scheltema & Holkema's Boekhandel 32
Schilp, Ernst 194, 195
Schippers, K. 183
Schippers, Wim T. 182
Schlesinger, Stefan 104, 105, 107, 108-111, 128,
    129, 151
Scholing, Alex 213
Schouwenburg, Nicole van 213
Schreuders, Piet 194
Schröder, Rob 204
Schrofer, Jurriaan 9, 144, 145, 146, 156, 158, 159,
    160-163, 175, 177, 198, 213
Schuitema 76, 80, 81, 82, 83, 84, 87, 88, 89, 92, 113,
    116, 120, 131, 133, 136, 167, 172
Schwarz, Dick 174
Schwarz, Paul 174
Schwitters, Kurt 58, 61, 62, 63, 76, 78, 91, 172
Senefelder, Drukkerij 35
Seuphor, Michel 68
Shannon, Charles 40
Sierman, Harry 146, 192
Simon, Oliver 128
Simons, Anna 51
Slothouber, Jan 213
Sluijters, Jan 42, 54, 55, 74, 113
Sluiter, Willy 55
Spiekermann, Erik 198
Spruyt, Drukkerij Mart. 179, 192
Stadsdrukkerij Amsterdam 192
Stam, Mart 114, 131, 136, 138, 179
Stam-Beese, Lotte 131
Steinitz, Käthe 62, 63
Steinlen, Th.-A. 35
Stoepman, Frits 146
Stofbergen, Leendert 146
Stolk, Swip 170, 176, 180, 182, 183, 184, 195, 213
Stols, A.A.M. 45, 46, 96, 103, 107, 126, 135, 144, 146,
    147
Strijbosch, Wim 140
Swart, Martijn 211
Swarte, Joost 213
Tak, P.L. 29
Tamminga, Fokke 135
Tatlin, Vladimir 172

Taut, Max 73
Teige, Karel 58
Tel Design 158, 170, 176, 186, 197
Thieme, Drukkerij G.J. 96, 144
Thijsse, Jac. P. 30
Thorn Prikker, Johan 16, 18, 35
Toorn, Jan van 145, 170, 178, 179, 180, 181, 183,
    192, 213
Toorn Vrijthoff, Jelle van der 175
Toorop, Jan 9, 10, 16, 20, 21, 26, 27, 35, 38, 39, 40, 74
Total Design 158, 160, 174, 175, 177, 180, 197
Toulouse-Lautrec, Henri de 29, 35, 55
Traast, E. 210
Treumann, Otto 114, 131, 136, 137, 141, 145, 152,
    153, 155, 156, 177, 180
Trio, Drukkerij 78, 104, 107, 135, 144, 192
Tschichold, Jan 58, 76, 103, 125, 131, 189
Tschinkel, Augustin 125
Unger, Gerard 10, 151, 198
Urban, Paul L. 114, 126, 127, 131
VANK 15, 19, 47, 56, 61, 94, 96, 101, 133
Vecht, N.J. van der 56
Veen, Uitgeverij L.J. 27
Veldheer, J.G. 24, 25
Verberne, Alexander 156, 157, 199
Verdonk, Esther 175
Verheul, Peter 199
Verkade, Eduard 53
Vermaas, Chris 192, 198
Vermeulen, Jan 135, 146, 147, 190, 199
Vermeulen, Rick 202
Versluys, Uitgeverij W. 27
Veth, Jan 25, 40
Vlugt, L.C. van der 74, 84
Vordemberge-Gildewart, Friedrich 91, 114, 131,
    134, 135
Voskuil, Jo 113, 120
Vossen, André van der 57, 129
Waals, Tessa van der 208, 209
Warmerdam, Mart 211
Weihs, Bertram 172
Weiss, E.R. 104
Wenckebach. L.W.R. 27
Werkman, H.N. 11, 58, 68-71, 114, 115, 134, 135,
    138
Wernars, Gerard 136
Wiegers, Jan 71
Wijdeveld, H. Th. 58, 67, 72-74, 99, 101
Wijnberg, Nicolaas 136
Wild Plakken 170, 204, 205, 213
Wilde, E.L.L. de 164, 180
Wildenhain, Franz 131
Wildenhain, Marguerite 131
Willink, A.C. 114
Wilmink, Machiel 94, 95, 133
Wils, Jan 66, 67
Wissing, Benno 136, 162, 163, 174
Witte, Aldert 146
Woestijne, Joost van de 146
Wouw, Jolijn van de 174, 175
Wright, Frank Lloyd 67, 74
Zapf, Hermann 105
Ziegelaar, Joke 213
Zon, Jac. 35, 36, 39
Zwart, Piet 10, 13, 58, 66, 67, 76, 78, 79, 82-87, 89,
    92, 94, 96, 97, 106, 107, 116, 119, 120, 125, 133,
    138, 152, 167, 172, 192

Photographs

Tom Haartsen, Ouderkerk a/d Amstel; Arthur Martin, Bussum;
Peter Couvee, Gemeentemuseum, The Hague;
Rijksmuseum Meermanno Westreenianum, The Hague;
Reproduction Department Stedelijk Museum, Amsterdam
Much material was also donated by various designers and design studios

This publication was partly made possible with the financial support of the
Dutch Ministry of Welfare, Health and Culture.
The publishers are grateful to thank the Rijksdienst Beeldende Kunst,
The Hague, and the Foundation for Dutch Graphic Design for all their
cooperation.

Every care has been taken in properly crediting the reproductions in this
book. Any persons who have not been correctly credited concerning the
photographs should appeal to the publisher.

Acknowledgements

Kees Broos, author and art historian, was born in 1940 in The Hague and studied art history and archeology at Leiden University. In 1971 he was appointed curator of drawings and graphic art at the Gemeentemuseum in The Hague, and in 1980 he became curator of its modern art department. From 1971–1981 he was editor of the *Kunsthistorisch* yearbook; *Museumjournaal*; *Simiolus Art Quarterly* and *Kunstschrift Openbaar Kunstbezit*. Since 1982 he has worked as a freelance art historian and published many books and articles on art and graphic design.

Paul Hefting, art critic, author and art historian, was born in 1933 in Eelde. After studying art history at Utrecht University, he obtained a PhD on a dissertation on the Dutch painter G. H. Breitner. From 1963–1966 he worked in the department of architecture of Delft Technical University. From 1966–1981 he was curator of the Rijksmuseum Kröller-Müller and from 1970–1974 he was editor of *Museumjournal*. He was published many books and articles, and since 1981 has been in charge of graphic design at the Royal PTT Nederland NV (Dutch Post Office).

Cees de Jong, designer and publisher, was born in 1945 in Amsterdam. In 1970 he graduated from the Gerrit Rietveld Academy and since 1975 has been director of V+K Publishing, which specialises in publishing and designing international co-editions on architecture and design. These include *Nooit gebouwd Nederland* (Never built Netherlands), *Het Rietveld Schröder Huis* (The Rietveld Schröder House), *The Image of a Company, De Nieuwe Fotografie* (The New Photography) and *Type & Typographers* – a number of which have received awards.

Jan Johan ter Poorten, graphic designer, was born in 1964 in Vlissingen. After graduating from the Royal Academy for Art and Design, Den Bosch, in 1988, he gained practical experience working for a Dutch publisher and two UK design studios. Since 1989 he has worked on various book projects for V+K Design, as well as on a range of other printed matter.